Queen of the Confederacy

The Innocent Deceits of Lucy Holcombe Pickens

by

Elizabeth Wittenmyer Lewis

University of North Texas Press
Denton, Texas

The paper in this book meets the minimum requirements of the American
National Standard for Permanence of Paper for Printed Library Materials,
Z39.48.1984

Permissions
University of North Texas Press
PO Box 311336
Denton, TX 76203-1336
940-565-2142

Library of Congress Cataloging-in-Publication Data
Lewis, Elizabeth Wittenmyer, 1919–
Queen of the Confederacy: the innocent deceits of Lucy Holcombe Pickens/
Elizabeth Wittenmyer Lewis.—1st ed.
p.   cm.
Includes bibliographical references (p.) and index.
ISBN 1-57441-146-2 (hardcover : alk. paper)
1. Pickens, Lucy Petway Holcombe. 2. Governors' spouses—South Carolina—
Biography. 3. Women—Confederate States of America—Biography. I. Title.
F273.P58 L49 2002
975.7'03'092—dc21

2002000645

Cover Photograph courtesy of the Davis/Little Collection

Design by Angela Schmitt

To my family—
past and present

Contents

vii—Preface

xi—Acknowledgments

xiv—Principal Characters

1—Chapter One • Changing Times • 1830–1840

8—Chapter Two • Riches have taken to themselves wings • 1840–1846

18—Chapter Three • If she wears blue stockings • 1846–1849

27—Chapter Four • A stranger in a strange land • 1850

36—Chapter Five • My spirit is restless • 1851

43—Chapter Six • The only kindred blood I ever knew • 1851

49—Chapter Seven • My home is in the prairied West • 1852–1857

62—Chapter Eight • The Marriage Mart of The South • 1857

73—Chapter Nine • The heart hath reason • 1858

79—Chapter Ten • Talking of elevated and mighty themes • 1858

87—Chapter Eleven • The confused sound • 1858

92—Chapter Twelve • It was very marked and not known • 1859
Illustrations

101—Chapter Thirteen • I suspect it will look more like a Muscovite • 1859–60

108—Chapter Fourteen • There is nothing real • 1860

116—Chapter Fifteen • I find myself going up the hill • 1860

126—Chapter Sixteen • I am where duty and honor demand • 1861

134—Chapter Seventeen • It was grand—it was awful • 1861

141—Chapter Eighteen • Submissiveness is not my role • 1862

148—Chapter Nineteen • The only comfort in all this misery • 1861–63

158—Chapter Twenty • A volcano under that exterior • 1863–65

165—Chapter Twenty-one • Out of the dead, cold ashes • 1865–69

177—Chapter Twenty-two • Rouse yourself • 1869–1875

184—Chapter Twenty-three • The Joan of Arc of Carolina • 1876–1893

192—Chapter Twenty-four • We do not forget! • 1894–1899

199—Epilogue

203—Appendix A   On Leaving Villa De Lanski

206—Appendix B   Pickens Genealogy

208—Appendix C   Holcombe Genealogy

211—Notes

235—Bibliography

243—Index

List of Illustrations following page 100

1. Philemon Holcombe
2. Dorothea Eugenia Hunt Holcombe
3. Anna Eliza and Lucy Petway Holcombe, circa 1846–48
4. Beverly Lafayette Holcombe and unknown man
5. Philemon Eugene Holcombe
6. Theodore John Hunt Holcombe
7. Helen Holcombe
8. Anna Eliza Holcombe Greer, circa 1851
9. Lucy Holcombe, circa 1850–58
10. Francis Wilkinson Pickens, circa 1858–60
11. Lucy Holcombe Pickens, circa 1858
12. Tsar Alexandra II
13. Tsarina Maria Alexandrovna
14. Lucy Holcombe Pickens and daughter, Douschka, 1859
15. Mumka with Douschka
16. Lucinda with Douschka in Russia, 1859
17. Lucy Holcombe Pickens and stepdaughter Jeannie reviewing troops of the Holcombe Legion, 1861
18. Lucy Holcombe Pickens, Confederate States of America one hundred dollar bill
19. Lucy Holcombe Pickens as a young widow, 1870
20. Wyalusing in winter, circa 1860s–70s
21. Lucinda with Lucy's granddaughter, Lucy Francis Dugas, circa 1883
22. Douschka with daughter, Adrienne Dorothea Rebecca Dugas, 1887
23. The Mount Vernon Ladies' Association Council, 1883
24. Lucy Holcombe Pickens in the1890s
25. Bust of Lucy Holcombe Pickens

Preface

Paul Rigali, a Civil war buff in Houston, Texas, told me that the only woman to have her image engraved on Confederate paper currency was a Texan. I dismissed the statement as another Texas brag. To prove his point, Mr. Rigali produced Confederate one dollar and one hundred-dollar bills engraved with the image of Lucy Holcombe Pickens of Marshall, Texas. Curiosity led me to Marshall's Harrison County Historical Museum. Their files contain numerous news clippings that reveal the adulation once given to this Texas girl who became the wife of the Confederate governor of South Carolina. Headlines heralded Lucy as the "Uncrowned Queen of the Confederacy." Other articles claimed a "Fleur de Luce" following that compared Lucy to Scarlett of *Gone With the Wind*. With such accolades, why had this nineteenth century woman slipped into obscurity?

A fortunate meeting with a reporter for the Marshall newspaper led me to Jefferson, Texas, to hear the fascinating monologue, "Miss Lucy," written and performed by Marcia Thomas. Captivated by "Miss Lucy," I sought out descendants in Texas and other Southern states, for Lucy was born in Tennessee and (when not in Texas or Russia) lived most of her adult life in South Carolina. These descendants shared letters, journals, and photographs that show Lucy Holcombe Pickens to be a woman of strong character with a fervent belief in woman's changing place in the hidebound patriarchal nineteenth century South.

A journal kept by Lucy's mother, Eugenia Dorothea Vaughan Hunt Holcombe, revealed family events and problems. This prompted further research. University library archives, museums, and historical societies gave access to a wealth of Holcombe and Pickens letters, Lucy's poetry, her collected writing, and her published historical novel written at age nineteen.

Lucy's character is shown in the letters of her mother, Eugenia

Dorothea Hunt Holcombe, who wrote in 1846, "Lucy is lively, full of imagination, has a great regard for truth and is sensitive to a fault." These accolades are buffered by further revelations that, "Lucy procrastinates . . . is rather lazy, has no order and is inclined to carelessness . . . "[1]

Her personality and physical attributes are seen through the eyes of many beaux and the courtship letters of Francis Wilkinson Pickens, the man she would marry. But it is Lucy's published historical novel, her unpublished manuscripts, and collected writings that are most significant. Written on numerous sheets of paper loosely bound together, Lucy penned her opinion of American womanhood, her ideals and ambitions, her attempts at novel writing, and her poetry. From these first-hand accounts, Lucy evolves from a precocious child and Southern belle to a woman of direction. Like other educated and privileged young women in the nineteenth century, she sought independence but within the framework of the patriarchal South. In so doing she tacitly resisted the pressure to fill merely a maternal role.

By her writings she showed herself to be in sympathy with Elizabeth Cady Stanton and other champions of Women's Rights, yet she did not share their political demands. Lucy held strongly to her conviction that a woman of intelligence should contribute to society in a creditable manner. In carrying out her convictions, she never sought to overthrow the network of loyalty to family, husband and the South, including an unquestioned acceptance of slavery. However, Lucy tempered that acceptance, and quite possibly salved her conscience, by teaching her slaves to read and write, an act that was outlawed in many Southern states.

This story of Lucy Holcombe Pickens's life begins with a look at her family heritage and her Southern plantation environment with its restrictions, privileges and its slavery. Education in the North exposed Lucy to a different culture, and marriage took her to the Imperial Court of Russia, where she enjoyed the attentions of Tsar Alexander II and numerous royal courtiers. Gossip and jealousy followed this fascinating American beauty, while periods of debilitating homesickness kept her in a constant state of emotional turmoil. Returning to America 6 November 1860, the eve of the Civil War, Lucy made a momentous decision that affected the rest of her life.

Patriotic to the South, she cast her lot with the Confederacy and unstintingly gave of her wealth to further the "Cause." Lucy enjoyed some amount of influence while her husband, Francis Wilkinson Pickens, the wartime governor of South Carolina, threw his state into secession and the catastrophe that followed. With the fall of the Confederacy her position faded. Reconstruction years and personal tragedies tore at the heart of this Southerner but Lucy never accepted defeat, remaining in her own embittered way, loyal to the "Cause."

Lucy was not alone in her suffering nor did she have a monopoly on beauty, brains, and ambition. Many Southern women of her time excelled in all these areas yet found themselves limited by a restrictive society. Mary Boykin Chesnut, the renowned diarist, Virginia Clay-Copton, former wife of Senator Clay from Alabama, and Varina Davis, wife of Jefferson Davis, all spoke out in testimony to the changing concept of women's place outside the home.

Perceptive of women's strengths and man's foibles, Lucy wrote, "A woman with liberal information, one who comprehends fully and correctly, the principles and propriety, not only of the intellectual but social world, may exert on society a great and good influence."[2] By exercising these principles, based on education and a belief in women's need for independence, Lucy gained the recognition that she so coveted. In so doing, she never let it be forgotten that "submission is not my role, but certain platitudes on certain occasions are the innocent deceits of the sex."[3]

It is hoped that by the recounting of her story Lucy Holcombe Pickens may once again be seen as a noteworthy participant in the restrictive nineteenth century society in which she lived.

Acknowledgments

A life story of Lucy Petway Holcombe Pickens would not have been possible without the interest and cooperation of Lucy's great, great grandnieces, Gretta Greer Davis and Cherry Ann Greer Little. These sisters showed me their cache of Holcombe/Greer family letters, memorabilia, photographs, and the book, *Leaves from a Family Album, Holcombe and Greer* written by their parents, Jack and Jane Judge Greer. They also brought out that indispensable genealogy, *The Holcombes, Nation Builders*, compiled by Elizabeth Weir McPherson in 1947. To have such cooperation and interest over a considerable period of time is rare indeed and I am much indebted to these descendants of Lucy and their spouses.

Great grandniece, May Margaret Touhey of Marshall, Texas, told me of her grandfather, Philemon Eugene Holcombe, Lucy's brother. She also introduced me to the mysterious Caddo Lake, and over the best fresh fish dinner in Harrison County, Miss Touhey recounted the story of the Holcombe's exciting arrival in Texas. Miss Touhey's nephew, Dr. John Touhey, has continued her interest by giving access to family photographs.

The volunteers at the Marshall, Texas, Historical Museum, particularly Genell Barclay, started me on my search for missing pieces, a search that began with the viewing of Marcia Thomas's stage production, "Miss Lucy," in Jefferson, Texas. From here my search took me to Tennessee, Pennsylvania, North and South Carolina, Virginia, Louisiana, and back to Texas.

A distant Pickens relative, the gracious Augustus Graydon, urged me to come to Columbia, South Carolina. He showed me the site of Edgewood, past and present, shared family letters, and led me to Lucy's great granddaughter, Dorothea Adrienne Sheppard Jenkins Weston. Dorothea welcomed me with true Southern hospitality, family portraits, and a treasure trove of memorabilia. Her daughter, Adrienne Dugas

Moore and husband, Dr. Austin Moore, Jr., continue her interest and help. Another great granddaughter, the late Lucy Holcombe Sheppard Bradley, remembered Edgewood from summer visits as a small child. Holcombe relatives, Dr. and Mrs. David Wyatt Aiken of New Orleans made available unpublished family memoirs filled with a genial look at the times and mores of nineteenth century southern plantation society. These contacts with Lucy's relatives resulted in instant friendships.

In La Grange, Tennessee, Mr. and Mrs. Stanley Allen, present owners of the house in which Lucy was born, graciously showed us through the house and recounted incidents in Lucy's childhood. Jamie Evans of the Hobart Ames Foundation, clued me into the logistics and location of Woodstock, the Holcombe property near La Grange.

I soon discovered that librarians and custodians of archival collections are a researcher's best ally, and my thanks go to those in the following institutions for their invaluable help: John E. White of the Southern Historical Collection at University of North Carolina; Henry Fulmer and Laura Costello at the South Caroliniana Library, University of South Carolina at Columbia; C. Vaughan Stanley of Washington and Lee University Library; Reverend Vernon Nelson at Moravian College, Bethlehem, Pennsylvania; and William R. Erwin, Jr., Special Collections Library, Duke University at Chapel Hill, North Carolina. At Rice University, Houston, Texas, Lynda Laswell Crist and Mary Seaton Dix of the Jefferson Davis Papers, and Nancy Boothe, director of the Woodson Archives, gave kindly advice.

The personnel at the Howard-Tilton Memorial Library of Tulane University, Hill Memorial Library at Louisiana State University, the Historical Society of Pennsylvania, South Carolina Historical Society, The James Buchanan Foundation, New Orleans Historical Collection, the Mount Vernon Ladies Association, the East Texas Baptist University Library, and the South Carolina Confederate Museum at Columbia; were all unstinting in their help. Personnel of Hardeman and Fayette County offices in Tennessee, Harrison County in Texas, and at the South Carolina State Archives, patiently steered me to the volumes of information that unraveled deeds, marriage records, and wills.

To put this wealth of information together was daunting. Armed with moral support and guidance gained from courses at Rice University taught by Christopher Woods, I dug in. The stack of rough drafts and revised manuscripts grew at an alarming rate. Reviewers comments spurred me on and I would like to thank especially the following academics and historians for their advice: Mary Robertson of Savannah, Georgia; Elizabeth John of Austin, Texas; Alexander Moore of South Carolina; William Seale of Washington, D. C.; Martha Swain of Mississippi; and Mary Lenn Dixon of College Station, Texas. Their interest and suggestions were invaluable.

Others not directly connected with universities and libraries have also encouraged me. Margaret Holley was determined that the story of Lucy's life and times should be told. The late Carmen Anderson, along with Joy Glass, Carolyn Wells, and all members of the Campanile Writers, listened and offered advice. Ed and Elsie Ekholm talked me through problems while the late Shirley Brooks Greene believed that "Lucy" showed great potential. However, it was my nephew, Samuel Wittenmyer Williams, who introduced me to the person who gave me the greatest boost, Elizabeth A. John.

My sons, daughters-in-law, and my grandchildren, Emily and Robert, pressed me to persevere. Robert, a future historian, helped me over the thornier paths of syntax but the publication of my first biography could not have been accomplished without the kind assistance of Ron Chrisman and Paula Oates. I look forward to being around long enough to work with Ron, Paula, and the University of North Texas Press again.

Through all the trials, disappointments, joys, and frustrations, my husband spurred me onward and faithfully joined me in trips across country. He tramped through cemeteries, suggested possible leads, drove up blind alleys, fed the parking meters, paid fines, read rough drafts, and all with few complaints, providing the end of the day's work would be rewarded by a gastronomic discovery.

To each and every one, and to those whom I have failed to name but who are known in my heart, I sincerely thank you for standing by in my pursuit of the real Lucy.

Elizabeth Wittenmyer Lewis

Principal Characters

Major Philemon Holcombe—Lucy's paternal grandfather, Revolutionary War hero

Lucy Maria Anderson Holcombe—Lucy's paternal grandmother, blood relation to Marie Antoinette

Beverly Lafayette Holcombe—Lucy's father, youngest son of Major and Lucy Maria Holcombe

Eugenia Dorothea Vaughn Hunt Holcombe—Lucy's mother, wife of Beverly Holcombe

John Hunt—Lucy's maternal grandfather, father of Eugenia

The children of Beverly and Eugenia Holcombe:
> Anna Eliza
> Lucy Petway Holcombe Pickens (non de plume H. M. Hardimann)
> John Theodore Hunt
> Martha Maria Edgeworth
> Philemon Eugene
> Helen, adopted

Elkanah Bracken Greer—husband of Anna Eliza

Beverly Holcombe Robertson—Lucy's first cousin and ardent admirer

Dr. William Henry Holcombe—Lucy's cousin, of Louisiana

Maria Hawley—governess to Holcombe children

Mr. C. H. Alexander—friend, builder, and entrepreneur.

Mr. S. H. Mathews—La Grange, Tennessee merchant and family friend

"Uncle" Nat Willis—friend, of La Grange, Tennessee

The Reverend Henry Shultz—Headmaster at the Moravian Female Academy

St. George S. Lee—an early suitor of Lucy's

Reverend Staples—Presbyterian preacher, of Marshall, Texas

Miss Arletta June—teacher and friend, of Marshall, Texas
Mr. Dunlap—friend, of Marshall, Texas
John Quitman—friend, Governor of Mississippi
General Narciso Lopez—leader of filibuster expedition to Cuba
Lieutenant William Logan Crittenden—member of expedition to
    Cuba and supposedly engaged to Lucy
Laurent J. Sigur—financial backer of Bahia Honda filibuster
    expedition
Ambrose Jose Gonzales—confidant and countryman of General Lopez
Fleming Gardner—suitor and fiancée of Lucy, "Mr. Darbey"
Mrs. Wilhelmina McCord—New Orleans editor
Jemine—dressmaker who lived with the Holcombes at Wyalusing
Mrs. Atha—friend, of Marshall, Texas

Holcombe House Servants:
    Lucinda—Lucy's personal maid
    Ned Hood—"Uncle Neelus"
    Aunt Viney
    Beatrice
    Honey
    Caroline
    Celah
    Charley—orphaned slave cared for by Holcombes
    Ernest

Francis Wilkinson Pickens—Lucy Petway Holcombe's husband,
    wealthy landowner, State Senator, U. S. Congressman, U. S.
    Minister to Russia, Governor of South Carolina
Susan Lipscomb—daughter by Pickens's first marriage
Eliza—daughter by Pickens's first marriage
Maria Pickens Butler—Pickens's daughter by first marriage
Rebecca Pickens Bacon—Pickens's daughter by first marriage
Jeannie Pickens Whately—Pickens's daughter by second marriage
Francis Eugenia Olga Neva "Douschka" Pickens—Pickens's daugh-
    ter by Lucy (third marriage)

Mathew Galbraith Butler—husband of Maria Pickens
John E. Bacon—husband of Rebecca Pickens
Tsar Alexander II and Tsarina Maria Alexandrovna of Russia.
James Buchanan, President of the United States—1856–1860
Duke de Osuna of Spain—Lucy's admirer
Clara Victoria Dargan MacLean—Lucy's friend, writer
Ellen Middleton—Lucy's friend
Floride Cunningham—Lucy's friend
Mary Boykin Chesnut—Civil War diarist and rival of Lucy

Pickens House Servants:
    Tom
    Uncle Harper
    Aunt Mary Johnson
    Aunt Betty
    Wallace
    Aunt Charlotte
    Caroline
    Alfred
    Bess

QUEEN OF THE CONFEDERACY

CHAPTER ONE

1830–1840

Changing Times

*L*ucy Petway Holcombe was nineteen when her fiancé was killed in a filibustering expedition to free Cuba from the bondage of Spanish rule. The year was 1851 and the young girl expressed her feelings by writing, "What life is more sublime than one given to a nation struggling for the principles of moral and political freedom?"[1] Sentiment such as this, typical of Victorian prose, was just as typically forgotten, but not by Lucy. She patterned her life on noble principles with an eye to her own interests and strove to be worthy of her patriotic heritage, a heritage that began in America in the seventeenth century with the arrival of William Holcombe of Pembrokeshire, Wales.

William Holcombe settled in the tidewater lands of Virginia.[2] Succeeding generations of Holcombes followed William's example of faith in this new land. Lucy's much-lauded grandfather, Philemon Holcombe III, served in General Washington's army and rose from the ranks to become a major. He saw action with General Harry Lee's Light Horse Brigade and served as aide-de-camp to the Marquis de Lafayette at the siege of Yorktown.[3] The Major's wartime tales of surviving on parched corn and sweet potatoes amused his grandchildren. Lucy, however, was more impressed by his marriage in 1781 to Lucy Maria Anderson, a blood relation of the French Queen, Marie Antionette.[4]

After the wars, Major Holcombe and Lucy Maria settled in Amelia County, Virginia, on his father's 800-acre plantation, The Oaks, near Seven Pines. Here they raised a large family of ten children, the last of whom, born in 1806, was Beverly Lafayette, the father of Lucy Holcombe Pickens. Years later, Lucy's older sister, Anna Eliza, was to say of their grandmother, "She petted especially her little namesake, my sister, Lucy, saying, 'There never was a sweeter child.'"[5]

The Holcombe plantation thrived until successive years of crop failure resulted in Major Philemon Holcombe's ruin as a farmer. In an effort to rebuild their fortune, Major Holcombe and Lucy Maria, now in their sixties, resolved to move to the "Congressional Reservation" of Western Tennessee. Here the soil was said to be rich and ideal for raising cotton.[6]

They left The Oaks in the care of an elder son, and with household belongings loaded onto wagons, headed westward early in January 1828. Their unmarried son, Beverly Lafayette, and two married daughters, Frances and husband Thomas Watkins, and Amanda with husband George Wyett, accompanied them.[7] The Holcombe caravan of many wagons, carriages, slaves, horses, and livestock traveled over rutted roads and unbroken land. At night the large party made a wondrous sight, bedded down in tents and wagons and ringed by numerous campfires, livestock, and dogs. Sometime in March of 1828, they reached Fayette County, Tennessee, and the village of La Grange on the Wolf River.[8] It would seem their destination was not chosen haphazardly. La Grange was named for the summer home of Major Holcombe's idol, the Marquis de Lafayette. Major Holcombe purchased an old house in the village and acreage to plant in cotton and wheat.

Sometime during that first year, possibly while wintering in New Orleans, Beverly Holcombe met seventeen-year-old Eugenia Dorothea Vaughan Hunt, elder daughter of John Hunt, a wealthy land-owner near La Grange.[9] They were married in July of 1829 by Wiley B. Peck, and Eugenia wrote in her journal, "Very happy prayed that my mother might know it, husband 24 years old, handsome, very erect, weight 156. Six feet high, brave, manly, generous, polite and courteous to all, a great favorite with my best of fathers, and idol of mine."[10]

It is presumed that the births of their five children took place at La Grange in the white frame house called Ingleside owned by Eugenia's father.[11] In this bucolic setting on 29 December 1830, their first born, Anna Eliza arrived.[12] The child showed promise of beauty at an early age. Her brown eyes looked serenely on the world, but beyond the quiet confines of "Ingleside," the nation experienced rapid, and not always welcome, changes under the presidency of Andrew Jackson.

The United States of America, consisting of twenty-four states in 1830, boasted thirteen million inhabitants sprinkled throughout cities, villages, and remote settlements. Trade and commerce flourished, bringing change economically, socially, and politically. Two competing political parties, the Whigs and the Democrats, emerged, splitting the people. Because of disputes with President Jackson over a national bank, the various local banks closed. Then Jackson, in a move that caused much grief, forcibly moved the Native American Indians, the Cherokees, from their home grounds in the southeast to reservations west of the Mississippi River.

During this time of turbulence and change, Anna Eliza's antithesis arrived. The Holcombes' second child, Lucy, was born 11 June 1832, a time when the sweet scent of magnolia blossoms lay heavy on the summer breeze. Eugenia Dorothea Vaughan Hunt Holcombe cradled her newborn daughter and examined each tiny feature. Satisfied that her "summer child" was perfect in every way, Eugenia kissed the babe and named her for her two grandmothers vowing, "that so fair a bud should not be reared in sin."[13]

Christened Lucy Petway Holcombe, this child began life in the slave-holding plantation society of western Tennessee. By dint of her personality, intellect, and desire for independence, she would gain some recognition in her time.

Lucy brought much joy to her family with her happy disposition and enthusiasm, a perfect foil for her older sister's serious, sensible ways. Her red-gold curls and large, deep-blue eyes marked her as a pretty child although her features were thought not to be as fine as those of her older sister. Lucy's personality made up for any physical flaws and she looked with eagerness on a world from which she excluded everything but beauty, happiness, and herself. Once reminded by her mother that one must have direction and usefulness to find happiness, Lucy replied, "No, Mama, happy people are the most useful because they haven't anything else to do. You may find an example in myself."

"Ah, but Lucy, my dear," her mother reminded, "one cannot walk through life with no better guide than its own rash dictates. Flowers grow in our path but thorns flourish there too."

"We need only pluck the flowers," the young Lucy answered. "But, you are right, Mama, and between you and Anna Eliza I have great hopes for myself."[14]

The Holcombes delighted in their two daughters but expressed great hopes for a son and two years after Lucy's birth, John Theodore Hunt was born 3 February 1834. Named for his maternal grandfather, "Thee" as he was affectionately known, possessed many of the happy traits of his sister Lucy. His mother prayed that Theodore might study for the church but the boy managed to avoid studious pursuits. Tall and handsome with the Holcombe blue eyes, Thee was more inclined to read novels and hunt with his dogs.[15] The third daughter, Martha Maria Edgeworth, arrived 16 November 1836. A precocious child, Martha Maria called herself "Ladybug." She died from the croup at three years of age. Her mother had her portrait painted showing a tiny ladybug on the hem of her dress.[16] Philemon Eugene was born 24 October 1838. Named for his paternal grandfather, Philemon suffered deafness at an early age, an affliction that later did not hinder the skill of this tall, athletic hunter.[17] Both parents encouraged the children to do well and bring honor to the family. Their gentle, loving mother, a devout Presbyterian, also instructed her children in reading, writing, arithmetic, and music.

The children's father made certain that each one "sat a horse" as befitted their Virginia ancestry. Emphasis was placed on their heritage and Lucy, impressed by her paternal great-grandmother's claim of royal lineage,[18] wrapped herself in a cocoon of pride. In the antebellum South, ancestry and honor ranked above wealth in determining social standing. Thus, other peoples' perception of her honorable ancestors gave Lucy her identity and strengthened her loyalty to her own family. It may also have accounted for her rebellious impatience with rule or rulers, said to be a characteristic of the Holcombes.[19]

In 1839 Beverly moved his family from the village of La Grange to a house called Westover in the settlement of Woodstock on the Wolf River.[20] This Fayette county site lay several miles north of La Grange and south of Somerville, the county seat.[21] On these nine hundred acres he established a cotton plantation and valued this productive land at twenty dollars an acre.[22] The greater part of his property was contiguous to that owned by John Hunt. Eugenia hinted in her diary that her "kind and good father" influenced or helped in the purchase.[23] Although John Hunt had children by another marriage, it is apparent from Eugenia's many references to her father's generosity that he favored her, his oldest child.

Isolated from the village of La Grange, the Holcombe children played with the young slave children. Some antebellum Southerners warned that slave playmates set bad examples and, conversely, close contact with slave children gave White children a demeaning sense of superiority.[24] This supposition did not seem to apply to the Holcombes who seemed to treat their slaves humanely. They clothed and housed them decently, and, in spite of the law forbidding teaching slaves, the Holcombes gave their slaves lessons in reading and writing and made a point of referring to them as "servants." Nevertheless, these servants were still human beings in bondage.[25]

In these first few years on their plantation, the physical stress of childbirth and the duties as plantation mistress severely taxed Eugenia's health. She employed Maria Hawley, a spinster teacher from

Kentucky, to serve as her companion and governess to the children.[26] Eugenia described the somewhat severe and opinionated Miss Hawley as, "one of the excellent of earth, yes lovely in person and character."[27] Lucy, then seven years of age, was allowed to accompany her governess on a visit to Louisville, Kentucky.[28]

Early on a windy March morning in 1840, Lucy embarked on her first adventure away from home and mother. High-wheeled stagecoaches followed the slightly graded Stage Road from Somerville to Bolivar, a distance of about fifteen miles. After Bolivar the condition of the roads changed from graded to little more than rough paths for the several hundred-mile trip to Louisville. From sunup to sunset passengers bounced about on the stiff-backed coach seats. Every ten to twenty miles the coachman pulled up for a rest and a change of team. By the end of each day, tired, shaken, and appalled by the crowded inns and the greasy, tasteless food, the travelers fell into fitful sleep in beds that very often accommodated other occupants. After four or five strenuous days and sleepless nights, under none too clean conditions, they reached Louisville.

A pall of smoke hung over this busy port town on the Kentucky and Ohio Rivers. With youthful enthusiasm, the child begged her governess to take her at once to see the sights. Miss Hawley, exhausted from the trip, resisted. Not used to being thwarted, Lucy's deep blue eyes overflowed with tears. She shook her curls, stamped her foot and screamed, all her sweet, endearing ways forgotten. Three days of Lucy's screaming fits sickened her hosts. Bribery and persuasion could not pacify the spoiled and now homesick child and Miss Hawley could no longer stand her temper tantrums. She took Lucy and boarded a steamboat for the trip down the Ohio and Mississippi rivers. At Memphis they took the coach for the fifty-mile drive to Somerville, Tennessee. Here Miss Hawley set the child on the back of a horse, behind a gentleman, and instructed him to take her home to Woodstock.[29]

They started off, the horse plodding along the ten miles of an old Indian path that led through the forest to the Holcombe property. Twigs snapped beneath the horse's hooves—gun shots in the child's imagination—just as each dark tree trunk hid an Indian. After what must have seemed an eternity to Lucy, the red glow of sunset lighted a clearing at the end of the trail. If she peeked around the gentleman's broad back, she would see the tall chimneys of her home and smell the wood smoke curling upward. When brother Thee came running through the fields with his dogs it would be like Lucy to slip down from the horse and run laughing and screaming to roll and tumble with her brother.

Home at last, petted and praised, Lucy did not let her mother out of her sight. "Poor child, so tender, so loving, so strangely devoted to me, her father thinks she will die if she is ever separated from me . . ."[30]

CHAPTER TWO

1840–1846

"Riches have taken to themselves wings and flown away."
Eugenia Dorothea Holcombe

*L*ucy, born into an antebellum, slave-holding society, would be aware of the responsibility and demands of this oppressive system that the mistress of the plantation helped maintain.[1] From dawn to dusk she would see her mother tend to the basic needs of the slaves and to the instruction and supervision of work. Everything was taught and done by hand on the premises—butchering, preserving, canning, soap making, butter churning, spinning, weaving, and sewing. The once-a-year supplies and storehouse of provisions were kept under locks, the keys fastened to the mistress's belt. Duties did not end with directing daily chores. Lucy might see her mother called out in the night to tend the sick, say prayers for the dying, or help with the birthing of a slave-child.

Slavery may have been essential to the South's economy and, as a social system, shaped the lives of its womenfolk.[2] The Southern plantation mistress found herself locked into a position of isolation, sometimes in a hostile environment. Very often she had only her children and female house slaves for company. Tired and often distraught with worry and concern, she might take comfort in her religion. Religious convictions lay at the heart of the countrywoman's struggle to know herself and to apply that knowledge so as to live and die a Christian woman.[3] Eugenia was no exception. With her prayers and Bible readings she imparted the tenets of the Presbyterian Church to her children and to her slaves.

Letter writing and journal keeping served as an emotional release and temporary respite from her responsibilities. Visits by relatives and friends, though welcomed, doubled the domestic demands, and travel away from the plantation was frowned upon unless accompanied by a male member of the family or an older friend. This situation was bound to stymie the personal development of the plantation mistress.

Before Eugenia Holcombe's marriage, she had received a fine classical education from Reverend Philip S. Fall, in Nashville, Tennessee.[4] Ambitious and talented, Eugenia's mental attainments overshadowed those of her husband. It is most likely that Beverly Lafayette Holcombe, as the youngest and favorite son, pursued his love of horse breeding and racing rather than scholastics. A handsome, soft-spoken, generous man, with quite possibly a roving eye, Beverly continued his role of master-in-absentia, leaving Eugenia in full charge of the plantation. Having provided his wife with a home, children, servants, and a place in society, it probably never occurred to him that she would want anything more from life. Eugenia, on the other hand, may have felt trapped. She writes in her journal, "Nine years has robbed this world of many of its charms and shown me men and women as they are not as imagination painted them."[5] Later she added, "A new year has commenced and with it a renewed desire to serve God better, to read the blessed Bible more, to pray more for my dear wayward thoughtless husband."[6]

Eugenia feared for her daughters and did not want them to experience this form of feminine defeat. She felt it critical that they receive a fine education and wrote in her journal, "I wish for my precious daughters to be carefully educated and thoroughly informed, so highly accomplished in all things that would add to their happiness. A good education will make them independent."[7] She began by introducing Anna Eliza and Lucy to the works of Robert Burns, Lord Byron, and Sir Walter Scott. Lucy, a bright, inquisitive child, added to these literary offerings her own favorites, *The Fanciful Tales of Fashionable Women* by Maria Edgeworth and *Godey's Lady's Book*.[8] Wishing her daughters to be musically accomplished, Eugenia taught them to play her prized piano. Anna Eliza showed a fine talent for the piano but Lucy, fondly called "Petty" or "Push," preferred to sing, admitting that she wanted to be admired facing an appreciative audience.[9]

In the winter of 1839, the third daughter, Martha Maria died. Crushed by the loss of her child, Eugenia took to her bed and relied on Miss Hawley for supervision of the children. Two years later, an entry in her diary mentions that Philemon suffered a glandular swelling under his right jaw, thought to be a scrofula caused by the whooping cough. Doctor Biggs of La Grange recommended a trip south to New Orleans for consultation. Before leaving 18 January 1841, Eugenia requested that, "Miss M. Hawley be given the entire control of my darling children." Then she added to her journal, "Farewell and God bless you dear ones. Adieu."[10]

Accompanied by a nursemaid, Eugenia and Philemon boarded the stern-wheeler *Lady of Lyons* at Memphis on 23 January 1841. As soon as the steamboat pulled away from shore, one passenger, a Dr. Martin from Louisville, paid particular attention to Eugenia and her child. Without consulting the mother, Dr. Martin took Philemon off and vaccinated him. The child burned with fever for several days. When the fever broke the scrofula had vanished, but Philemon would suffer from deafness.[11]

After several weeks of rest and visiting with relatives in New Orleans, Eugenia, on some whim or possibly deliberately, went to the New Orleans Orphanage. The matron entered with a small child in her arms. The child looked at Eugenia, held out her arms, and cried, "Mama, Mama." Tears poured down Eugenia's cheeks and she could barely control her emotions. The matron said the child came to the orphanage after losing her parents and home in a violent tornado that swept through Natchez.[12] Amazed at this child's resemblance to her own lost babe, Eugenia begged the matron to let her take the child. She believed that Providence had sent her to the orphanage and she promised to advertise for the parents. Apparently no one answered and the Holcombes, although they never formally adopted the foundling, raised her as their own daughter. They named her Helen.[13]

On returning home with a recovered Philemon and a new daughter, Eugenia's joy was short-lived. The cash box was empty and their wealth, measured by the cotton harvest, had dwindled owing to her husband's folly. Beverly Lafayette, singularly generous and impetuous of nature, had attended the horse races at Holly Springs, Mississippi. The performance of a certain horse so excited him that he sprang to his feet and bet the yield of his entire cotton crop on that horse to win the race. The bet was taken, the horse beaten, and Beverly Holcombe lost thousands of dollars.[14]

Shortly after this depletion of the family's wealth, Mr. C. H. Alexander, a family friend and entrepreneur who dealt in Texas properties, prevailed upon Beverly to co-sign a bank loan. Beverly complied, giving his Woodstock home as collateral. Alexander defaulted on payment. Beverly lost their home, and Eugenia took to her sick bed. The Woodstock property that Beverly lost was most likely given to Eugenia by her father, John Hunt, but on marriage, antebellum law decreed that all property belonged to the husband. However, this law did not apply to Texas. In 1837, Mr. Alexander had sold "for the consideration of eight thousand dollars,"[15] sixteen acres of land in Marshall, Texas, to Eugenia Dorothea Hunt Holcombe.

The loss of the family wealth made a profound impression on Lucy.

Eugenia blamed their misfortunes on her husband's refusal to attend church. His frequent absences from home distressed her. No doubt aware that she was the better manager, but following her designated role in society, she acquiesced to her husband's judgment. With admirable tact she told him what to do in a lengthy, undated letter probably written sometime in the year 1841. A portion of the letter follows.

"Dearly beloved Companion and Husband, . . . I have and do love you, as well as woman ever lovd [*sic*], and I have frequently thought since you left: if our blessed Maker, sees proper to remove me, and be denied the sight of you again, and for you, not to Smooth my pillow while dying it will be just Punishment for us both . . . I often think my death would be the sacrifice to be offered up, before you would embrace Religion . . . and pray and hope you may be a bright and shining Christian."[16]

Much affected by his wife's confession of love, Beverly Lafayette Holcombe wrote on the outside of the letter, "To be kept sacred for my wife's sake." He then joined the church and, for good measure, took the Temperance Pledge.[17]

Fearing for her children's education, Eugenia turned to Miss Hawley for advice. The resourceful governess proposed enrolling the girls in a school in New Albany, Indiana, taught by her brother-in-law. Miss Hawley reminded Eugenia that Anna, a budding beauty at twelve years of age, would be away from her Uncle George Wyett, whose attentions were not as innocent as they should be.[18] Lucy, with childish determination, refused to go. Perhaps she remembered a previous unhappy trip with the governess.

Soon homesick letters arrived from Anna. Miss Hawley, insolent and intruding, appended a message, "My Dear Madam, Mr Wyatt [*sic*] informed me that Mr H [Holcombe] was obligated to pay thirty five hundred dollars per year to the bank—and he thought or feared he could not do it—I more than fear it —I think I know it, so if all your hopes of eight years prosperity depend upon that contingency—farewell to the delusive idea. You will be disappointed. I am sorry to write unpleasant things but still more sorry to see you trusting to a broken reed. Yours ever, Maria"[19]

Miss Hawley is never again mentioned in letters or journals. Anna returned home and her mother wrote in her journal, "Great have been my worldly afflictions, riches have taken to themselves wings and flown away, summer friends went with them. My home is changed, all is gone."[20]

Faced with the loss of income and home, Eugenia turned to her father, John Hunt, for help over this difficult period. He provided for their use the two story clapboard house called Ingleside, now known as Westover, and located in La Grange.[21]

Double front porches with unusual fan-shaped windows above the wide doors distinguished Ingleside from the other fine homes in La Grange. Ship-lapped cypress board covered the house, and tall, brick chimneys at either end provided draft for fireplaces in each of the four large rooms. An L-shaped extension along one side served as storage. At the end of the spacious center hall, a curving staircase led to the upstairs rooms. Anna Eliza's initials remain carved into the mantelpiece in the bedroom she claimed for herself and her sisters.[22] The kitchen, a separate building behind the house, was built with a brick floor as a fire preventive. Washing and cooking kettles hung from iron pegs over the large, open fireplace.

Once settled at Ingleside, Lucy and Anna enrolled in the first La Grange Female Seminary. Mr. T. Booth, the schoolmaster, charged $7.50 per quarter for each girl and gave lessons in simple mathematics, English grammar, and penmanship.[23] Classes were held in the students' home as a facility for the La Grange Female Seminary was not built until 1851. Eugenia continued to supervise the girls' religious instruction mentioning in her journal attending Bethany Presbyterian Church in Glade Springs. This church is no longer standing and, according to Bolivar County Records and Presbyterian Church Historical files, all records have been lost. It is probable that the Holcombes also attended services at Immanuel Episcopal Church in La Grange, the oldest Episcopal Church in West Tennessee. It was common practice for people of different faiths to worship wherever they could be accommodated until their own church was built.

Having a place to worship on the Sabbath and living closer to her father and members of the Hunt family must have pleased Eugenia. Falling into the daily pattern of social calls, she found many friends among the inhabitants of the village. Lucy and Anna Eliza busied themselves with parties, carriage rides, picnics, attending the medieval tournaments enacted by the young men, and taking part in the popular May Day Fete. For this yearly event, virginal white dresses trimmed in colorful ribbons, white kidskin slippers and gloves to match replaced the usual dress of pinafores and coveralls.[24] As evening darkened the sky, feet tapped out the rhythm of "Shoo-fly Girl" and fiddles marked time for the strenuous dance called a "German" and for the more sedate quadrilles.

Suitors from La Grange and neighboring Holly Springs, Mississippi, found their way to Ingleside. They called with flowers, hastily plucked from the garden, to be placed in the adored one's hair or pressed between the leaves of a book of poems. Daguerreotypes and locks of hair tied in ribbons found their way into gold lockets worn about the neck or held in vest pockets. The girls were always chaperoned by their mother, a female relative, or an older household slave, while the gentlemen callers joined in the entertainment of poetry readings, games of whist, charades, or musical accomplishments.

Lucy no doubt preferred to ride her horse with her brothers or wander through the fields picking berries with the slave children. Sometimes she accompanied her mother to the "black peoples' graveyard" and laid flowers on the moss covered mounds.[25] Returning from these excursions, blue eyes dark and wild with excitement, she laughed and sang—

> I've been -
> Down the lake
> Up the hill
> To the quarter
> And over the mill[26]

Eugenia, noting Lucy's carefree, impulsive behavior and Anna Eliza's emergence into young womanhood, decided the time had come to send them to a school of higher education. An education would confer a mark of gentility and make her daughters worthy of protection, admiration and chivalry. It would also better equip them for marriage and motherhood.[27] The idea of education for females had already escalated in the Northern states. Emma Willard's Seminary in Troy, New York, had offered higher education to females since 1821. Mount Holyoke in Massachusetts and Oberlin College in Ohio had admitted women by 1837. These institutions were followed in the South by a spurt of "French Schools" emphasizing what was known as a polite education and accomplishments.[28] Later called "Academies," the schools offered a formal curriculum of liberal arts, French and German language, instruction in ladylike values and etiquette, and the ornamental branches of needlework.

Many schools were church-related, notably the Moravian Seminaries for Young Females in Salem, North Carolina, and at Bethlehem, Pennsylvania. This religious sect from Bohemia had sought refuge in America in the early 1700s. By hard work, self-denial and application of the teachings of Christ, they established communities and schools for their own brethren and worked hard to convert the Indians to Christianity.[29] The Moravians stood high in the estimation of the Holcombe family. Lucy's grandfather, Major Philemon Holcombe, and his idol, the Marquis de Lafayette, had been cared for by this religious sect at Bethlehem during the American Revolutionary War. Impressed by their kindness and methods of education, these patriots implored the Moravians to open their schools to girls of other faiths. They did so at Bethlehem in 1785 and a little later at Salem.

The Moravians' regimen of moral and religious training and their austerity appealed to Eugenia. She wanted Lucy and Anna to have exposure to other cultures and favored the Bethlehem school over the one at Salem in the slave-holding South, expressing the desire that her daughters be self sufficient and not dependent on servants.[30] It is interesting to note that Eugenia recognized problems with the patriarchal slave-holding South. At one time she remarks after visiting their graves, "Oh that I may meet them in the world to come with a clear conscience."[31]

While Eugenia worried about her daughter's education and her slaves, Beverly's attention centered on news of territory west of the Mississippi River. Stephen Austin, the entrepreneur who had obtained a sizeable land grant from the Mexican government, called this territory the Republic of Texas. Austin traveled to Kentucky, and in stirring speeches promised acreage to those who would help protect these lands from the Indians and keep the Mexicans from taking them back.[32] The offer interested Beverly Holcombe. He wanted to add to the tract of Texas land deeded to Eugenia Holcombe "in consideration of eight thousand dollars" paid to Mr. Charles H. Alexander.[33] He would plant the Texas acreage in cotton and wheat in hopes of recouping his lost fortune.

When Anna and Lucy received a letter from Texas written by Thomas N. Polk, a friend of theirs from La Grange, their father's interest heightened. The letter, dated 13 December 1845, is written from Washington City, Texas, later named Washington-on-the Brazos. Polk writes—

> "I will give you a short sketch of our travel after getting in Texas . . . We joined the balance of the Party at San Augustine and there we met with some rough customers. It is rather a mean looking town and not many inhabitants . . . We went on to Nacogdoches . . . where we met with some of the ranghers [*sic*]—and most uncivilized and perfect rowdys that ever lived—that is the town in which the Fredonia war was fought in 1826 . . . On yesterday we came into the most beautiful and lovely-looking country under the blue canopy of Heaven . . . the country to feast the eyes upon—it is a large Prairie that we traveled all day and yesterday . . . . on our right hand we could see as far as the eye could reach over live woodland with cedar and other evergreens interspersed and on the other hand extended the immense Prairie with clumps of Live Oak in Places and cedar in others—
>
> We will go from Bastrop to the City of Austin which is the capital of the Republic and at which place the supreme court is now in session—Some of the United States forces are stationed now at Austin to run off the Indians and the Lawyers have to go in crowds when they go to court—The Indians come down at night—between Bastrop and Austin and steal a great many horses and get out of the settlements before day— some few murders have been committed lately—We will try and ride through from Bastrop to Austin in one day . . . . The

baby of Flowers and the Sacred rock I will tell you of when I return. We will visit the Battleground of San Jacinto where there are many sculls [*sic*] to be seen now and I will pick up some musket balls to play checks with you and Lucy. We are now in about twelve miles of the region of wild horses and about thirty miles from a great many Buffalo which have been run down in this country by the Indians, but understand it is dangerous to go after them on account of Indians. We will go to La Grange [Texas] tomorrow . . . . We will spend Christmas in Bastrop."[34]

Beverly Holcombe's wanderlust was fired. He made frequent trips to Texas and bought more land in Harrison County with the intention of building a home in this new Republic.[35] While Beverly Holcombe's interests turned West toward Texas, his daughters began preparations to go North to school in Pennsylvania. The following year promised to be one that Lucy and Anna Eliza would never forget.

CHAPTER THREE

1846–1849

"If she wears blue stockings she contrives to let her petticoats hide them."
Lucy Petway Holcombe

*E*arly on a February morning in 1846, Lucy and Anna started their journey to the Moravian Seminary for Young Ladies in Bethlehem, Pennsylvania.[1] Shivering from cold and excitement, they'd be urged to hurry, as their father waited with the carriage. Off to the side, Mr. S. H. Mathews, entrusted as guardian to the Holcombe sisters on this voyage east, watched as the girls said their good-byes. A dry goods merchant in La Grange, Mathews traveled at least twice a year to Philadelphia for supplies including bolts of material and pattern pieces for the ladies. The fusty, aging bachelor would see that his "dear girls" received his undivided attention, particularly Miss Anna.

Hours later the travelers arrived at Memphis and boarded a paddle wheel steamboat, a relatively safe transport except for danger from exploding boilers. The novelty of the large, ornately decorated, three-decked boat would occupy the girls' attention as well as the ever-changing river scenery. They steamed up the Mississippi and Ohio rivers to the port at Wheeling in western Virginia and continued their journey by train and stage across the lush farmlands of Pennsylvania. Mr. Mathews told them of the sights they'd see in the big cities of the East and Lucy finally stopped her pouting and sniveling.[2] Three weeks after leaving La Grange, Tennessee, the tired travelers arrived in Philadelphia. The Holcombes had relatives in this city, in particular, Cousin Willie, a medical student at Philadelphia's Homeopathic Hospital. The hospital building was tucked among brick houses faced by cobblestone streets. Not far away stood Independence Hall and the newly built Carpenter's Hall. These sights and the numerous tall churches with needle-sharp spires would be new to the girls. Lucy, with her fondness for fashion, probably noticed the elegantly dressed women swishing by in bell-shaped skirts stiffened with layers of crinoline and hoops, and the top-hatted gentlemen in embroidered waistcoats and tight doeskin trousers.

The following Tuesday they boarded the Mail Stage for the fifty-mile ride to Bethlehem. The twelve-passenger stagecoach left promptly at 4:00 A.M. from Mr. George Yohe's Hotel, at the sign of General Washington, No. 6 North 4th Street.[3] The four-horse team raced across the countryside past snow-covered haystacks and columns of frozen corn stalks resembling scarecrows in the dimming light. At every ten to twenty mile way station, passengers eased their cold, cramped bodies, while a fresh team pawed the frozen ground, anxious to be off. As shades of night fell, the thrilling notes of the post horn announced their arrival at the Sun Hotel in Bethlehem.[4]

Sleepy, bewildered and already homesick, Lucy and Anna must have wept with gratitude when Mrs. Brock, the wife of the German innkeeper, gathered them in a motherly embrace.[5] Round, rosy-cheeked Mrs. Brock, speaking in the unfamiliar sing-song German accent, fussed like a mother hen over the little Southerners. A fire crackled in the hearth of the best chamber with its high, poster bed covered in quilts of red and green patterns. From the small, third-story windows, the girls could see the sleepy town dominated by the stone church, the Bell House and a cluster of large, four-story stone and brick buildings, the houses of the Sisters and the Brethren. These, Mrs. Brock informed them, were also used as classrooms and dormitories for the Seminary.

Reverend Henry Shultz presided as principal of the Seminary in 1846. Herr Shultz and his good wife were responsible for the education of the female boarders and their emotional, moral, and religious well being. As surrogate parents, they counseled the students and administered discipline when necessary. Forewarned of Lucy's tendency to homesickness, Herr Shultz assigned her a room with her sister in the older girls' dormitory.[6] Here, in the red brick building formerly used as the Brethren's House, they shared sleeping accommodations with twenty-two girls ranging in age from sixteen to eighteen. The 1846 roster listed 100 students, some of whom came from England, the West Indies, South America, and Canada, with the remainder from twenty-four of the United States.[7]

The required tuition for the Bethlehem Seminary in 1846 amounted to twenty pounds Pennsylvania currency[8] per student to cover courses in reading, writing, grammar, history, geography, arithmetic, plain sewing, and knitting. Further monies were required for the study of French, German and Italian, music instruction, drawing, and fancy embroidery.[9] Lucy's mother advised that they not take the "ornamental arts" but concentrate on learning German and French languages, and English grammar, reminding her daughters that grammar is to intellect as bones are to bodies.

The school day began at five o'clock in the morning with a clanging of bells. Shivering with cold and excitement, the students marched two-by-two to the washing room. Talking was forbidden. The breakfast bell rang at six and the girls' first complaint home concerned the steaming bowls of heavy Dutch food. Unperturbed, Eugenia advised her daughters to take out the tucks in their dresses. As a post-script she added, "Your dear Father says he has less fears for his children's health since he has heard of the fare . . . just how much did you weigh? Did you have many petticoats on when you weighed?"[10]

The rigid school program left little time for inner speculation and homesickness. Each afternoon at four o'clock, students assembled for what was called the "love feast," consisting of tea, ginger cookies, mail, and sociability.[11] The Holcombe sisters' first letter came from their faithful guardian and companion, Mr. S. H. Mathews, who requested, "Of Miss Anna I must claim the fulfilment [*sic*] of her promise, the wearing my likeness 'till we meet again."[12] Anna opened the gold and ruby locket to find a thick strand of hair and a likeness of Mr. Mathews. One can imagine the girls' giggles when they learned from their mother that bald Mr. Mathews had obtained the hairpiece from the local hairdresser. For Lucy, Mr. Mathews included a small gold pencil dangling from a gold chain. Letters to and from home sometimes took six to eight weeks for delivery and undoubtedly brought on tears and fresh bouts of homesickness.

In early April, their mother, not having heard from the girls for several weeks, wrote to Herr Shultz imploring him to look after her daughters.[13] Afraid the Headmaster would not understand their needs, Eugenia detailed their characteristics and personalities. While Anna was known to be selfish yet religiously inclined and always truthful, Lucy was impetuous, careless, a procrastinator but very bright and loving. Eugenia left their religious and moral training in Herr Shultz's capable hands but requested that her girls be allowed to write home without submitting their letters for his perusal. She explains—

"There are some things regarding their health and constitution which would not be proper for your inspection. Lucy, suffers from weak lungs and back and has never passed a summer without a short spell of sickness. For this we have been in the habit of giving a simple emetic and a little simple medicine. Anna, is very healthy with the exception of determination of blood to the head . . . . Anna is subject to something similar to nightmares and should be allowed to sleep with Lucy, as the touch of another person will cause an immediate reaction in the system."

When Lucy finally wrote home, she requested more spending money. Her mother put an end to this by reminding her daughter that their brothers were growing in ignorance for lack of the money

to send them to school. Anna wrote cheerful, gossipy letters, sometimes complaining that sister Lucy had again lost her trunk key and
would not answer her letters.[14] Their mother, sensing sisterly quar-
rels, advised Lucy to consult sister Anna as confidant and friend
whether she took her advice or not.[15] Eugenia expressed in her April
1846 letter to Herr Shultz that she feared that her daughters might
not use good judgement in selecting friends, as they had been shel-
tered in the family all their young lives. Letters to her daughters also
chronicled her own frail health and loneliness, confiding in a letter
to Lucy, "When a kind heart comes forth and offers the word of sympathy then my heart flows & I could kneel at their feet."[16]

Anna Eliza's letters from school days exist in the family collection, particularly the one in which she admits to her father that she
had written to the honorable Henry Clay, United States Senator from
Kentucky known as "the Great Pacificator." Anna, honest and chatty
writes, "I can't think what made me do it. Don't scold me for it was
the influence of the moment and I saw sister Lucy working him a
splendid pair of shoes[17] and I thought I would write to him."[18] Henry
Clay responded with a letter to Anna's mother and hoped that her
daughters would someday call on him at Ashland.[19]

None of Lucy's letters survive from that period. That Lucy did
write home while at school is known by such references as, "the flowers lost out of your letter . . . and your father received your letter."[20]
By applying herself to her studies and particularly to English literature and French and German languages, Lucy weathered her frequent
bouts of homesickness. As representing Southern culture and tradition perhaps Lucy felt obliged to excel, yet she was acutely aware that
scholastic excellence was not always considered ladylike in the nineteenth century and wrote in her copybook, "If she wears blue stockings she contrives to let her petticoats hide them."[21] This is an early
note of Lucy's desire to be independent yet not upset tradition.

Anna may have socialized with school friends, while Lucy preferred to read, stroll in the garden or visit God's Acre, the Moravian
cemetery where each grave is marked by a large stone, "a breast stone,"
that lies flat on the flower-covered mound. Of particular interest to

Lucy was the grave of the highly respected Mohican Indian, Tschoop, converted to Christianity by the Moravians in 1742.[22] Her mother had praised this Indian for his humanity, and perhaps visiting his grave gave this homesick child a feeling of closeness to her mother.

Both girls joined in school-supervised calisthenics, sometimes rowing the school's boat, *Zinfandel,* along the little Monocacy River to an island frequently used for school picnics. Anchoring in the midst of lily pads, Anna strummed her guitar and sang sweet sentimental songs, while Lucy lay back in the boat, fingers trailing in the water to pluck the waxy, white water lilies. One day Herr Shultz strolled by. Struck by the sight of Lucy's titian hair adorned with water lilies, he called her "Undine," the water nymph who was said to become mortal when she married a human and bore a child.[23] Knowing her fondness for flowers, Anna and Herr Shultz were puzzled by Lucy's refusal to dissect the parts of a flower in botany class. "Beauty should be seen and appreciated as God presented it," Lucy explained, "and not destroyed to discover the reason for being."[24]

The girls knew they must remain at the school for the entire term of three years and their happiness knew no bounds when their mother made her first visit to them in February 1847. Eugenia introduced her daughters to friends in New York and they took the boat up the Hudson River to visit cousin Beverly Holcombe Robertson, a West Point cadet, the son of Beverly Holcombe's older sister, Martha Maria Holcombe Robertson. Lucy and Anna made many friends among the cadets, some of whom they would meet years later under very different circumstances. Their mother also introduced them to her friends in New York. Lucy wrote that they went out a good deal, "and if I were not so modest I might tell you what a sensation we made . . . "[25]

Eugenia's visit with her daughters would certainly include detailed descriptions of home, friends, and the latest news of their father's involvement in Texas. That state had been admitted to the Union, 29 December 1845. President James K. Polk signed the bill claiming the southern border of Texas to be the Rio Grande. The Mexicans disagreed. They did not recognize Texas independence but had allowed settlers to come into their territory with the Nueces River as the boundary. The loss of Texas infuriated them and they threatened to recover it by force if necessary.

President Polk was willing to exchange the amount Mexico owed the United States for property damage to United States citizens in return for Mexico's recognition of the border as the Rio Grande. Mexico perceived this offer as a threat and January 1846 Polk sent General Zachary Taylor with five thousand troops to Corpus Christi. He also sent John Slidell as a representative to Mexico to attempt further negotiations. Polk had campaigned for President on a platform advocating westward expansion and those who supported him clamored for "Manifest Destiny." When Slidell was refused an audience with Mexican President Herrera, Polk took action and in April ordered Taylor and his troops to advance to the Rio Grande. This precipitated the start of armed conflict and 13 May 1846, the United States declared war with Mexico.[26]

At home, political battles over slavery erupted. In the North women organized anti-slavery societies but little was accomplished. Women's Suffrage, however, was another issue of concern. Under the leadership of two women from the North, Lucretia Mott and Elizabeth Cady Stanton, the first Women's Convention was held at Seneca Falls, New York, in 1848. Thus began the struggle for recognition of women's equality. Susan B. Anthony joined her "sisters in struggle," giving lectures and organizing meetings to further women's education, their right to vote, and a place in the courts. Singly and together, women rebelled against those who spoke only of women's softness, purity, and spirituality yet denied them intellectual capacity. Woman's Suffrage was hotly debated in many male-dominated homes. These political and moral problems probably infiltrated the quiet peacefulness of the Moravian Community and Lucy and Anna must have been aware of the issues. Certainly Lucy would have found them interesting.

The three years spent under the tutelage of the Moravians would transform both girls into poised young ladies. Their departure in December, 1848, coincided with the traditional Moravian Christmas Vigil, a celebration of the birth of Jesus.

For this occasion, pine boughs and candles graced each window of the Moravian church. The mingled fragrance of pine and hot beeswax gave the illusion of warmth in the unheated church. When the blast of trombones sounded from the bell tower, announcing the beginning of the service, a hush fell over the congregation of parents and friends. Eighty young girls, their simple white dresses brushing the tops of sensible shoes, took their places on benches facing the congregation. Small white bonnets covered the heads of those girls of the Moravian faith while the well brushed and braided hair of the others was unadorned. After a service of antiphon singing and the awarding of prizes for scholastic excellence, light within the church grew dim, and a clear, sweet soprano voice sang the opening lines to that favorite of Moravian Christmas songs—

> Morning Star, O cheering sight!
> Ere Thou cam'st how dark earth's night!

The last hushed note drifted into the darkness. Candles were re-lit and passed down the line of students. With faces aglow in the soft golden light, the schoolgirls exited the church singing that glorious recessional, "On This Day Earth Shall Ring."[27] Touched by the beauty and solemnity of the moment, the congregation responded, their voices joined by the joyous tones of the trumpet choir.

The leave-taking of schoolmates and of Miss Bernade and Miss Niese, their tutors, brought tears and promises from Lucy and Anna. They in turn would miss the soft voices and gentle ways of these Southern sisters. The girls returned home, not, as their mother feared, "more uncouth with stiff Dutch manners" but fulfilling her hopes of eloquence and excellence.[28] When asked if she had not become "strong-minded," a reference to the Northern women's rights activists, Lucy countered, "It is not knowledge that makes women strong-minded but the want of it or rather the affectation of it."[29] At the same time she blithely described herself as "vivacious, bubbling, vain, confident, lazy, beautiful, careless, impulsive, generous yet sometimes not charitable, strong in prejudices, but often forgetting to be just."[30]

At home in La Grange Lucy found a kindred spirit in their talented friend, St. George Lee, a handsome Irishman fifteen years her senior. St. George had emigrated from Ireland with his several sisters and brothers about 1830 and assumed the role of protector and provider to his siblings.[31] The affable Mr. Lee persevered in his pursuit of Lucy, encouraging her to continue her writing of poetry. But Lucy, at fifteen, saw life as an exciting confusion of conquests and could not be bothered to commit herself to any one person. She gave little serious thought to the future, although she must have been aware of the worsening financial problems that plagued her parents.

Beverly Holcombe, like his father before him, decided to make a new start in a different location. In 1848, on the acreage he owned in Harrison County, east Texas, he planted wheat and cotton and began the construction of a house in the nearby town of Marshall. Two years later he summoned his family to join him. Eugenia held back, reluctant to leave civilized La Grange, Tennessee, for the unknown new state of Texas. Friends sympathized and the elderly Uncle Nat Willis urged her to take her fine rosewood piano. Eugenia refused.[32] Texas was a country of savages and she would not have her piano destroyed. On a tearful day in early January, 1850, Lucy, Anna, Helen, their mother, and the house servants said goodbye to friends and relatives in Tennessee, and began their long journey to their new home in Texas.

CHAPTER FOUR

1850

"A stranger in a strange land."
Eugenia Dorothea Holcombe

The town of Memphis, Tennessee, sat on clay banks high above the Mississippi River. Below the town the noisy, whiskey-soaked waterfront of saloons, brothels, and warehouses waited for the trade brought by steamboats. On this January morning in 1850 all action centered on the steamboat *Eclipse*. The shriek of its steam whistle warned loiterers off the gangplank as wood smoke billowed from its twin stacks. The buckets of the boat's double paddle wheels slapped the water and, pushing free of the wharf, the *Eclipse* headed downriver to Vicksburg.

High above, on the white-railed gallery deck, Lucy and Anna Eliza pulled their woolen capes about them and waved kisses toward friends on shore who came to bid them farewell. The wind off the river whipped the girls' capes about their high-laced shoes and tugged at the ribbons of their bonnets. Barely eighteen months apart in age, both girls were beauties. Anna Eliza possessed the more perfect features and the sweet, sad expression of the Madonna. Fittingly, Anna's horizons stretched to motherhood, home, and church. Lucy's beauty lay in her vivaciousness and flirtatious smile. Admirers described her deep blue eyes as pansies fringed by dark lashes with delicate straight black eyebrows drawn like wings across her forehead. Their gushing sentiments compared her hair to threads of molten gold with fire at the end. Nor did they forget her small Grecian nose and determined chin.[1] It was not surprising that the two sisters left broken hearts in the wake of the steamboat carrying them toward new conquests in Texas.

They watched the shoreline fade in the distance and tears dampened Anna Eliza's perfect oval face. She worried that she should have given her daguerreotype to handsome Colonel Greer or to that amusing Robert Dortch. Instead she gave it to Alex Kirkpatrick.[2] But to Lucy, life was a series of amusing flirtations and was not to be taken seriously. Besides, hadn't Robert addressed his last letter to her as the "dove of my heart"?[3] Impulsive and sometimes imprudent, where Anna was cautious and reasoning, Lucy caused her older sister much concern which only seemed to strengthen their devotion to each other shared now by mutual anxiety for their beloved mother.[4]

For Eugenia, leaving her three dear ones—little "Tinker" (Martha Maria), her father, and a beloved brother—buried in Tennessee was far worse than the embarrassment caused by financial problems. Down on the main deck the Holcombe house slaves pressed close to the stacks of crated furniture, the baskets and boxes filled with "Mistrus's" best china, glass, and the trunks of clothing. Most of the cargo was marked "Beverly Lafayette Holcombe"; some wag had inked "G. T. T." (Gone to Texas) on the canvas covering the cargo. The trip was purposely delayed by stays of weeks that lengthened into months while the girls and their mother visited in Vicksburg, Natchez, and New Orleans.[5]

Lucy, no longer the child who preferred the outdoors to the attention of youthful swains, made the most of each visit. Both girls caused many hearts to flutter as they filled dance cards, rode about in fine carriages, and attended levees. St. George Lee met them in

Vicksburg and the gallant Irishman escorted the sisters to the theater. Lucy carelessly lost her cherry-colored gloves, and when St.
George found them, he folded them carefully and kept them in his
vest pocket close to his heart.[6] On the more serious side, Anna painted
but Lucy, barely still a moment, played the Southern belle to perfection. She possessed all the prerequisites—family connections, apparent wealth, intelligence, accomplishments, and beauty. She also had
a natural charm that made the endless small talk and the paying and
receiving of calls endurable.[7]

After months of visiting, Eugenia and her daughters left New Orleans for Point Coupee. From here, at this juncture of the Mississippi
and the Red rivers, their boat steamed up the deep and narrow Red
River to Shreveport, Louisiana. They found space on the crowded,
paddle wheel boat and when night fell, the steady thump of the buckets and splash of the water lulled them to a fitful sleep, interrupted by
the warning calls of the boatswain. Oil lanterns swayed at the bow
and stern casting strange shadows on the water where dark shapes
rose and sank with the current. By daylight, passengers watched the
water for snags and alligators and waved to the ragged settlers standing by their poor dwellings, or polling their flatboats loaded with firewood for the boat's steam boiler.

Near Shreveport, the Holcombes transferred to a narrow, stern-
wheeled riverboat for the long journey across Caddo Lake to Swanson's
Landing on the Texas shore. Their household goods, loaded on a
flatboat, trailed behind. Caddo Lake was more swamp than lake. Tall
cypress trees extended far out into the dark water, their knees pro-
truding above the water's surface. Gray moss shrouded tree limbs
and shadowed dark passages of stagnant water where alligators lay in
wait for small animals. Long-necked cormorants perched on stumps
and stretched their triangular-shaped wings to dry like clothes on a
line. Nothing stirred in the dank-smelling air. Only the sharp cry of a
water bird broke the oppressive silence.

Eugenia might have likened this part of the journey to crossing
the River Styx and prayed for guidance and salvation in the land beyond. While the girls looked to the western horizon for sight of Texas,

they doubtless chatted about the prospects of new beaux. Little Helen snuggled next to their mother and watched the black clouds gathering on the horizon. With the first ominous rumbling of thunder the ten-year-old hid her head under Eugenia's shawl.

The boat's captain wet his finger and held it up to test the wind, but the air was unusually still. He looked back at the flatboat overloaded with furniture and shook his head. The five Holcombe slaves—cook, Aunt Viney, butler and valet, Uncle Ned, and housemaids Lucinda, Beatrice, and Celah—bundled in the stern. Frightened by the jagged streaks of lightning that flashed above the shore trees, their moans added to the rising tension. Sudden gusts of cold wind blew spray into the boat and churned the surface water into white caps. "It's sure a blue norther', Ma'am," the Captain shouted into the doorway of the cabin. Eugenia, huddled against the chilling wind, nodded stiffly, not comprehending.

The boat began to toss and take on water. Thoroughly frightened, the servants sought the shelter of the boat's small cabin, while their mistress prayed for the salvation of all. Eugenia, fearing for the lives of those near and dear to her, sank to her knees, oblivious to the fury of the wind whipping rain against her face. Calling on the Lord for help, she prayed, and Uncle Ned shouted into the turmoil, "Amen" and "Lord, have mercy!" Their fear turned to panic as the wind roared and the waves broke over the boat's side. The nine passengers clung to each other and watched in terror as pieces of the cabin, broken apart by the tremendous force of the wind and waves, disappeared over the sides. Then, with the suddenness of its coming, the wind died and a pale, forgiving sun peeped through the trees. The girls looked back toward the flat boat that carried their household goods. Only the top of boxes and crates showed above water but the storm had pushed both boats across Caddo Lake to the Texas shore.[8]

Boatmen and slaves hauled on the lines and pulled the swamped boat up Big Cypress Bayou to the busy port of Jefferson. All was bustle and industry at this internal port in Texas that handled shipments to and from the northwest. Huge bales of cotton, stacks of lumber from the pine forests of East Texas, bags of seed from the native Osage Orange trees, and kiln-dried bricks lined the wharf, waiting for transport to New Orleans. The smell of sawdust filled the air as mill blades tore into enormous pine logs. Above the noise, stevedores shouted orders to unload the Holcombes' cargo.

Lucy was seventeen when she set foot on Texas soil.[9] The storm had soaked her clothing and whipped the braids of her hair loose from the poufed circlets around her ears. With each step onto the plank dock her ankle boots of fine kidskin squished and pulled tighter on her feet.

Most everyone in sight sported an arsenal of guns and knives, the latter being exercised in whittling while their owners eyed the ladies. "Evening, Ma'am," soft, deep voices welcomed the bedraggled and exhausted passengers. A few of these admirers offered to escort Eugenia and her daughters to the stage line while Uncle Ned loaded wagons for the twenty-five mile journey south to the town of Marshall. Eugenia refused to leave until Uncle Ned uncrated the portraits of little "Tinker" and the likeness of Major James Philemon Holcombe.[10] The paintings suffered only minor damage, but Eugenia was more concerned about them than her rosewood sofa and chairs that stood on the wharf oozing mud and water through their velvet cushions.[11] Trunks of clothing and the two portraits would be strapped to the back and top of the bright green stagecoach with the golden eagle painted on the doors.

Two hours later, with a great fanfare of horn blowing, the stagecoach rolled into the town of Marshall. A red brick courthouse under construction dominated the slightly elevated center of the town. Businesses, some with store fronts, surrounded the square, giving evidence to Marshall's wealth of lawyers, its optics store, grocers, chair manufactory, drug store, confectionery, saddle shop, jewelers, and a haberdashery.[12] The town seemed to support ample businesses for its population of little more than one thousand, including four hundred twenty-one slaves.[13]

When the coach pulled up to the mounting block, passengers stepped down onto the plank walk. Eugenia and her daughters looked about with mixed emotions of dismay and relief. Beyond the square, tree-shaded dirt roads led to the residential section of fine frame houses and two of brick. It was inevitable that the Holcombe women would compare the sight before them with the more settled village of La Grange, Tennessee. That night Eugenia wrote in her journal, "A stranger in a strange land. What a shadow seems hanging over my future life."[14]

The Holcombes were certainly not the first plantation owners to arrive in Marshall, Texas. A steady influx, many from the planter class of Tennessee, Virginia, and the Carolinas, had already settled in Marshall because of the area's fertile soil, the abundance of pine and hardwood forests, and accessibility to navigable waterways. These families brought with them wealth, influence, and scholarly interests. As the county seat and the fourth largest town in Texas in 1850, Marshall became a literary center referred to as the "Athens of East Texas." [15] At least in this way Marshall resembled La Grange but at the moment Eugenia was more concerned about where they might live. The house she fully expected to move into was not finished.

Tired and ailing, glad to be together again as a family with her husband and sons, yet disappointed not to have a home to move into, the Holcombes took rooms at the Marshall House, a three story frame building on the south side of the square. Eugenia made the acquaintance of fellow boarders, the Reverend Moses. W. Staples and his wife. Rev. Staples had been sent to Marshall on behalf of the Presbyterian Board of Domestic Missions. With his help, Eugenia and Beverly organized a church in their hotel rooms, forming the nucleus for the First Presbyterian Church of Marshall, Texas.[16] Lucy's name is noticeably missing from its first roster.

It is not known how long they stayed at the hotel, but in time they moved to their new home—an imposing structure of Grecian temple design sitting on sixteen acres of hillside and commanding a view of the town from the end of Burleson Street. Built of native brick fired on the site by slave labor, its two stories were supported by tall columns on all four sides.[17] The front of the house had an evenness of design, with three front doors, all opening into large rooms that could be thrown together for receptions. Windows extended from floor to ceiling and closed with green shutters. All exterior and interior wood was native pine from the trees felled to clear the land. Handmade wooden shingles covered the roof. Five large rooms on the first floor had brick fireplaces that connected with fireplaces in the five bedrooms on the second floor. The upstairs rooms and hallway led onto a balcony that overlooked the flower garden. The kitchen stood apart from the house as a fire precaution. White plaster covered the interior walls. [18] Great care was taken to procure the best materials from the New Orleans supplier, Edw. H. Pomroy.[19]

They called their home Wyalusing, an Indian word that translated as "friend to the friendless" or "home for the wayfarer.[20] Lucy and Anna Eliza may have chosen the name because of their great respect for the Moravians' work with the Indians. It was an appropriate choice. The Holcombes opened their house and larder to anyone who seemed in the slightest need of care or a meal and these guests sometimes stayed for months or years.

Once again taking up the reins of a plantation mistress, Eugenia made certain that her daughters understood that to whom much is given, much is required. Daily rounds were made of the slave quarters with baskets containing liniment, salves, medicinal herbal concoctions, linens for bandages, the well-used book, *Buchanan's Domestic Medicine*, published in 1798, and a Bible. These books remain in descendants' libraries.

As Thomas Nelson Page put it, "The Southern woman's life on a plantation was one long act of devotion—to God, her husband, children, servants, the poor, and humanity." [21]

A direct descendant of the Holcombes, the late Miss Anna Smith of Marshall, described a typical Sunday at Wyalusing in her unpublished reminiscences, "Every Sunday a bell called the slaves to worship. They gathered around the back porch where Eugenia read and explained passages from the Bible. Old Auntie Delia and the mothers with babes in arms sat on the front bench." When the lesson and prayers ended, Lucy and Anna led the singing. The slaves dutifully sang their "Mistrus's" hymns and then, with ebony faces lifted toward

Heaven, they swayed and clapped rhythmically to their own songs of hope.[22]

Once settled in their new home, the ritual of calling began, and news spread quickly of the two lovely Holcombe sisters. Letters arrived from suitors left behind in Tennessee, Mississippi, Louisiana, and Alabama. Lucy saved one from Robert Dortch, who humorously described himself as being "hors en combat" after being thrown by a malicious and wicked horse. "I can scarcely walk over my room," he explained, "and must therefore for at least a month forgo [*sic*] the pleasure of seeing you.[23]

Lucy thrived on admiration and wrote, "Admiration is a pleasant thing after all, if we would only be candid about it."[24] Later she received a letter from her old flame, St. George Lee, encouraging her to write. He was fond of illustrating his own writing with caricatures of humans and sketches of animals. Many of his lighthearted yet poignant stories were published in the *Old Knickerbocker* Magazine and signed "Jasper Smoothly" or sometimes "Lunar Caustic."[25] Mr. Lee authored the satirical poem about their friends and acquaintances in La Grange. He titled it, "Harp with a Thousand Strings With Waifs of Wit and Pathos." An acute observer of human nature, Lee also wrote short articles of human interest published in the Galveston paper during the Civil War.[26]

About the time the Holcombes moved to Texas, St. George and his four siblings left Mobile, Alabama, and settled on ranch land in Victoria County, Texas. To eke out a meager living he raised and raced greyhounds. In spite of his family responsibilities, St. George Lee showed concern for Lucy's welfare as in the following letter—

"My dearest . . . you are too irresistibly [*sic*] fascinating and too generous, your imprudence and forgetfulness of self whenever your sympathies are aroused will lead you into a labyrinth of troubles. . . . you have no idea of the scrapes in which you will be involved—I say all this because I love you . . . What could have possessed you to take chloroform?" [27]

Chloroform was first introduced and used by dentists in 1847. Perhaps Lucy had some dental problem that necessitated its use. Mr.

Lee continued to fuss like an older brother, but Lucy's increasing ambition for fame, recognition, and wealth prohibited her from taking a poor dirt farmer seriously. For old time's sake she promised to write to St. George, for he said he'd bring her a pair of greyhounds. At the moment, however, new beaux kept her too busy to bother about old flames.

CHAPTER FIVE

1851

"My spirit is restless and longs for activity."
Lucy Petway Holcombe

*L*ucy traveled to New Orleans with her mother and sister to shop for Anna Eliza's trousseau and while there she met her old suitor, St. George Lee. The meeting was not by accident but, when the time came for Lucy to return home to Marshall, St. George refused to accompany her as she requested. No explanation of his need to return to his business in Mobile satisfied the self-centered Lucy. The unhappy suitor left and poured out his emotions in a letter written on board the steamboat *Florida,* "I lay awake all night thinking of how I left you like a broken lily drooping your fair head in utter prostration. I felt almost criminal . . . I am on the rack 'till I hear from you."[1]

Lucy left him on the rack. She broke off their long-standing friendship and told him she'd never marry. It would be many years before she forgave St. George but at the moment the excitement of Anna's wedding demanded her attention. On 14 January 1851, Anna Eliza, twenty years of age, married Elkanah Bracken Greer, a young lawyer from Paris, Tennessee.

It was the first marriage held at Wyalusing. The high-ceilinged rooms, decorated with pine boughs and holly and lit by numerous candles, glowed with warmth and hospitality. But the most beautiful glow came from Anna. Her thick, light brown hair, was parted in the center and drawn back in large rolls over her ears and capped by dainty white lace. Her gown of white brocaded silk, adorned with tiny bows of seed pearls and satin ribbons, was looped and gathered over hoops. Lucy, her sister's attendant, wore a yellow silk ball dress, and little Helen carried the ring on a small velvet pillow.[2]

The Marshall weekly newspaper, *The Texas Republican*, noted the marriage, "Anna Eliza Holcombe, one of the beautiful and accomplished sisters, to Elkanah Bracken Greer. May their sea of life be without a ripple."[3]

This was not to be for Anna. Elkanah had charmed the Holcombe women with his manners, ready wit, and penetrating blue eyes, but his temper and wild ideas were more familiar to his male contemporaries. As a soldier with the 1st. Mississippi Volunteers commanded by Jefferson Davis, Elkanah saw action in the War with Mexico. He performed nobly and Lucy admired his patriotic zeal, although later she would fault him for his irresponsibility. Illness marred the couple's honeymoon trip to Elkanah's former home in Tennessee. Anna, always frail, was tired from traveling, and stayed with her in-laws while Elkanah attended to business in Natchez. He also heard the sensational Swedish songstress, Jenny Lind, in concert and viewed the controversial nude statue, "The Greek Slave," sculpted by Hiram Powers.[4] Anna, experiencing a lonely honeymoon, implored Lucy to write, but her sister was too busy attending dances and being the flirtatious Southern belle.

In the nineteenth century South it was tacitly understood that marriage was the ultimate goal of a Southern belle but Lucy had other plans. She savored her independence and held to her belief that, "A woman with liberal information, one who comprehends, fully and correctly, the principles and propriety, not only of the intellectual but social world, may exert on society a great and good influence."[5] She began by taking an active interest in politics.

No doubt Lucy's admiration and devotion to her mother, coupled with her education and exposure to Northern culture, had taken root. Extending her comprehension of the intellectual world, Lucy began to study the style and delivery of political speakers. She traveled to Jackson, Mississippi, to hear the debates at the State House. In 1851 this handsome pillared building commanded a view of the mud streets and boardwalks of Jackson. Mounting the winding staircase to the third floor gallery, Lucy chose a seat by the railing and leaned forward to listen. The speaker acknowledged her presence and soon all attention turned to the attractive titian-haired, blue-eyed beauty in the balcony. Lucy acknowledged her admirers and left the chamber. The mesmerized legislators rose as a body and met her at the foot of the stairs. Unwilling to let any one member monopolize "Miss Lucy," the solons escorted her to the train station. Lucy no doubt reverted to her flirtatious Southern belle role and exchanged pleasantries with her admirers. She boarded the train and turned to wave goodbye to her following. The conductor called "all aboard" and a grand rush was made to procure a seat next to this fascinating belle. Back at the State House, the session was dismissed for the day for lack of a quorum.[6]

Flirtations were amusing but not without purpose. Lucy's list of suitors was legend yet she continued to keep her options opened for the right combination of wealth and position. Along the way she enjoyed the attentions of her first cousin, Beverly Holcombe Robertson, a West Point graduate and the son of her father's older sister. Eugenia, noting signs that Lucy and cousin Beverly were becoming too fond of one another, took her daughter off to Natchez. The diversion worked—for the moment.

The trip may have been made by carriage across northern Louisiana to Lake Providence, a pretty hamlet on the Mississippi River. Crossing over the river, old friends welcomed them at La Grange and at their old homestead, Woodstock. Beverly Holcombe continued eastward to take Theodore to school at Bethlehem and Eugenia and Lucy proceeded southward to Natchez to visit Dr. William Henry Holcombe, the son of Beverly's older brother, Dr. William James Holcombe.[7] "Cousin Willie" practiced homeopathic medicine and explained the reason why in his autobiography. "Nature fitted me for an Editor but a contrary and unlucky wind wafted me into the pill business and I am compromising with my disgust at all medicine by giving as little ones as possible."[8]

Employing this philosophy, Dr. Holcombe gained a reputation for his unorthodox but seemingly successful treatment of yellow fever.[9] At this time little was known of the cause of this malady and less about the treatment. Dr. Holcombe prescribed the extremely dilute solution of ten-thousandth grain of silver nitrate in one-half glass of water in the second stage of severe illness. It had a remarkable effect. Only thirty-three of the 555 patients treated died. This caused the skeptics to question their preferred method of giving large doses of calomel.[10]

The good doctor did not limit his accomplishments to the practice of homeopathic medicine. His published volumes of poetry were much admired in the South. Soon after the Holcombes arrived, he escorted his cousin Lucy to the only ice cream parlor in Natchez. Over dishes of what he termed a "lemon-saccharine-glacial-lacteal compound," he read his poems and discussed his interest in the philosophy of Swedenborgianism.[11] No doubt Lucy enjoyed the poetry but may have found his mystical worship of the spirit world unacceptable to her Presbyterian background. Unfazed, Dr. Holcombe greatly admired his cousin and wrote in his diary, "I was almost abashed by her resplendent beauty, so magnificent was her dress, carriage and personal appearance."[12]

The Holcombes also visited their friends, the Quitmans, in Natchez. John A. Quitman, the son of a minister in Rhinebeck, New York, came to Natchez in 1820 to seek his fortune. Educated for the law, he dabbled in Mississippi politics and married Eliza Turner, a wealthy Natchez belle. Quitman brought his bride to the handsome pillared house built in 1818 on a hill overlooking a lake. They called the house Monmouth and its size and splendor fit the physique of its handsome owner.[13] After arriving at Monmouth and taking a short rest, the ladies dressed for dinner and, at the appropriate time, entered the parlor with its carved rosewood furniture upholstered in blue velvet. Several dignified-looking men in high stiff collars and flowing cravats came forward to be presented. Perhaps Lucy's eyes lingered on the swarthy, handsome man with the silvery hair and military bearing. Introduced as General Narciso Lopez, he bowed low over Lucy's small white hand, his black eyes devouring this young beauty before him.[14]

The conversation that followed centered on Cuba, the emerald isle belonging to Spain. The rich coffee and sugar plantations of the island, with its strategic position in the Caribbean, made it most desirable to the United States.[15] The Federal government tendered an offer for purchase but the Spanish Minister declared, "The people of Spain would prefer seeing it sunk in the ocean."[16] Stung by this retort and fired with the greed of Manifest Destiny, America looked to other land to the south—South America, Mexico, and the islands in the Caribbean. But, to the Southerners, and particularly the pro-slavery expansionists, the island of Cuba continued to present a prime target for aggressive speculation.

On this night, Lopez, his voice breaking with emotion, spoke of his plans to take an expedition to the island of Cuba. Two previous expeditions led by Lopez had failed miserably. Undeterred, the General appealed to his friends in the South who considered him a hero and overlooked his earlier failures. He told General Quitman and his guests how the natives he called Creoles, natives of Cuba with European parentage, had long been subjugated to harsh laws and barbaric torture. It was his intent to invade the island and wrest it from Spain's tenacious grip. This done, Lopez would set up a republic or annex the island to the United States.[17] Plans were underway for a third expedition but Lopez needed a leader.[18]

Early in 1851, General Lopez had approached Senator Jefferson Davis and offered him the leadership of an expedition to Cuba. Lopez padded his offer with a promise of depositing $100,000 in Mrs. Davis' name and, on the success of the expedition, another $100,000 or a coffee plantation.[19] Davis refused the offer on grounds that it would not be ethical, but recommended Lieutenant Robert E. Lee, who also declined.[20] Lopez, ever confident of success, asked his friend, General John A. Quitman, to assume leadership of a third expedition.[21] Quitman, too, refused. To invade another country, without government sanction, would be considered filibustering. But, more to the point, freeing natives would be contrary to Quitman's admitted pro-slavery stance.

Lucy, the romantic idealist, had read of General Lopez's previous attempts to invade Cuba. Her father disapproved of the ex-patriot's efforts to recruit Americans for an attack on Cuba without official sanction. President Fillmore went a step farther and proclaimed that the United States would not be responsible for the lives of filibusters and would not aid them if captured. He called them pirates.[22] Lucy disagreed. "What life is more sublime," she asked, "than one given to a nation struggling for the principles of moral and political freedom?"[23]

Did Lucy not realize that the ultimate goal of the expedition was to extend the Southern slave economy to the Caribbean and Mexico? Her enthusiasm for the filibusters contradicts her supposed sympathy for the plight of slaves. Perhaps adulation for the filibuster's leader appealed to her romantic Victorian ideals, fueled by her voracious reading of the romantic Victorian novels. Her reaction was gratifying to the men present, particularly to Mr. Laurent J. Sigur, the financial backer of this proposed third expedition.

Mr. Sigur, an ex-Cuban and publisher-owner of the *New Orleans Delta News*, would furnish the ship, *Pampero*, to transport the filibusters to the island.[24] A circle of admiring men gathered about Lucy. Among them stood Ambrosio Jose Gonzalez, a countryman and confidant of Lopez. Gonzalez seemed particularly impressed by the ardor of this young woman with the soft, musical voice. He had been with the general on the second expedition and came tonight with word that the Creoles were becoming restless under Spanish rule. Time was running out, he said, and urged that the expedition embark within the next few days. General Quitman advised waiting until

their force of volunteers could be increased. But Gonzalez was ada-
mant. The volunteers must leave at once, he said, before the Creoles
tired of waiting and dispersed.[25]

While the men argued the possibilities, General Lopez focused
his attention on Lucy, fascinated by her expressive eyes. No doubt
responding to his magnetism, Lucy likened this dark-eyed foreigner
to her idol, the Marquis de Lafayette. As the evening drew to a close,
General Lopez, whose face showed the "passionate splendor of a
Southern clime," bowed low over her hand.[26] Holding it a bit longer
than usual, he raised it to his lips in farewell and whispered the wish
that she would meet him again at the rendezvous before sailing to
Cuba.

CHAPTER SIX

1851

"The only kindred blood I ever knew, stains the green shore of Cuba."

Lucy Petway Holcombe

*T*he rendezvous, as described by Lucy in *The Free Flag of Cuba,* took place Friday, 31 July 1851, at Old Hickory, the plantation owned by the Sigur family, which was close to the Mississippi River and New Orleans.[1] A group of men sat in the center of the room, their attention on a large map spread out on the table. General Narciso Lopez hovered nearby while the handsome Colonel William Logan Crittenden sat at some distance.

Although Colonel Crittenden had not previously been mentioned in letters, he apparently was one of Lucy's beaus. Later, it was reported that she was engaged to Crittenden. Whether this was a serious engagement or one of Lucy's flirtations is not known. General Lopez, noting that everyone was present, began to inform the gathering of his intended expedition.

Once again General Quitman urged delay, stressing that five hundred volunteers would not be enough to carry out a successful expedition. His caution went unheeded. The assembled officers, tired of waiting, hailed the earliest departure as expedient. With much bravado they toasted the ladies present, their host, and the success of what was to be known as the Bahia Honda Expedition. The party continued until the officers left for New Orleans to join their men on board the *Pampero*.

Before daybreak, 3 August 1851, five hundred soldiers crowded the decks of the *Pampero*.[2] Seasoned soldiers from Kentucky, adventurers, and a good number of Hungarian refugees had signed on. Excitement ran high. Honor and glory overshadowed all thought of danger. They called themselves filibusters, even if President Millard Fillmore considered them "pirates."[3] The expedition seemed doomed from the very start. The *Pampero*'s engines would not turn over. Towed to the mouth of the river, the ship wallowed in the swells while mechanics among the volunteer soldiers worked to repair the engines.[4]

On the third day, the engines repaired, the ship steamed to Key West. Unable to get a pilot to guide him north and into St. John's River to pick up artillery and extra ammunition, Lopez ordered the Captain to make a run for the coast of Cuba. The volunteers stacked their muskets against the ship's compass and continued their card games. The magnetic needle of the compass, attracted to the metal gun barrels, led to a false reading and the ship went off course. The next morning they awoke to see the menacing walls of Morro Castle guarding the entrance to Havana's harbor.

Captain Lewis turned the *Pampero* and immediately steamed northwest toward Bahia Honda. When close to land, the Captain hailed a pilot from a passing ship. He came on board under duress and ordered full steam ahead, racing the *Pampero* toward shore and grounding the ship on a coral reef. The men grabbed their weapons and rowed ashore to be met not by friendly natives but by hostile gunfire.

By two o'clock in the morning, 453 volunteers had landed at the coastal village of Murillo, twelve miles west of Bahia Honda. The *Pampero* returned to Key West. Lopez, anxious to press inland, took 323 men and headed through the jungle-like terrain to Las Pozas. Colonel Crittenden, with 130 men to guard the supplies, ammunition, and personal luggage, followed as soon as he could commandeer wagons for transportation. Late that night, Crittenden and his men headed for the mountains but were cut off by the Spanish Militia under General Enna. Crittenden's company fell back and split. Half of his men made it through General Enna's line and to Las Pozas. They begged Lopez to send relief to Crittenden and the rest of their company, but the General refused.

Crittenden and the remaining fifty men hid in the dense undergrowth. Eventually they made their way to the shore. Scrambling into four abandoned fishing boats they pushed out to sea only to be apprehended by the Spanish ship *Habanero*. The captain threw them in chains and delivered Crittenden and his men to the authorities in Havana on 16 August.[5]

Without benefit of trial or contact with the American Consul, Mr. Allen F. Owens, the prisoners were condemned to be shot. One concession was granted them. They were allowed time to write letters to their loved ones. Colonel William Logan Crittenden wrote to his uncle, Honorable John J. Crittenden, who at that time was Attorney General of the United States. He then addressed a letter to a friend, Dr. Lucien Hensley.[6] A portion of this letter read, "Ship of War Esperanza, August 16, 1851—Dear Lucien: In half an hour I with fifty others am to be shot. We were taken prisoners yesterday . . . The odds were too great, . . . have not the heart to write to any of my family . . . I will die like a man . . . Communicate with my family. Farewell. My love to all my family . . . Yours, Strong in Heart, W. L. Crittenden."

The men were marched to the public plaza in chains. The crowd jeered and spit on them as they mounted the execution platform. Spanish soldiers prodded them with bayonets and ordered them to kneel. Colonel Crittenden refused. His words rang out across the plaza, "A Kentuckian kneels to none except his God, and always dies facing his enemy!"[7] Captain Victor Ker also refused to kneel and over the shouting of the crowd the guns of the firing squad downed the two brave men. The crowd, roused to bloodthirsty extremes, grossly mutilated the bodies of all fifty executed men. A week later, General Lopez and those men who had remained with him were captured. The General met death by the garrote after shouting to the multitude watching, "I die for my beloved Cuba. Farewell!"[8]

The execution of Crittenden and his fifty men created an outburst of indignation in the United States. When news of the executions reached New Orleans, men stormed the Spanish Consulate shouting "Revenge!" The building housing the Spanish newspaper, *La Union,* was ransacked and the presses flung into the street. The mob's fury was such that the New Orleans Artillery Battalion was called out to restore order.[9]

The other prisoners, shackled, shaved, and divested of all their belongings, were sent to Spain in irons. Mr. John Thrasher, an American citizen living in Havana and publisher of the newspaper *El Faro,* tried to intercede but the Spanish militia charged him with espionage.[10]

The American public clamored for President Fillmore to obtain the prisoners' release. The situation became rife with political and international problems. Finally, Fillmore wired congratulations to the Queen of Spain on the birth of the Infanta in December of 1851 and ordered the Spanish flag at New Orleans to be saluted. Mollified, the Queen granted the release of the prisoners. Fillmore's action did not sit well with many in the South. Colonel Jefferson Davis, in a postcampaign speech at Jackson, Mississippi, in June of 1852, called Fillmore's action "the truckling spirit of the administration."[11]

And where was Lucy at this time? If one is to take the actions of her novel counterpart, "Mabel," she waited at a friend's plantation near New Orleans. When news reached her of the expedition's failure she was devastated and saddened by the death of the men. She had championed Lopez's cause and rumors were rife with talk of her engagement to Colonel Crittenden. Gossip also linked her with the ill-fated General Lopez. She withdrew to the haven of her family and remained in her room, refusing all company save that of her dearest friend, her mother. Finding solace in the bosom of her family, she roused herself to write of the ill-fated expedition.

Determined to vindicate the heroic deeds of the soldiers and the pure motives of the Cuban General, she sat at the carved walnut writing desk by the window in her bedroom and wrote. In graceful Spencerian script she wove a tale of romance around the historical facts of the expedition. The resulting manuscript bore the title *The Free Flag of Cuba or the Martyrdom of General Narciso Lopez.* Lucy was nineteen at the time and signed her novel, "By H. M. Hardimann." This nom de plume, an obvious reference to her royal ancestor, Henrietta Marie Hardeman, tightened her link to royalty and the ill-fated Marie Antoinette, Queen of France. Lucy dedicated her book to General John A. Quitman stating, "My characters are not all fictitious; some of them have, or have had, living originals in the actual world."

The characters are easily identifiable. "Mabel," is, by admission, Lucy. The other main female character, "Genevieve," is a copy of Anna Eliza, and Genevieve's sweetheart, "Ralph Dudley," fits Elkanah's character very nicely. Lucy gave the manuscript to a friend in New York known only by the name Gerard. After succeeding in placing the manuscript with a publishing company, Gerard wrote to Lucy addressing her as "Lulu."

"January 16, 1855. Cheer thee beautiful beloved—there is nothing to regret, much to rejoice at . . . The Free Flag is neatly got up. It has the name of a respectable publishing house on it—Dewitt and Davenport . . . I have found her whom my soul loveth, [*sic*] who freely responds to my devotion by giving me the warmest love of her heart, who is, heaven willing, to be my partner my happiness through life . . . I have gained far more than I can lose . . . Our book will take it . . ."[12]

It would seem that Lucy imposed her charm on Gerard with no intention of carrying through. Perhaps she resented his claim to "our book." There is no further mention of Gerard. A newspaper review noted, "*The Free Flag of Cuba*—This is the title of a little Romance, recently published by Dewitt & Davenport. The author is 'H. M. Hardimann,' which besides sounding very unlike the writer of so much pathos, eloquence and graphic elegance, for other reasons and impressions seemeth [*sic*)] to us a nom de plume. The book is redolent of female taste, fancy and sentiment . . . A gifted, spirited, pure-minded and warm-hearted Southern woman alone could have so handled such a theme."[13]

It is interesting to note that Lucy writes page after page of glowing description and tribute to General Narciso Lopez in her historical novel yet devotes only one paragraph to Crittenden to whom she was supposedly engaged. And Crittenden chose to write only to his uncle and to his friend, Dr. Lucien Henley, whose identity remains a mystery. It is suggested that the name, Lucien Henley, with corresponding initials, may have been chosen to mask identity and avoid embarrassment for Lucy Holcombe.

Mrs. Murray, Colonel Crittenden's mother, believed that General Narciso Lopez was deceived by a Spanish officer in whom he had implicit confidence. Lucy agreed. Mr. Charles Spalding Wyley said that Lucy wrote another book titled, *The White Diamond*, in which she openly blames Ambrosio Jose Gonzalez, the confidante and fellow countryman of Lopez.[14] Wyley thought the book was bright but dismissed Lucy's charges as "a woman's unjust aspersions." However, he added, "When I was on Tupelo Island shortly after the execution of Lopez and Crittenden, I saw General Gonzalez. The General's extreme nervousness was most noticeable when the Spanish steamer, *Pampero,* cleared into Florida Sound and anchored in front of the town."[15]

A few supported Lucy's claim that Gonzalez was the traitor but were reluctant to come forth and blame this popular and respected man who gained the confidence and friendship of many in government circles. Ambrosio Jose Gonzalez settled in Beaufort, South Carolina, and married Harriet Rutledge Elliott.[16] During the Civil War, Gonzalez was appointed Colonel in the Confederate Army and was accepted into Southern society. Such is the verdict of history.

CHAPTER SEVEN

1852–1857

"My home is in the prairied West and God is nearer us than fashion."
Lucy Petway Holcombe

*L*ucy spent much of the following year at home, and, as her mother wrote to Theodore, she was occupied with, "sleeping, reading, writing and music."[1] Comforted by the love of her family, she probably enjoyed the daily pleasures of gardening with her mother and riding out to the farm at Fern Lake with her father. Although Colonel Holcombe may not have been a practical businessman, he was a respected farmer known for his fine horses and his generosity. When his faithful valet, Ned Hood, missed his wife, a slave owned by a Mr. Hood of Tennessee, Beverly Holcombe sent Ned back to Tennessee with eight hundred dollars to buy his wife. Mr. Hood refused to sell but did allow two of the couple's children to return with Ned to Texas. This trusted servant stayed with the Holcombe family until his death, past the age of one hundred years.[2]

The concern of the Holcombe family now centered on the education of their sons. Philemon, the younger of the two, attended schools in Marshall. Because of his deafness, he may have been encouraged to do manual rather than cerebral labor. John Theodore, the favored older son, was expected to bear the Holcombe name with honor. They sent him to the Moravian Seminary for male students in Bethlehem, Pennsylvania. His mother wrote weekly letters full of advice and gently admonishing him for his lack of studious and pious habits. Lucy wrote the following letter 26 July 1852.

> My dearest Theodore!
>
> We received a letter from you last week which greatly relieved our anxiety, our precious mother was suffering very much from anxiousness. She was fearing a thousand things about which no one else would have imagined. Her only thought—only anxiety, only hope of life seems centred [*sic*] in <u>you</u> her first born son. Your future moral and intellectual character is the <u>theme</u> of her hearts study, and now my dearest brother, I fear you do not appreciate all this deep devotion and interest as you ought. Do you read her beautiful letters so full of nice useful and heartfelt advice over and over again? Ponder on and strive to profit by them? Such letters any statesman might look to for counsel, then my brother do not throw them carelessly aside, reflect on them, take them to base your character on, and to guide you in life. Remember, the faults and inconsistencies of character which may <u>now</u> appear cannot be attributed to the <u>thoughtlessness</u> of a boy for you are now fast approaching manhood when you will be responsible for every step! When you enter the world you must take a <u>stand</u>, a <u>position</u>, whether it be high or low rests with <u>yourself</u>! This my dear brother is what our beloved mother is striving to impress on you, and oh let not her labor of love be in vain.
>
> When you write could you not have sweet affectionate letters neater? Let them look as tho [*sic*] you were striving to

gain her approbation in everything. You should respect her too much to send a carelessly written letter. Not that she has complained, (for she is always too happy to hear from you) but I thought I should mention it to you.

Now my own dear brother you must not think sister Lucy is scolding you, far from [it]. She is just giving you one of her long talks! I know you love mother very dearly but sometimes I fear none of us love her enough, as <u>deeply</u> as she should be loved. You must <u>often</u> write long serious letters for she <u>will</u> prize them.

Our dear father has been very ill but is now entirely well, sends his best love to you and says he wants to be proud of his boy. He often talks to me about you! Our family is very well, tho [*sic*] we have had some sickness in M. [Marshall]. Col. McCown and Mr. Burnside are dead.

There is nothing more in the village. Mrs. Pullam writes that uncle Dug has been very ill for some time and Mr. Tucker is in Lamar where he will stay till fall then go to New Orleans. Next week we go to Dr. Field. I will on my return write you how I like Mrs. F son Dorinan whether I wish my brother may resemble him. For the present I will say goodby [*sic*] write very soon my darling brother to your devoted sister . . .

Do not forget to tell me all I asked in my last letter or to send me the 'forget me not' seed and flowers. You must take the enclosed to Miss Z <u>your self.</u>

How does Dr Wilson like the nomination. Tell him Whigs make very wry faces at <u>Scott</u>, but <u>take</u> the dose. <u>All send love to you</u>—your sister.[3]

Helene who writes poetry is Lucy. [written sideways on the first page, right border]

Finally, in May of 1853 it was decided to bring the errant son home, but Theodore had already taken matters into his own hands and left school in January of that year.[4] Eugenia was frantic and wrote her son in February.

Theodore

My darling child are you still in Memphis with your friends
or where are you my precious boy? I received your letter last
night which had been written a month. I know you must have
suffered a great deal from anxiety in not knowing how to act.
If you are in Memphis start directly on the first Memphis Packet
for New Orleans. If you are in La Grange go over and see
Capt. Hullum and he will tell you what to do for by this same
mail I write to him. My son you can never repay me for the
great anxiety I feel for you, both as to your moral and intellectual course through life. After encountering many difficulties, I succeeded in carrying you so far on your way to an
Institution in which I had every confidence in its training your
moral and intellectual faculties in the way best calculated to
make you an eminent and usefull [*sic*] man . . .

Inquire in New Orleans for Dr. Williams. Do not stay there
longer than necessity may compel you. Thank all those who
have been kind to you and continue always to acknowledge to
God his great mercy to you. Your only Mother—E.D.H.[5]

By some circuitous route that no doubt included the theaters of
Philadelphia, Memphis, and New Orleans, the prodigal son returned
to Marshall, Texas, the summer of 1853. Handsome, petted, and indulged, Theodore shared a love of the arts with Lucy, but he did not
have her zest for life and ambition. Irresponsible and lazy, and much
attracted to the ladies, Thee remained single and singly devoted to
Lucy. Only after her death did he express regret for his lack of attention in earlier years and his great love for his parents, sisters, and
brother.[6]

The attention paid to the oldest son shifted to Anna Eliza with
the arrival of her first-born, Beverly Holcombe Greer. Three years
later, another baby, Eugenia Markoleta Greer, arrived. About this time,
in 1855, the town of Marshall was hit with railroad fever. The state
legislature granted funds and lands for the laying of track for the
Texas Western Railroad. Elkanah, Anna's husband, stayed home in

hopes of securing a position. Engineers and surveyors descended on Marshall, and with them came Fleming Gardner, a civil engineer.

This distinguished Virginian boasted more pride than wealth. A courtly and dignified man, he readily displayed his intellect and sardonic wit. Lucy referred to him as "Mr. Darbey" possibly a reference to the haughty "Mr. Darcy" who succumbed to the brilliant Elizabeth Bennett in Jane Austen's novel, *Pride and Prejudice*. Fleming Gardner, twenty years Lucy's senior, soon made it known that he adored her.

Sometimes Lucy addressed Gardner as "My Lord Baron Munchausen," referring to his exaggerated and magnified daydreams. He called her "Lady Bird" and they filled their letters with discussions of politics, economics, and local affairs, spicing them with light-hearted humor and the fantasy of dreams. Their correspondence began in 1855 and for two years Fleming Gardner courted Lucy in Marshall. By February of 1855, Fleming Gardner was writing, "Where shall I find another Lady-Bird? Where find one who wayward and wilful [*sic*] as she sometimes can be; is always so high souled, [*sic*] generous and gentle? Who whether in a mood for the sad and sober or kindled with enthusiasms, is alike interesting—But most of all, where again meet with one so beautiful and gifted? Who will look upon me with the kindness and treat me with the trustful confiding friendship which she has ever manifested toward me. It were vain even to hope it—worse than vain to expect it—I hope to see you again before long . . . " [7]

It was rumored that they were engaged, although Lucy continued her minor flirtations with other hopeful suitors.[8] She wrote to Fleming Gardner in August 1856.

> My dear Mr Darbey—
>
> I received by last mail your kind letter of July 4th. I have just written you but—is it flattery to myself to think Lady-Bird cannot write too often! So you were not sick, but I was—My friend Madame Blanche, the fortune teller, told me I would have a very severe spell of sickness this summer—I hope her other predictions may 'come true' likewise. Do you know I have been looking for you every day—I know that I am a very

stupid little goose. Now Mr. Darbey, there is one thing I want to tell you seriously—You say you will come in January—I will not be at home for we are going to leave in Dec.—I shall be in Washington 1ˢᵗ Jan so you see there is nothing left for you to do, but to come in November . . .

The railroad is going on swimmingly—Maj. B [Barstow?] is jubilant—the legislature has passed the extension bill over the gov[ernor's] head (he vetoed it) also the loan bill which lends the company $8000 per mile—So the prospects are to say the least good . . . I withdraw my appeal in behalf of Nicaragua. But when I am the Lady Dutchess [*sic*] of Munchausen, we will make Gen. Walker a visit & you shall tell him what a great friend I have always been to his cause.[9]

I assure you I had nothing to do with Mr Bryson's going—to be candid & confidential (as Lady Bird always is with Mr. Darbey) I don't think he would have 'done me any credit.' I suppose you are now at the Springs—perhaps at the feet of 'the old love'—No! you shall not dare to love any one else beyond a respectable friendship. You can flirt but be sure you don't go beyond the 'whispered nothings.'

Please believe that I am what I shall always be—Your sincere & affectionate—Lady Bird[10]

The coming of the railroad to East Texas boosted the social life of Marshall and the young people gathered on Wyalusing's wide porches many a summer evening. Lucy dressed carefully for these evening socials in a full-skirted frock that complimented her perfectly proportioned five foot four inch figure. Always inclined to the dramatic, she received suitors from a half-reclining position on a rustic couch placed on the south side of the wide verandah. Affecting a regal manner, Lucy would extend her dainty hand and accept the numerous tokens of love, the flowers, fruit, and carefully penned poems.[11] These indications of love and admiration were not taken seriously for she continued to tease and flirt, totaling up proposals as though marking a dance card.

When Lucy felt that ardor on the part of the male exceeded propriety she rose from her reclining position and, in her best theatrical manner, pointed to the fading sunset. Turning to the mesmerized male at her side, she lowered her deep blue eyes and gently reminded him that way beyond the swell of the Gulf waters lay the only love she had ever known.[12] She told her mother, "Only perfect truth from me alone would retain his [their] affectionate esteem and admiration."[13]

Lucy endeared herself to many men by her respect for their pride. Her masterful tact and ambiguity is shown in a letter written to a rejected suitor, Colonel William Bell.

"I have acted hastily, very hastily, by my reason I am condemmed [*sic*]. We are little less than strangers and did you know me better you might love me less! . . . Col. Bell I know you are noble and good and kind and of it my heart tells me that my lips have uttered only what they would repeat again. If it be wrong to love you I am at least sincere in my error for whatever be the future in that I shall always be unchanged. L. P. H." [14]

Although Lucy told St. George Lee that she would never marry, she could not have been serious. She may have feared that love for any man would create burdens. Besides, she craved recognition for her talents and once again turned to her writing. Her poems were published under the pen name of "Helene." An undated news article from the *Memphis Eagle and Enquirer of Tennessee* mentions, "the many gems she has furnished in years gone by to our own columns."[15]

Lucy was fond of reading the *New Harper's Monthly Magazine,* and wrote to the "Easy Chair Editor" signing the letter with her initials, L. P. H. The letter written in 1857 was published in Vol.16, March, 1858. Writing in the flowery style prevalent in the nineteenth century, Lucy describes herself as, "wearing neither hoops nor paint, and my hair has a style quite its own . . . Mine is a worshiping nature, and sorrows over fallen idols. It is something, in these days, not to be disappointed in things one has set apart as being better than other things."

In the next volume of the magazine, an unidentified writer attests to Lucy's charms, addressing her by her christened name, Lucy Petway, "Her forehead is too high—her chin is too small—she is over-pale for beauty, but that may be the moonlight—and now I see her eyes, I find it does not matter about the rest . . . I have seen those chains of gossamer and iron woven before. Ah! Lucy Petway, Lucy Petway! Spare Him!"[16]

Perhaps Lucy thought she would prefer spinster-hood to the inferior role of wives in the patriarchal Southern society but she left herself a loophole. "A woman," she reasoned, "with wealth or prestige garnered from her husband's position, could attain great power."[17] Once again she looked to politics as an entrée to a society that might offer a distinguished and acceptable suitor. In 1856 she openly campaigned for Millard Fillmore, the presidential nominee on the Know-Nothing (split from the Whig party) ticket, who objected to foreigners and/or Roman Catholics holding government positions. Fillmore, with his running mate, Andrew Jackson Donelson, opposed the Democratic Party's nominees, James Buchanan and John Breckenridge, of the popular "Buck & Breck" slogan.

With true political form Lucy spoke on behalf of the Ladies of Marshall to the Fillmore-Donelson Club. It was quite unprecedented for a woman in 1856 to voice her political opinions in public but the residents of Marshall, Texas, were not tied by convention. However, to avoid controversy, Lucy committed political compromise. She began her speech by acknowledging that women were proscribed rightly and properly from participating in actual duties of politics. Yet, she said, "She is by no means prohibited from watching with intense solicitude, those great national movements which result in our country's weal or woe . . . "[18]

Once again, Lucy was careful not to upset the status quo. Unlike her more outspoken Northern sisters, she catered to her audience, politically and politely stating her opinion. That Lucy would support Millard Fillmore, the man whom she once castigated for not coming to the aid of the filibusters in Cuba, shows again that she played both sides. When Fillmore lost the election she turned her attentions to his successful opponent and made plans to attend James Buchanan's inaugural. In her quest for recognition, Lucy seemed to attach her affiliation to whatever star might be rising.

In December of 1856, she traveled to New Orleans with Jemine C. Duncan, friend and dressmaker to the Holcombe household.[19] While in New Orleans they purchased materials suitable for Lucy's introduction to Washington's society. New Orleans was also home to Holcombe relatives and many friends. The Crescent City, the fifth largest city in the nation according to the 1850 U.S. Census, had 116,375 inhabitants. They were predominantly Catholic, foreign, and urban, giving the city the flavor of a European capitol. Life was to be enjoyed in New Orleans and its inhabitants had mastered the art. Hours and sometimes days of pleasant conversation, tempered with numerous cups of fragrant coffee or cooling and potent drinks, passed before completing business transactions. Behind shutters, in the hidden courtyards, or on the balconies with their ornate and intricate ironwork, families watched, gossiped, and applauded the haunting melodies of the street musicians. Throughout this cosmopolitan city, the sweet fragrance of flowers mingled with the piquant spices of cinnamon and clove. It was a city made fascinating by the mix of cultures, languages, and color, and enlivened with an appreciation of life.[20]

While in New Orleans, Lucy called on Mrs. Wilhelmina McCord, editor of the *Southern Parlor Magazine and Ladies Book*.[21] She wrote to her mother of the visit and how she had taken a carriage to Mrs. McCord's domicile, the Delta Book Room of the St. Charles Hotel. After making polite inquiries of their mutual friend, Governor Quitman, Mrs. McCord offered refreshment and handed Lucy a copy of the *Southern Parlor Magazine.*"[22] Lucy glanced through the magazine while Mrs. McCord prattled on between sips of tea. "I do believe that there is sufficient feminine intellect in the South to sustain a magazine, and without flattery, Dear Miss Holcombe, I know of no one who could do more in that respect than you."[23]

Lucy hesitated before answering. "I am a great one to say 'yes,' dear Mrs. McCord, but I am determined never to make a promise unless I am certain of fulfilling it. I expect to be a great deal in society for the next few months. My time and thoughts will be much occupied, Mrs. McCord, but I'll try now and then to send you something."[24]

The next issue of the magazine appeared with "Miss Lucy P. Holcombe, authoress, and contributor." Lucy was not pleased and immediately had it changed to read, "H. M. H., author."[25] To claim a public voice rested uneasily with some women, and although Lucy wanted recognition, she realized that she might not advance in society if perceived as too independent. It is also interesting to note that her choice of pen name again harks back to her ties with royalty.

Continuing her plans to attend the inaugural of James Buchanan, Lucy, Jemine, and cousin Lollie, wife of Lucy's cousin, Dr. Willie Holcombe, boarded a steamboat in New Orleans on 10 January 1857. They reached Point Coupee twenty-four hours later and while her companions laughed and gossiped Lucy, full of introspection, wrote to her mother.[26] She mentioned her visit to New Orleans as being quiet and pleasant, with many callers during the day but going out only three nights, accompanied by cousin Lollie. She was more pained than pleased, she told her mother, by Judge Spoffard's confessions of love. "I felt I could never marry him," she wrote, "and my frankness cost me tears but I am sure he did not think less kindly of me for them."

She had also called on her mother's old friend, a Mr. Honfleur, and described the meeting, "He took the veil from my bonnet and looked earnestly into my face while the tears came rapidly into his eyes. At last he said, 'It is her child.' I literally gushed into tears and remarked, 'You must please forgive me sir, I love my mother so, that I can never love her enough.'"

Lucy continued her letter with plans that she meet her parents at cousin Willie's home in Waterproof, Louisiana, and together they would proceed by boat, train, and possibly stagecoach to Washington. With consideration for her sister's children, Lucy suggested that they bring little Beverly with them. She wanted "Doctor Willie" to examine the child and treat him for some facial aberration although she does not indicate in her letter what this might have been. Soon after her parents' arrival, the group continued on its way, reaching Washington in time for the inauguration of President James Buchanan, 4 March 1857.

An air of festivity filled the city. Red, white, and blue bunting, wrapped around the newly installed lampposts, flapped in the wind. Pedestrians overflowed the walkways. Carriages, calashes, drays, and commercial wagons jammed the streets. Excitement was rampant. The city of Washington looked forward to this new administration. James Buchanan, a bachelor from Pennsylvania with strong ties to the South, enjoyed the social paradise the Southerners made of the Federal City. They held the majority of seats in the Senate and the House of Representatives. Some of these positions had passed from generation to generation in the same family. Southern wives and daughters, known for their flawless complexions and sweet charm, spent the winter months at Brown's Hotel or the Ebbitt House, favorite strongholds of the Southern contingent. Social activity blossomed while political battles continued to be hotly contested in the Senate Chamber and the House. Competition for political office increased and elections turned violent, but the economy prospered and building continued along Pennsylvania Avenue.

Mrs. Clement Clay, wife of the Senator from Alabama and doyenne of society, wrote of the reckless gaiety and the elaborate parties that feted those in government circles, "People were mad with rivalry and vanity."[27] It is no wonder that Lucy longed to spend a season amongst this glitter of wealth and wit. Although she pictured herself as an intellectual, she took great interest in fashion and the celebrated balls whose cost and brilliance set capital matrons buzzing. Much impressed by the Inaugural ball, she wrote of a singular woman guest to whom she gave the fictitious name, Clotilde.[28] "I like to think of her tall slender form in the rich robes & better still of radiant brow upon which was shadowed forth that nameless mystic power which is seldom seen in the face of woman . . . She felt her power & used it with a relish & extent truly feminine for which act of justice to her sex I thank her with all my heart . . . "

Lucy's romantic fantasy presents a more serious side of one so willful and graciously spoiled. Being in the midst of society, she used every opportunity to observe those around her. What she saw did not always please and she recorded her impression of American women in general, "I had a sorrowful understanding of Mrs. Bremer's appreciation of America en mass.[29] I saw every day the graceful fragile forms withering even in their spring, & the delicate features innocent of vital energy or intellectual activity. I saw too that eager grasping at monetary pleasure, that great want of inner cultivation & development which causes American women to be, if so sad a truth may be spoken, unworthy of American institutions." [30]

These observations speak much for Lucy's need to excel intellectually, to be worthy of her heritage and patriotic to her country. Serious as they may sound, Lucy's observations did not deter her from enjoying Washington social life and, after the inaugural festivities, she and her mother left the Capital to visit friends and relatives in Virginia. Letters from Anna Eliza awaited them. Sweet, dependable, chatty Anna Eliza seemed to be floundering in difficulties. An errant husband, financial difficulties, and a third pregnancy, multiplied her miseries. She missed her oldest child, Beverly, who was still with Doctor Willie at Waterproof, Louisiana. No doubt Anna envied her sister's freedom and missed her companionship. In a letter written from Marshall, Texas, dated 7 February 1857, she instructs Lucy to care for their mother's health, "Attend to mother at once if she shows any sign of sickness and on no account forget the mustard plasters on her breast & feet, and the hot bath. She can take Morphine very well when she is in extreme danger but only then." [31]

Lucy and her mother returned home to find a thoroughly distraught Anna. Whooping cough raged through the servants' quarters and Anna, alone with her children, tried to cope with the management of the house and the troublesome conditions at their father's Fern Lake farm. Anna's husband, Elkanah, a born soldier possessed by a desire for action and recognition, had gone off to recruit members for the suspect organization called the Knights of the Golden Circle.

This secret order of militant Southerners and Northern subversives was organized about 1854 by George Washington Lamb Bickley, a man professing to be a medical doctor. The organization was patterned on the lines of the old Southern Rights clubs of the 1830s.

Under Bickley's management, lodges or "Castles," as the Knights called them, sprouted throughout the Deep South and in a great number of Northern states.[32] Beneath a facade of secret codes, passwords, handshakes and rituals lay their subversive plan to colonize the northern provinces of Mexico and enter them into the Union as slave states.[33] Their ultimate goal, in cooperation with the secessionists, would be to establish a grand empire on the foundation of slavery.[34] With Bickley's urging and Elkanah's help, thousands of men were recruited in Texas and Louisiana.

Saner minds knew Bickley to be a dangerous humbug, a charlatan with a glib tongue. "General" Bickley was exposed as a "scoundrel."[35] But Elkanah would not give up. Determined that Bickley's "glorious undertaking" would not fail he traveled about the country enlisting "knights." Elkanah's subsequent neglect of Anna and his children and his influence on Theodore worried the Holcombes, causing a rift in the family.[36]

Worry and lack of Elkanah's presence and financial support told on Anna's health. In her inimitable way, the girls' mother took command. With Lucy, Anna Eliza, two young grandchildren, Beverly and Markoleta, their nurse, and a lady's maid, Eugenia set off for the "Springs" in Virginia to take the cure. Quite possibly she hoped not only for Anna's restored health but that a suitable husband for Lucy would be found at the so-called "Marriage Mart" of the South.

CHAPTER EIGHT

1857

The Marriage Mart
of the South

*T*he mountains of western Virginia provided a welcome summer retreat for residents of the fever-infested lowlands and coastal regions of the Southern States. Resort hotels and cottages were clustered in valleys ringed by numerous mountains and mineral springs. The grandest of these hotels, White Sulphur Springs, known as "The White," ruled over lush green lawns against a backdrop of mountains criss-crossed by trails for riding and hiking. Romance flourished in this setting and The White enjoyed a reputation far and wide as the Marriage Mart of the South.[1]

Families made yearly pilgrimages to the springs in search of social distraction and health and, more importantly to some, to launch their daughters into society at one of the coveted balls in The White's ballroom with its magnificent chandeliers. Many arrived in elegant carriages trailed by wagons loaded with servants and trunks of finery. Some took up residence in the cottages surrounding the main building on streets with names of Virginia, South Carolina, Alabama, and Georgia.

Upon arrival of the Holcombe entourage in 1857, a tired Eugenia, distracted by the "oompah" of the German band's afternoon lawn concert, found that all the rooms in the main building were occupied and all cottages taken. The manager accommodated them at the comfortable but less elegant Sweet Springs Hotel seventeen miles farther east, with the understanding that they would return to The White for the ball.

Eugenia's disappointment may have been alleviated when she read the next day's notice in the 15 August 1857 *Charleston Courier,* "The sweet poetess, Miss Lucy Holcombe of Texas,—better known in the literary world by the Nom-de-plume of 'H. M. Hardimann'—has arrived." The reporter mentioned that Lucy was too much admired as a woman to be spoken of merely as a writer and added, "Her clear blue eyes, from which she looks out with such a calm inquiry, are by no means to be imposed upon; they detect at once the true meaning of the scene before her."[2]

Once settled into the Sweet Springs Hotel, it was customary for guests to sit on the long gallery sipping lemonade and cooling themselves with palm fans. Acquaintances from earlier visits waved. Men, young and old, dressed in doeskin trousers, with white shirts billowing from embroidered vests, doffed their hats and stopped to pay their respects. Younger girls, new to the scene, watched with envy and practiced indifference. Etiquette would demand that pretty Anna Eliza, a married lady unaccompanied by her husband, be relegated to the ranks of the chaperones. This would define her role at the balls as one who could only take part as an observer from the sidelines.

In the hotel room, Lucinda, the Holcombes servant, unpacked Lucy's extensive wardrobe for husband-catching.[3] She warmed the flat-irons, hung the filmy fichus and lace berthas, thin substitutes for modesty, and bent the skirt hoops into shape. The ten yards of embroidered silk and brocade fashioned into Lucy's ball gown had to be smoothed and fussed over until each fold and loop hung correctly. The early training of a slave as a personal maid sometimes made for a bond of closeness to her mistress. Lucinda's feelings are not known but it is quite possible that she held a certain pride for this mistress who was dependent on her services.

The slow descent of the sun behind the mountains bathed the trees and grassy lawn in a golden glow. Young couples returned from walks and games of croquet to dress for dinner and for the dance that would follow. Most of the young ladies chose gowns of pink or blue for their entrance to the celebrated ballroom. But Lucy, as an older debutante of twenty-five, would not care to look or act the ingenue. With a high sense of drama, she glided across the ball room floor dressed in a golden-bronze gown that matched the color of her hair. Her entrance had its desired impact as noted by Lucy's friend, Sallie Simkin who recounted Lucy's meeting and courtship at the Springs. "Francis Wilkinson Pickens watched with speechless admiration as this vision in gold floated toward him, and the twice-widowed congressman from South Carolina knew immediately that he wanted this woman to be his wife. Regaining his poise, he asked Miss Holcombe for the first dance and launched his pursuit by begging her to ride with him early the next morning"[4]. Typically punctual, Pickens called for Lucy before the sun had burned the mist from the valley. Exhilarated by the cool, clean air, Lucy tucked the long skirt of her bottle-green habit under the horn of the sidesaddle and started off at a brisk canter without waiting for Mr. Pickens to mount his horse.

Later, they walked in the gardens. Hopelessly lost in the notorious maze, they paused to rest on a discreetly placed bench behind a screen of sweet olive trees. Mr. Pickens, breathing heavily from exertion, or from excitement, poured out his life and his love and proposed marriage. Lucy demurred, professing they had only just met and scarcely knew each other. Mr. Pickens persisted, "Do you think giving you more time, you could love me?"

"Oh, it is possible," she answered.

The Honorable Mr. Pickens mentioned that he'd been asked by President Tyler to serve as ambassador to France. Also, President Polk had wanted him to represent America at the court of St. James in

Great Britain. He had refused both positions. Lucy coyly mentioned that she often dreamed of living abroad. "Perhaps," she remarked with modest hesitancy, "if President Buchanan appoints you to an interesting place I might consider your proposal."

Pickens's reaction was immediate. He left for Washington the next morning. The journalists in the *Charleston Courier* of August 1857, exulted, "It is whispered that a certain distinguished gentleman from South Carolina has become deeply affected by the fascinations of this lady."

Francis Wilkinson Pickens of Edgefield, South Carolina, was descended from a family of statesmen and patriots. Born in 1807 at Tupelo, Colleton District, South Carolina, he was the son of Susannah Smith Wilkinson and Governor Andrew Pickens.[5] As a brilliant young lawyer under the tutelage of South Carolina's revered statesman, John Calhoun, Francis's stellar rise in politics assured him a high position in government. As a state legislator he ran successfully for United States Congress winning his seat in 1853. A devout Episcopalian, Francis Pickens was reputed to be the wealthiest man in South Carolina with over 500 slaves on plantations in Alabama, Mississippi, and his native state.

Pickens spoke freely of his wealth, his political leadership, his social connections, and the fact that he was twice a widower with five grown daughters. Of square build, a large open face, intelligent brown eyes and formal manners, Pickens considered himself a good catch at the age of fifty-one. When he returned to the Springs and found that his love had left with her mother to visit relatives in nearby Lynchburg, Virginia, he sat down to write the following letter.[6]

Sweet Spring—Wednesday 18 August 1857
My dear Miss Lucy

We arrived safely last night and I would have called then on your sister, Anna Eliza, but I was confused and put out very much from having left my trunk at the White Sulphur, and when I began to complain about it, I found that was not the worst of it, for I had left my heart also at that sweet birth place of soft & passionate love . . .

I called however this morning directly after breakfast & found her & children well. She says she has no idea of going back to the White for she is so comfortably fixed here. I told her that you seemed so delighted with your new beaux that I supposed you wanted to remain where you were. She replied "Ah! Sister Lucy says a great many things she does not mean, but Ma rules and controls her. She indulged her sometimes but not always!"[7]

I do hope it will suit you to come, but if you do not please my dear Miss Lucy—remember what you promised me faithfully to do, that is—that you would be careful not to remain out in the dew late at night again or expose yourself to colds. I beg this of you not from any selfishness so much as from the love I fondly bear you and the deep deep interest I take in your welfare. You are delicate & sensitive to the last degree. Your nervous system is so finely strung that it requires the softest zephyr of the balmy South to play forever on it, & the slightest blast, from the North, chills & sickens it . . .

Several who know you, say that you are engaged & have been for sometime. I hardly think any man worthy of you . . .

The scarlet fever, in the very mildest form, is on two children in one of the brick cottages. There is some panic, but in reality no danger, if children are kept from going near to it. Your sister is in the new hotel & there is no danger unless it gets into it . . . I saw your sister this evening again, & she does not seem alarmed.

Make my particular & kindest respects to your mother & for yourself the most disinterested admiration of one who loves you dearly   F. W. Pickens

P. S. . . . I suppose you enjoy yourself very much, but please do not let any one prejudice you against me by any ridicule to which a proud & beautiful young girl is always so sensative [*sic*]. F W P [8]

The letters of Francis Pickens, written in the accepted formal and sentimental Victorian style, show him as idealistic, didactic, and romantic with an over-riding paternalism. Lucy did return to Sweet Springs and remained there about a week. During that time she saw a great deal of Francis. They rode horseback in the mornings, walked on the mountain paths, wandered in the rose gardens, took tea, and called on friends. Francis wanted Lucy to meet a particular friend, Mrs. McCord, a widow from Columbia, South Carolina, who had written the tragedy, *Caius Gracchus.*

Louisa Susannah Cheves McCord also wrote many articles defending slavery, free trade, and arguing that a woman's sphere lay within the home. Mary Chesnut writes of Lucy's meeting with Mrs. McCord. "Lucy the fair was not slow and low-voiced and languid then. She was bright and fluttering. Unfortunately Mrs. McCord directed her conversation to Mr. Pickens. As they left the room, Miss Lucy Holcombe, who was not accustomed to play second fiddle or to be overlooked, was on her high horse and gave Mrs. McCord a Parthian shot. 'I came here supposing you were my friend, Mrs. Wilhelmina McCord, who is the editress [*sic*] of a New Orleans newspaper.'"9

On 27 August 1857, Lucy and her mother left the Springs. Francis, with the vanity of an older man, accompanied them as far as Richmond, Virginia. Eugenia tried to dissuade her daughter's ardent suitor by saying that her grandson, Beverly, would inherit her money.10 She underestimated Francis. Hopelessly in love, he sent Lucy a gift of pearls and penned a long, sentimental poem ending with the following stanza—

> Why did we meet? I dream of thee by night
> And think of thee by day; the morning light
> Wakes me to breathe thy name, the evening hour
> Brings memories of thee; thou hast the power
> To bind my spirit unto thine, till thought
> becomes a dream with remembrance fraught.11

Heaving with the love-sick pangs of an adolescent, Francis wrote in his diary, "She is so beautiful & sweet & her hair so soft—We became engaged at Sweet Springs, Va, last week in August." Then he carefully folded a thick strand of titian hair in his vest locket and curled a few strands into his large signet ring.[12] If Lucy knew that he considered them engaged she made no mention of it and, in all probability, she viewed this as just another one of her conquests to be forgotten momentarily.

Lucy and her mother left Francis and journeyed to New York City, possibly by train. It was late September of 1857 when they arrived home making the trip by both train and steamboat. Francis returned to Edgewood, his South Carolina plantation, in October.[13] Three letters from Lucy awaited him. He answered immediately, pouring out his feelings in flowery expressions of love to, "Miss Lucy who has joy in her eye and peace upon her radiant brow." On the envelope of one of Lucy's letters, Francis wrote, "The affection of a beautiful woman, spoiled yet noble & intelligent."[14]

Much can be learned about Lucy in Francis's letters. In a pedagogic manner, he repeats her statement or question before answering. She confesses that she is nothing but a petulant child and will never bear restraint. "If I want to go to the North Pole and you objected, I would go anyway." Francis may have chuckled to himself when he answered as a father might to a child, "All I beg is that you don't expect me to go with you."[15]

She expressed interest in his possible election to the United States Senate and discreetly inquired about his property. Francis, who inherited his wealth, answered, "I never made any money in my life. Wealth I never esteemed essential to happiness, on the contrary it enslaves the soul when it becomes overgrown."[16] It is doubtful that Lucy shared this attitude.

When Francis heard that she had stayed up to all hours of the morning in the Cincinnati hotel lobby with her cousin Beverly Robertson, he rebuked her. Lucy criticized him for being jealous. He tried to dodge the accusation by claiming he was only interested in her health. But Lucy would not let it go and wrote, "If I were your wife and you were not happy, I am quite sure it would be because you were very unreasonable and did not love me!"[17]

In schoolboy fashion, Francis declared his love and confessed that he was petulant, inferior, tyrannical, selfish, close, stingy, hard, and exacting. But, with exasperating pomposity he countered this with his noble traits of patriotism, consideration, intelligence, and love of virtue, fame, and public devotion. He reminded Lucy that he expected to be elected by state legislators to the United States Senate.[18] By now the prospect of life in Washington as a Senator's wife had paled and Lucy gambled for higher stakes. She reminded him that she preferred foreign travel and that President Buchanan had offered him the post of Minister to Russia.[19] At this point Francis seemed willing to move mountains to win Lucy, yet he desperately wanted to be elected to the United States Senate. Playing both sides, he asked President Buchanan that his offer of the post of Minister to Russia be kept open pending the January election results of 1858.

Once again Francis implored Lucy to give her father the letter he had written requesting permission to marry her. Anna Eliza had advised her sister to wait. Lucy further entreated Francis not to complain or give her lectures, as she could not bear criticism. Francis sent her a beautiful edition of Shakespeare. Lucy refused the gift saying she did not appreciate being given lectures through another and declared that she would never condescend to him or to anyone to justify herself.[20] It is not known which of Shakespeare's works Francis chose as a subtle example or lesson.

Hopelessly in love, Francis bared his soul to Lucy. He wrote of his wealth, his concern for his slaves, his love of nature, his children, and his political views, and occasionally meandered into philosophy with frequent quotes from the classics. Indeed, he told all, except a misalliance he'd made as a young man. Francis told his friend, Milledge Bonham, that he did not really think he was the father of "the boy."[21] Pickens salved his conscience by sending money yearly to his illegitimate child and seeing to his education. Years later, an obituary notice of unknown source or date, found tucked into a family album, notes the death of "Frank Pickens, son of the former Minister to Russia, Francis W. Pickens."[22]

Lucy, spoiled, petulant, and admitting to loving admiration, warned Francis that if married she would not expect to be "neglected and avoided as if I'd committed some great sin."[23] He pledged undying attention. But Pickens did not realize that Lucy craved constant admiration beyond the nuptial ties. Friends and acquaintances warned Francis that Lucy was engaged. He seemed to think they referred to cousin Beverly Robertson and was confident that Eugenia would not permit a marriage of first cousins. What he didn't know of was Lucy's fondness for Fleming Gardner, who called her his "Lady-Bird," nor that Lucy was reputedly engaged to Mr. Gardner.

Soon after her visit to the Springs, Lucy wrote to Gardner. The fragmented letter is barely decipherable.

> I have been looking anxiously for a letter. Why don't [you] write me? Some good reason I know, for [you] would not willingly neglect me—I am afraid you are sick, if so, how I wish you were here that I might nurse you. That I might show you how patient & gentle Lady-Bird can be . . . But I should really never for[give you if] you left without coming to kiss Lady Bird goodbye . . .
>
> I wish you would pack your trunk & start tomorrow for Wyalusing. Dear Mr. Darbey, I want so much to see you—
>
> Mr . . . has not so strong & tender a claim on me . . . It does not seem one year since I saw you, but twenty . . . Dear dear Mr Darbey, I am with the most sincere love—
> Your affectionate Lady-Bird.[24]

Gardner apparently failed to carry out Lucy's wishes and her ardor cooled. He wrote in 1857 to his "Ever loved Lady-Bird" and told her of his strange dream in which they were sitting side by side. Lucy requested to lay her head upon his heart and be shot in that position. Gardner agreed, knowing that the same shot would kill both of them. With horror at the thought he awoke, but could not put the dream out of his mind; he felt something of indefinable happiness in the thought that they were to die together.[25] Did Lucy interpret this dream as rejection? There is no evidence of further correspondence on her part with Gardner.

Although Lucy vacillated between affairs of the heart with the conscience of a temperamental, endearing, and spoiled child, she never lost sight of her ambition to be recognized, worshiped, adored, and wealthy. Meanwhile, Francis continued his paternalistic concern and verbose confessions of undying love. Time was of great concern to Francis. He must make decisions about his daughter Maria's coming marriage; he wanted to take his youngest daughters to Europe; and he needed to go to Washington to consult with President Buchanan on his promised appointment as Minister to Russia. Once again he urged Lucy to "go like a woman to your father and give that letter."[26] Offended and angered by his orders, Lucy retaliated, "Mother says, 'It is impossible that you [Lucy] can care for one so much your senior. I would rather see you die in your beauty and innocence than marry anyone you did not feel affection for.'"[27] In his next letter he quotes her as saying, "Furthermore, Cousin Bev says I am too proud and ambitious to throw myself away on a disappointed politician."[28]

Lucy may have been encouraged to write these harsh and cutting words by Louis Wigfall, their outspoken, trouble-making friend and neighbor in Marshall. A hard drinker and fast talker, Wigfall had once been a political rival and near neighbor of Francis Pickens in Edgefield, South Carolina. He made no secret of his dislike for his fellow Carolinian. While Wigfall gossiped, Lucy played for time and enjoyed the attention of other suitors. With no apparent effort, she turned on the charm as the situation demanded and softened her words with romantic idealism, as shown in this poem that she sent to Francis.

> Come sit a while beside me
> Beneath the stars soft light
> And oh! forbear to chide me,
> For I am sad tonight.
> The shadow of tomorrow
> Is stealing o'er my heart
> And a voice of milder sorrow
> Is whispering, 'we must part.' [29]

If Lucy was trying to tell Francis that all was over, her efforts had the opposite affect. In bold, slanting strokes of the pen he answered passionately, "I love you dearly, deeply, wildly, madly, I love you with painful solicitude."[30] Furthermore he promised to take her "through scenes abroad that will deeply interest you and make you one of the brightest of this earth."[31]

Francis may have been blind with love, but he was canny. He offered her a position in the midst of cultured and brilliant minds—with the price tag of marriage. Perhaps Lucy continued to hope for her ideal mate, whom she described on page eighty-four of her historical novel, *The Free Flag of Cuba*, as, "tall and good looking, with cold, quiet manner, and large commanding eyes—a perfect prince of knowledge, at whose feet I would sit with timid wonder and love."

By mid-January, time and patience ran out for Francis. He accepted the position as Minister to Russia with orders to leave by early April. In desperation he wrote directly to Beverly Lafayette Holcombe stating his desire to marry his daughter.[32] When he did not hear from Lucy for fifty-six days he sent a curt note, "I'll be walking amid marble palaces under gilded domes . . . Farewell, farewell."[33] And on 4 March 1858, he added a parting shot, "Nothing but your own words your own wish can ever break my faith with you . . . I will not dip my pen in my heart. I shall go in a few days to Washington. Farewell."[34]

It worked. Lucy sent for him. Francis, the triumphant bridegroom, arrived in Marshall, Texas, Saturday, 24 April 1858.[35]

CHAPTER NINE

1858

"The heart hath reason which reason knows nothing of."
Blaise Pascal (1623–1662)

It was April and Wyalusing never looked prettier. Yellow jessamine twined about the tall white pillars and filled the air with a sweet scent. From the swing on the wide verandah the singsong laughter of sister Anna's children rippled on the breeze. The clopping of horse hooves signaled the town's only carriage for hire coming up the curving driveway. A shiver of panic may have seized Lucy as she recognized the stocky passenger, an ill-fitting wig covering his bald pate. Regaining her composure, perhaps she tucked a rose in her hair, as was her habit, before smiling a greeting to Francis Wilkinson Pickens, her passport to fame and fortune.

Her mother's reception of the Honorable Mr. Pickens was less cordial. Only Anna Eliza received him with affection, remembering his kind concern for her children during the scarlet fever epidemic at Sweet Springs the previous August. But Lucy's parents resented this interloper who wished to marry their beloved second daughter and take her away from home. Eugenia especially regretted that her daughter would consider a marriage without love. And the age—yes, the age—how could she bear to have a fifty-one year old man, no matter how famous he was, call her "Mother" when she, herself, was only forty-seven!

Lucy may have reminded her parents of Mr. Pickens's illustrious South Carolina parentage—he was honorable, highly intelligent, a respected lawyer, a United States congressman, and landowner of considerable wealth. Francis, not insensitive to the family's misgivings, would be quick to present the letter from his friend, President Buchanan, appointing him United States Minister to the highest and most opulent court in Europe. Lucy's brothers were not impressed, although aware that Mr. Pickens's influence might aid in securing a government position for Theodore. Nevertheless, Lucy's determination to marry this man older than her own father won grudging consents from her parents. The former congressman reminded Lucy that time was at a premium. He had orders from the President to leave for the Russian court by mid-May at the latest. The wedding must take place two days hence. Relatives and friends should be notified immediately and multiple arrangements made.

The afternoon of 26 April 1858, a steady procession of buggies, wagons, and horses circled the tree-shaded driveway to Wyalusing. Within the house, the glow of many candles shone on polished wood and silver. White roses from the garden, yellow jessamine, and ferns filled the deep windowsills of the three adjoining parlors now crowded with guests. Their chattering hushed as Miss Arletta June, seated at the newly purchased rosewood piano, struck the familiar chords of the wedding march. Outside, barefoot slave children, no doubt happy with the thought of their own promised party, ran to the tall windows for a glimpse of Missy Lucy and the "Colonel."

Lucinda brushed Lucy's hair into a simple style and crowned the mass of titian waves with blossoms. It is quite probable that Lucy wore Anna Eliza's wedding dress of heavy white brocaded silk. No doubt her hands trembled as she fastened the tiny buttons of the bodice, for it is inevitable that Lucy would regret going against her beloved parents' wishes. She may have reconciled her marriage as a personal sacrifice, a means of aiding her father and possibly brother Theodore. Perhaps she realized that marriage for prestige and wealth might be a delusion but, ever the consummate actress, she began the hesitant walk through the three rooms. Dr. Thomas B. Wilson, the Episcopal Rector, stood by the altar fashioned of ferns and smiled encouragement. Francis stood beside him. Dr. Wilson's voice boomed across the room. "Dearly Beloved, we are gathered together here in the sight of God . . . ."

Francis reached for her hand just as Dr. Wilson addressed the family and guests, "If any man can show just cause why they may not lawfully be joined together . . . " Heads turned and a noticeable murmur rose. Tension mounted as the endless seconds ticked on. Some would glance discreetly toward the back to see if one might come forth. When no audible objection was heard, the Rector motioned to the ring bearer. Little Charley strutted forward in Philemon's outgrown velvet trousers and frilly white shirt. His black face glistened and his eyes riveted on the plain, wide gold band in the center of the satin pillow he'd been instructed to carry.[1] As Dr. Wilson pronounced Francis and Lucy man and wife, ladies wiped their eyes, smiled, and sniffed daintily. To all appearances it was a happy occasion, but Lucy knew otherwise. Her mother's heart was broken, for Eugenia wrote in her journal that night, "My precious darling Lucy so long my companion, is married and nearly broken my poor heart."[2]

Guests strolled onto the verandah to admire Eugenia's rose garden. They sipped lemonade and champagne and tasted Aunt Viney's wedding cake. Toasts were proposed, and disappointed suitors tried to drown their sorrows. A hush fell as Mr. R. W. Loughrey, editor and publisher of *The Texas Republican*, Marshall's weekly newspaper, rose to present a toast to the bride. With gallant gestures, and in his finest baritone, he recited a stanza of Lord Byron's *Hebrew Melodies*—

> She walks in beauty like the night
> of cloudless climes and starry skies . . .

The smitten editor wrote an account of the wedding for his paper, titling it, "An Angel Visit."[3] During the reception, Francis, puffed with pleasure, charmed the ladies with his attentions and old-world manners. The following day another reception for the couple, subscribed to by twenty-four men of the Holcombe's acquaintance, was held at the newly opened Adkins House, Marshall's grand hotel.[4]

Two days later, the newlyweds started their long journey to South Carolina accompanied by the servant, Lucinda, whom the Holcombes gave to Lucy as a wedding gift. It is assumed that Lucinda had no other family when John Hunt willed her to his daughter, Eugenia, in 1849.[5] As a slave Lucinda had no choice in the matter. Trained to be a maid and companion to her mistress, one can only hope Lucinda enjoyed the privileges of this position although she remained in bondage.

The three boarded the New Orleans packet boat at Shreveport. Lucy, despite any misgivings, smiled radiantly and the captain, charmed by her presence and the importance of the occasion, hastily renamed his boat the *Lucy Holcombe*.[6] Approximately twelve days later the newlyweds arrived at Edgefield, South Carolina, and hastened by carriage to Edgewood, the Pickens's plantation.

A long, raised gallery extended across the front of the rambling white frame house. House slaves flanked the wide front door, their barefoot children peeping from behind long skirts and trousers. Rebecca Simkins Pickens, the twenty-four year old daughter of Francis's first marriage, waited at the top of the steps. Francis carried his bride up the ten steps and across the verandah to set her down in the wide hallway. Introducing each of the house servants by name, he guided Lucy through the library and the newly-built small greenhouse that adjoined her bedroom. Edgewood had a look of homey comfort with book-lined walls and many deep chairs for reading but Lucy had little time to enjoy her new home. Within a week, they left by train for Washington. Rebecca, Jeannie Dearing Pickens (the twelve-year-old daughter of Francis's second wife), and two servants, Lucinda and Tom, Pickens's man-servant, accompanied them.[7]

In Washington, President James Buchanan received them with every courtesy. A bachelor, the President had his niece, the beautiful

Miss Harriet Lane, act as his hostess. Although lovely to look at, Miss Lane presented a "gracious chill."[8] While Francis received his orders from the President, Mrs. Clement Clay, the pretty wife of the Senator from Alabama, took Lucy on a shopping expedition. Mrs. Clay referred to Lucy in her memoirs as, "a sweet little nun of a woman." She went on to say that Lucy had arrived in the city with a wardrobe consisting of garments cut of the costliest fabrics but ridiculously made. Fearing that Lucy might be subjected to derision from the more heartless females, Mrs. Clay undertook to remedy the situation by a shopping trip to a more sophisticated seamstress.

Mrs. Clay wrote of an observation made as they were about to step out of the carriage to enter the shop, "I was startled by the appearance, above a shapely foot, of a bright, yes! a brilliant indigo-blue stocking! I held my breath in alarm! What if the eye of the more scornful fashionables should detect its mate! I hurried my charge back into the vehicle at once & summoned our good friend Mrs. Rich to the door and our errand that morning was accomplished by the aid of a trim apprentice who brought to our calash boxes of samples & fashion plates for our scanning."[9]

Perhaps Lucy wore the blue stockings to impress people with her intellectual pursuits. Or, she might possibly be rebelling against Francis's infuriating stuffiness and constant directions. Whatever the reason, Lucy made an inimitable impression in the Capital City before leaving for New York.

Passage was booked on the British steamship *Persia*, scheduled to leave the New York docks on 28 May 1858. When that day arrived, Lucy had a sudden change of heart. The magnitude of the step she had taken and its immediate consequences overwhelmed her. She could not possibly bring herself to go so far away as Russia. Fear that something might happen to her beloved family paralyzed all thought. Her dearly loved mother constantly courted illness, and at such a distance Lucy feared that she might not be able to return in time. Terrified by the thought, she refused to budge and nothing would induce her to leave the New York hotel and America.[10]

Lucinda did her best to soothe her mistress, reminding her that Tom needed to take the luggage down to the steamship. But Lucy feared that if she left the country she might never see her mother again. Francis pleaded, mentioning that the Captain sent word that they were holding up sailing. The ship must leave on time. It must sail with the tides. Beside himself with worry, Francis ordered Tom to take the trunks and hold the cab. Still Lucy refused to budge.

Lucy's family recounted that the famous Captain Charles Judkins, commander of the ship *Persia*, appeared in Lucy's hotel room at this moment. A man of about forty years, most of them spent on the sea, Charles Judkins was well liked by those who served with him and was not averse to charming the ladies. A man of great determination and a rare character, this captain would not care to forfeit his fine reputation by a delayed sailing or conversely to chance the ire of a United States Minister.[11]

Lucy wiped her tears and confided her fears of leaving home. The good captain, smitten by the sad but lovely blue eyes and gentle voice, pulled his chair a bit closer and leaned forward. In a soft yet commanding tone, he assured Madame Pickens that if she continued to feel this way when they landed, he and his ship would bring her right back. The *Persia*, Judkins told her, was built in 1856 with iron in its hull, making it the safest of the Mail Fleet. His sea-blue eyes glistened as he described his command with all the feeling one might give to the love of a beautiful woman. Judkins would note that the staterooms were appointed with every detail fit for comfort and the Ladies Salon was exquisitely furnished in Oriental fashion. Undoubtedly he told Lucy that the *Persia* was the most beautiful as well as the swiftest of the Cunard's mail fleet.[12]

Lucy rose. With head held high she took Captain Judkins's arm and departed to board the *Persia*, now delayed from its scheduled sailing time by two hours. The next day the *New York Times* noted in its Shipping News of 29 May 1858, "The British Steamship *Persia* sailed. Col. & Mrs. F. W. Pickens & two servants. U. S. Minister to Russia [from] South Carolina."

CHAPTER TEN

1858

"talking of elevated and mighty themes . . ."
Francis W. Pickens

Francis, with Lucy by his side, was about to realize his fondest dream of crossing the ocean with his love, "Holding each others hands, looking at the stars and to the heavens, talking of elevated and mighty themes . . . mingling our souls together in the rapture of holy and consecrated love."[1]

The dream ended abruptly with the first sharp roll of the ship. All in their party became violently ill that first day out except the new Mrs. Pickens. Invigorated by the air and enjoying the attention of the officers and other passengers, Lucy promenaded with friends and especially with Mrs. Gwin, wife of the senator from California, who was embarking on the "grand tour" of Europe with her daughter.[2]

Seated at the captain's table, the Honorable Minister to Russia and his lady were introduced to passengers whom Lucy found most interesting.[3] After seven days at sea they reached Liverpool, England.

Rooms were engaged for them at the Queen's Hotel. Lucy was pleased with the private parlor and rooms but thought the food inferior and was happy to leave the morning of 9 June for London. She had much to write about in her letters home, letters that show Lucy to be acutely observant of her surroundings. Extracts from these letters were printed in the Memphis, Tennessee, *Eagle and Enquirer* newspaper in 1858. Lucy wrote—

> I must confess myself a little disappointed in the appear-
> ance of 'Old England' although it is beautiful. It has very much
> the appearance of Pennsylvania and the New England States
> with its patches of green, its running water and grazing cattle.
> But there is one thing lovely beyond description, I mean the
> daisies and butter-cups that sprinkle the earth as a shower of
> silver and gold; the brilliant hues of the red poppy, growing
> wild as it does among the rye, oats, etc., gives a picturesque
> effect, especially when relieved now and then by bunches of
> gay dandallions [*sic*].
>
> I saw also the famous hawthorn hedges, those hedges
> which, in novels, the handsome young man in hunting cos-
> tume always springs over, followed by his dog, and through
> which villains creep to hear important conversations; they are
> very pretty, but I much more admire the Cherokee [Rose],
> and more especially the wild peach hedge seen in my own
> dear South. I was glad enough to see the smoke of London,
> for the car was uncomfortable and I was greatly fatigued. Gen.
> Campbell, the Consul,[4] met us at the depot and told Col. P.
> that he had taken rooms for him at Fenton's Hotel, St. James
> Street, so to Fenton's we came, and it certainly is the gloomi-
> est place in the world. My parlor, in which we dine, is large,
> solemn and musty, bedroom small and five flights up. We or-
> dered dinner at 6 and after dinner drove to St. James' and
> then to Hyde Park. I was disappointed in Hyde Park. It is cer-
> tainly vast and extensive, like a young country in the heart of
> London, and is doubtless the greatest blessing the lower classes

of London have, but the grounds are not, to my taste, hand-somely laid off, nor are there many trees.

St. James' Park has more, and on the whole, I like that better. Hyde Park was filled with the splendid equipages of the nobility, and the more modest vehicles of the commonal-ity, to say nothing of the hundreds on foot who crowded every path. The nobility I think, do not go out in very much finer style than ourselves, only a greater display of servants. The carriages are open (like those in New York) summer, and the coachman and footman in livery. The handsomest livery I saw was black hat with gold band, green coat with gold lace and buttons, crimson plush knee-breeches, and white silk stock-ings.

Unhappy with their accommodations, Francis set out early the next morning, 10 June, to secure more agreeable rooms at the Morley Hotel on Trafalgar Square. Lucy, pleased with the new parlor and bedroom elegantly furnished in rosewood and damask with pier glass mirrors, noted the marvelous view of the fountains in the square. She identified a statue as that of Sir Robert Peel. She could not help but see the imposing facade of the National Gallery dominating the north side of the square.[5] Its dome over the magnificent raised portico and turrets on side pavilions gave it the look of a palace. Britisher Sir John Summerson wrote of the sight, "[It] gives the effect of a mantel-piece with domed clock in center and vases on either side only it is less useful."[6]

The morning of 11 June dawned and Lucy awoke, realizing that she would spend her twenty-sixth birthday in a foreign land, "without those dear faces that have gladdened all my life."[7] A great wave of homesickness made her momentarily miserable until something caught her eye. A basket of pink and white tulips, yellow daffodils, and dainty baby's breath sat on the bedside table. Francis stood at the foot of the bed in his dressing gown and urged her to look within the basket. Wide-eyed with excitement and pleasure, Lucy pulled out a small box and opened it slowly, savoring the moment. Within were earrings, breastpin, and bracelet of wrought gold, with bunches of enameled violets, a tiny diamond in each blossom. Another basket held grapes, peaches, nectarines, cherries, and a fine cantaloupe.[8]

That evening they attended the Royal Haymarket Theatre and saw William Shakespeare's *Macbeth*, played by Charles John Kean, the second son of the famous actor Edmund Kean. Lucy thought the theater dark and dingy and inferior to those at home but she appreciated Kean's splendid performance.[9] The next night they heard Charles Dickens read his *Story of Little Dombey*. He read with singular beauty and pathos but Lucy described his pronunciation as "rather cockneyish." His performance, she thought, was not up to his intellectual ability and reputation and added to her letter of June 1858 to her mother, "He read more like an Englishman than a scholar and was more like an actor than an orator."[10]

On 13 June, Lucy and Francis with Rebecca and Jeannie took their seats in Westminster Abbey for the evening service. Lucy gazed about the grand, old church, its walls lined with the busts of the illustrious dead. The solemn tones of the organ heralded the procession of priests and choir-boys in their vestments. The service was chanted and the sermon, given by the Bishop of Kent, dwelt on the vanity and insufficiency of worldly joys and honors, and the great necessity of true repentance.[11]

The sermon made Francis happy for he enjoyed pontificating on what he termed a corrupt and base world.[12] Before leaving London, the newly appointed Minister to Russia was presented to Queen Victoria. Lucy, however, did not attend as it was a levee for gentlemen only. Francis described the young Queen as dressed plainly with point lace around the neck and a diadem of diamonds and emeralds on her head. She stood beside Prince Albert and bowed to each one presented.

After a week in London the Pickens entourage took the train cars and traveled to Folkestone on the Channel. Lucy was glad enough to leave London for although she admired and enjoyed its many beauties, she thought that nothing was more barren than the comfort of an English hotel. "An American, especially a Southerner," she wrote, "must leave his appetite at home for experience teaches me that it is not easily satisfied with the cold bread and tough mutton which you get in England."[13]

Lucy continues her description—

> On the 16th we left London, after two hours in the cars reached Folkstone where we embarked for Boulogne, at which place we took the cars for Paris. I thought England beautiful, but France is enchantment. I must at once acknowledge Paris to be the lovely capital of fairy land and pleasure. I will mention one of the beauties of this charming city: The little village of Boulogne is three miles from Paris. The government bought the land between the two cities, laid it out in walks, drives, parks and flower grounds, artificial lakes, on which boats rock, swans swim and disappear in the dense shade made by elms and other trees. There is one spot of peculiar beauty. It is a little made mountain, one side of which is entirely rock, over which water brought from the Seine and piped under ground rushes in a beautiful cascade, falling in a lake bordered by grass and flowers. Last night we rode in an open carriage through this wood and its beauty was ravishing, all illuminated by lights in colors.[14] France may be unhappily governed[15], but it certainly has not that appearance for the streets and the gardens and other pleasure grounds are thronged with the gayest, happiest looking people I ever saw.

When Lucy's shipboard companion Mrs. Gwin arrived, the two ladies walked in the Tuileries, rested on benches under the chestnut trees, and took tea in the pavilions. They visited the Louvre with its magnificent paintings and sculpture. Lucy was especially impressed by a landscape painted by Claude Lorraine which the guide book described as, "The sky bathed in that strange, sapphire light, that glorious almost divine light that is said to have brought tears of ectasy [sic] or despair to Claude Lorraine's eyes."

Lucy and Francis were invited to dine with the American Minister, Mr. John Y. Mason, a Virginian, who had been appointed Minister to France by President Pierce. Mason served nobly in this post for six years until his death in 1859. Through him, Francis and Lucy were presented to Emperor Louis Napoleon III. "Of course you will like to know what my dress will be," she wrote to her family, "a blue silk glace ball gown with three point lace sprigs, jewels of the same, breastpin, earrings and bracelet."[16] Francis undoubtedly beamed with pride as his lovely young wife graciously sailed through the introductions in flawless French, a result of her education at the Moravian Seminary. Lucy and stepdaughter Jeannie, both fluent in the language, would find this talent invaluable at the Russian court of Alexander II, where only French or German was spoken.

It would be unusual for any fashionable woman to leave Paris without spending time and money at a couturier's salon. Lucy Pickens was no exception. She spent lavishly and her husband indulged her every whim, though cautioning her to "buy good linens to last a life time."[17] Lucy admitted to purchasing four gowns in Paris and as if excusing herself, wrote to her family, "My stay in Paris was not very pleasant for it was nothing but dresses and bills and etc. and you know how uncongenial all that is to me. I will make an inventory of my clothes when I get to Petersburg and send you little samples of dresses."[18]

From Paris they took the train to Berlin with an overnight stop at Cologne. The Honorable Joseph A. Wright, the tall, agreeable Minister to Prussia who had served as Indiana's governor, welcomed them. They stayed two nights in Berlin before hastening on to Russia. Two and a half months had passed since their marriage and Lucy, although enjoying the limelight, was experiencing more than a moment of longing for the dear ones at home. On their last day in Prussia she felt unwell and curling up by the window that looked out onto a garden, began a letter to her mother whom she called, "The mistress of my heart."

> You once said that you feared European life and court associations might change me, let me tell you dearest mother about that. The longer I am from home, the more ardently I

love and pine for its simplicity and endearments. My greatest enjoyment is to imagine home and where you all are.

Sometimes I see you in your room and the children are playing around you, and Bev. asks 'Ma when is my Lu-lu comin home?' or Sister Anna tells Daughtie to say 'Taudy tum back Annie.'[19] Sometimes I see you all on the front steps and again you and Mr. Dunlap[20] tying up the roses. Oh, dearest Mother, Mr. Pickens says if I loved heaven one third as well as I do home, I would go up to heaven without dying like the prophet of old. I have seen no roses anywhere to compare with yours. In Paris they call the Madam Laffay, La Centerfalia. I went to all the gardens and saw no new variety. I saw at the Jardin des Plant in Paris the grand glorious Cedar of Lebanon said to be the oldest in the world. I pressed my lips to the trunk for I thought of dear Mr. Dunlap. You remember how you laughed at Mr. D. about the ivy border? Well they border the beds here and in France with it and the effect is lovely.

Col. P. has come home and dinner is ready, so good bye for awhile. Friday night Gov. Wright came just as we got up from dinner (8 o'clock) and took me in his handsome carriage to ride in the royal park. I found him a real warm hearted western man but he stayed so late (having just gone and it is now after twelve) that I must shorten my letter for I get up and start for Stettin at 6, in the morning. I do not feel that I have yet written you but when I get to Petersburg I can then have leisure from hurry to lay my heart bare to you.

I got the morning I left Paris Jemime's dear and kind letter. It was like a whole shower of sunshine. God bless you Jemime. I will write when I have rested at Petersburg. Lilac is the fashionable color and bonnets worn large . . . I read parts of yours Annie's and Jemime's letters to him [Francis] and Cinda [Lucinda] and we all cried. Please dear mother write him one of your kind noble affectionate letters for he loves you dearly. All of you. He speaks so often and kindly of brother Theodore and of Father and all, my dear brother. Oh! My mother I think of him night and day with bitter tears and my poor sister! My heart and life, what is her condition? God help us and minister to our need. Love to each one everyone all. I kneel by your side and kiss you ten thousand times and beg you to know and feel my Mother, that as God is my judge no one steps into my heart before you or beside you. You are my first and dearest love and nothing can change or weaken my soul's tender devotion . . .

Kiss my Father my precious little Helen and my own sweet children and love to all friends. Write me. Your own fond child, Lucy P. H. Pickens[21]

CHAPTER ELEVEN

1858

"The confused sound of an unknown language . . . made me feel my isolation."

Lucy Holcombe Pickens

They boarded a ship at Stettin, on the Baltic, and sailed to the Russian port of Kronstadt, docking the morning of 6 July 1858.[1] Francis paced the cluttered stateroom, pocket-watch in hand. Lucy, her new Paris bonnet shading the whiteness of her face, may have mollified her husband with a light kiss to his cheek and handed him the enameled violet and diamond breast pin to fasten her Valencian Lace shawl. With a final click to the trunk latches, Francis ordered Tom to take them to the purser and, with his lady on his arm, the new Minister to Russia, puffed with pride and smiling in the secret way of newlyweds, sallied forth to meet the world. Governor Thomas Hart Seymour, retiring Minister, and John E. Bacon, American Secretary of the Legation, waited on the dock to welcome them.[2]

When Lucy stepped for the first time on Russian soil her excitement turned to panic. She confessed in her letter home, "It was the confused sound of an unknown language, the long beard, and singular costume that made me feel my isolation in full force."[3] Grateful that the bonnet's veil hid her tear-filled eyes, she accepted Governor Seymour's arm and stepped up to the waiting carriage. The smooth-riding vehicle bore them toward St. Petersburg, the "City of Palaces." Approaching the wide avenues and well-kept grounds of the aristocracy's residences, the driver pulled his team to an exaggerated prancing gait. Lucy might have made note that her father would take particular pleasure in the performance of these horses, a cross between Arabian and Cossack from the looks of their short, powerful necks and sturdy legs. He would also be amused at the driver dressed in an ankle length coat, sashed and padded at the waist to give the affect of portliness so favored by the Russians.

Governor Seymour called her attention to the Imperial Palace stretching along the river Neva, the magnificent fountains, avenues of trees, and gardens with flowers blooming in their summer splendor. The sight increased the ache in her heart knowing how much her mother would enjoy this beauty. She could barely hold back the tears, and when they arrived at the Hotel de Russia, Lucy collapsed in the privacy of their rooms to have what she described as a "comfortable cry" until time to dress for dinner.[4]

That evening the retiring minister sent his calash, a small, open carriage with two seats, one for the passengers and a very high one for the driver. They were driven over numerous stone bridges to the Point, the last in a group of small islands that make up St. Petersburg. From here they looked across the Gulf of Finland.[5] The air was brisk and chilly and not like the hot July of summers at home in Texas. By Francis's pocket watch it was almost nine in the evening, yet the sun continued to hang above the horizon while stars shone in the azure sky. Eyes reflected the soft glow of this enchanting twilight. Other carriages drew alongside, the occupants in evening dress. It seemed quite obvious that the aristocrats of Russian society drove to the Point to take the air and to see and be seen. The women laughed and flirted, hair sparkling with jewels, fur capes caressing their bare shoulders. Their tall, bearded escorts rose to the occasion with roving eyes and attentions. The sight very likely raised Lucy's spirits in anticipation of being a part of this elegant milieu.

Protocol demanded that the new minister present his credentials to Prince Alexander Gorchakof, the Russian Minister of Foreign Affairs, and request an audience with the Emperor.[6] Prince Gorchakof accentuated his venerable appearance by habitually wearing old-fashioned garments. To the comments this caused, the Prince replied, "I do not need to dress, I am clever. I do not need sartorial ornament, I read Horace in the original."[7] Prince Gorchakof sent word that Emperor Alexander II would receive his Excellency and Madame on Sunday at one o'clock. Lucy declined. She was unaccustomed to taking part in festivities on the Lord's Day. Francis would attend without her.

The Emperor and Empress were in residence at Peterhof, the favorite summer palace of Alexander's father, Nicholas I. The Honorable Mr. Pickens and Governor Seymour boarded the train at ten o'clock for the eighteen mile ride to Peterhof. The Emperor's carriage met them at the station and Francis confessed he'd never seen anything quite so grand. The large carriage adorned with the royal crest was drawn by four white horses, their manes braided with scarlet ribbons. A coachman and two footmen in royal scarlet livery trimmed with gold and black lace sat on high benches fore and aft. The sight must have amused Francis whose own blue carriage and matched team were considered quite grand in Edgefield, South Carolina.

On arrival at the palace, the Master of Entertainment conducted them to rooms where they could rest and prepare for the formal presentation at one o'clock. In due time the trumpeting of heralds summoned the new and retiring ministers and a stern-faced courier conducted them to their audience. Their footsteps echoed on the marble floors of the seemingly endless halls lined with golden pillars, statuary, and portraits of the nobility. At the entrance to the Audience Chamber, the Grand Master of Ceremonies formally announced their presence to their Imperial Majesties, Tsar Alexander II and Tsarina Maria Alexandrovna.[8]

The Tsar greeted them in English. Francis must have sighed in relief for he had not yet mastered French, the accepted language of the court. Tsar Alexander may have noted the resemblance in banal respectability of Francis to James Buchanan, the Minister during his father's reign.[9] Although only a young boy at that time, he remembered his father's admonition to Buchanan at the end of this minister's tenure, "Tell your President to send me another one just like you."

When Francis returned to their hotel he regaled Lucy with a recital of every moment of his audience and the lavish dinner and musical entertainment that followed. Lucy determined that she would not be left out again, even on a Sunday, and Russia, after all, might prove a very pleasant stay.

For the time being the Pickens family must remain at the Hotel de Russia until an official residence became available. The offices of the foreign delegation seemed confused about the new Minister's duties, his pay, and living quarters. This apparent mismanagement upset Francis but Lucy seemed grateful to settle into the rather grand-appearing hotel. Fluent in the French language, she made their needs known to the staff until Francis was able to speak the language with confidence. Lucy, having an ear for languages, was soon teaching French and Russian phrases to their slaves, Lucinda and Tom.[10]

The immediate effect of the move to Russia on the two slaves is not known but it is assumed they were as much impressed by the splendor and pomp and ceremony as their mistress. Tom, aware of his master's exalted position of representing America, passed judgment on the four Black men of the Emperor's court who dressed in Oriental costume and served as waiters. He spoke of these men as nothing but "Africans and no 'count."[11]

Both Tom and Lucinda enjoyed some amount of social intercourse among the Russians. Lucinda received several proposals of marriage and, with dignity and pride, this fine-looking woman refused them all. Tom, handsome in his blue livery with red and white trim, was in demand to escort Russian girls to dances and other festivities. He confessed to his master that the Russians thought, "the Colonel a king in his country and that he [Tom] is prime minister."[12]

Lucy took an interest in everything. Even the matter of having tea was an occasion not to be missed. Brewed in the strange, rumbling Samovar of silver or copper, teatime became an impressive occasion. Lucy made note of all the furnishings that she would purchase for her home and for her family. She first purchased a beautiful tea set of Russian china costing ninety American dollars for her mother. Lucy warned Anna Eliza not to mention this in letters as Francis found fault with her extravagance.[13] However, Francis often surprised her with gifts quite beyond the frugal habits he preached. She vented her distress in a letter to her sister, "Col. P. bought me the other day a lace pocket handkerchief at $40.00 and I almost cried with vexation. I thought of Mother so often saying 'if I had a million, I would never be so foolish as to give $50 for a handkerchief.' He of course thought I was delighted."[14]

CHAPTER TWELVE

1858

"It was very marked and not known to happen before to a foreigner."

Francis Wilkinson Pickens

*H*aving arrived at St. Petersburg in the summer, they saw the city built by Peter the Great at its best, its construction a marvel of engineering. Thousands of serfs from Russia's vast regions had driven piles deep under the marshy ground and laid on them great slabs of granite to form the city's foundation. On these slabs rose magnificent palaces and churches with walls three and four feet thick as protection against the six months of severe winter weather. The problem of flooding was avoided by a system of canals, dividing the city into numerous islands. Two principal landmarks sat on these islands—the Winter Palace, on the Neva River, and not far away, St. Isaac's Church with its magnificent gold dome. At that time, St. Isaac's Church was the third largest in size compared to St. Paul's in London and Notre Dame in Paris.

On Lucy's first visit to St. Isaacs, her carriage rolled along streets paved with smooth blocks of granite, yet the driver stopped the carriage frequently to avoid hitting the numerous pigeons feeding in the streets. Irritated by the jerky ride, Lucy ordered him to keep the horses going. The driver turned and gravely informed his passenger that Russians love the pigeons for they are considered the "bird of the Holy Ghost."[1]

From a distance she saw St. Isaac's immense gold dome gleaming in the sunlight and from its pinnacle a large gold cross pointing to a cloudless blue sky. The four porticoes, supported by highly polished columns of granite, dominated the vast St.Isaac's Place. Lucy found the interior of the church to be even more breathtaking, with its sparkling jewels and the mysterious scent of incense. Pillars of dark green malachite, red, yellow, and brown jasper, and the reddish-purple porphyry stone lined the white marble interior walls and supported the vaulted ceiling. Paintings of the Virgin and saints, their frames sparkling with diamonds, pearls, emeralds, and other gems, hung above the side altars. Silver and gold bars and precious gems made up the central altar. Lucy saw no seats or pews or cushions to rest on and no organ was visible, yet she heard the "most heavenly" music ever listened to and described her experience in letters to her family.[2] "All kneel or stand and come and go as they please. Priests walk through the church, swinging their incense filled censors, mumbling prayers and blessing all who approach but no sermons are preached . . . They profess not to worship images yet you see a prince of the blood and the poorest serf prostrate themselves, side by side, before the Virgin or some saint, rise, light their offering of wax candle at the altar, drop some coins in the alms-box, and go out, crossing themselves devoutly."[3]

This was unlike anything she had ever witnessed in her Presbyterian background. In Russia the Tsar was the head of the church. Its support came from extensive land holdings as well as voluntary contributions. The wealth so blatantly apparent within the church contrasted sharply with the abject poverty and ignorance of the masses. This appalled both Lucy and Francis. "Little regard is felt for the great masses," Francis wrote to his friend, Milledge Bonham. "God grant that our beloved country and free institutions may long be preserved. . ."[4]

Neither Francis nor Lucy recognized, or wished to recognize, the parallel between the masses, of whom serfs were in the majority, and the slaves in America. Possibly they reasoned that ideally, slaves in the United States were housed, fed, clothed, and cared for by their masters. This, unfortunately, was not always the case. Serfs, however, were accepted as chattel and had to take care of themselves as best they could.

Francis was also alarmed to see thousands of Russian soldiers being drilled or passed in review before the equestrian statue of Peter the Great in the center of Admiralty Place. It did not seem in keeping with the present emperor's advocacy of freedom.[5] When Alexander II succeeded his father in 1855, Russia was reeling from the embarrassment of a failed war in the Crimea. Although Alexander often eschewed military action, he was no coward. Advised by both Prince Alexander Gorchakof and Count Nicholas Miliutin, he astutely kept the military in evidence and successfully warded off the post-war schemes of France's Napoleon III and the baiting of the Englishman, Lord Russell.[6] The rest of the world would discover in Alexander II of Russia an utterly honorable personality, truly the most intelligent of all the Romanovs and the most humane as well.[7]

Lucy's curiosity was piqued. If this Tsar demanded and condoned such a show of strength, wealth and magnificent splendor in public places, what might she see at the Imperial Palace? She did not have long to wait. The royal summons arrived within days and Lucy and Francis, with daughter Rebecca, boarded the train for the thirty-minute ride to Peterhof, the summer palace. The Grand Chamberlain met them at the depot with the court carriage. The swaying motion of the huge, gilded carriage was barely perceptible as they proceeded toward the palace grounds. Soldiers lined the driveway in double file, forming a barricade against the swarms of peasants crowding to get a glimpse of royalty. As the carriage drew alongside, the anonymous sea of heads, faces hidden behind straggly red or black beards, bowed almost to the ground in respectful obeisance to the Imperial insignia.[8]

The Grand Master of Ceremonies and two courtiers led them from the carriage up the stairs to the Hall. The sweet, high note of a trumpet announced their presence, and Lucy must have tingled with pleasure as she heard, "His Excellency, Monsieur Pickens, Ambassador of America, Madame the Ambassadress, and Mademoiselle."[9]

The diplomatic corps, royal courtiers, and honored dignitaries filled the grand salon. Men of various stature and rank milled about dressed in the white or deep purplish-blue uniform of court attire. Heels clicked and swords jingled as courtiers bowed low over the hands of grand dames, wives, sweethearts, and daughters. When dinner was announced, Lucy found herself being taken in by Chevalier Regina, the Neapolitan Minister, and seated next to Count Folstoz, Master of the Household.[10]

The state dinner was held in the yellow banqueting hall of the Catherine Block, one of the more intimate palaces at Peterhof. The room glowed with Baroque opulence and richness beyond imagination. The long table shone with gold cutlery, fragile crystal, and the exquisite Gouvier hand-painted Imperial porcelain, each red and gold plate painted with figures of the various Russian peoples in their native dress. Large wine coolers enameled with scenes of Russia lined the table, and centerpieces of tall fruit compotes in the same pattern were placed so as not to obscure the view of the Emperor and Empress on their slightly raised dais at the center of the table.

An oil portrait of Tsar Nicholas I dominated one wall of the dining hall and a very large tapestry hung at the far end of the room. This revered tapestry depicts Peter the Great rescuing two fishermen from the raging waters of the Lagoda Sea.[11] Huge chandeliers with hundreds of candles gave light to the room. Footmen in royal livery stood behind each chair as stewards hurried back and forth keeping glasses filled with wines for every course, courses that changed so rapidly there was barely time to sample all the enticing and unusual dishes of fish, game, and other viands.

While Lucy listened attentively to her dinner partner, she no doubt discreetly noted her handsome host and hostess and the elegant dress and jewels worn by men and women alike. Diamond tiaras, necklaces, brooches, earrings, and hair ornaments shone like fire in the candle-light. Never before, she admitted to Anna Eliza, had she seen such a lavish display. Her daydreams ended abruptly when Count Folstov rose to toast the health of her Imperial Majesty on her birthday. All guests stood to drink to the health of the blonde, full-cheeked Empress Maria Alexandrovna[12] who, about the age of Lucy's mother, had lost her bloom of youthful beauty. As she watched the Empress her dinner partner rose again. Startled by the commotion, Lucy turned to look into the smiling, gray-blue eyes of the Tsar. With a courtly bow he asked her if the dinner was satisfactory.[13] The gallant Tsar raised her hand to his lips and brushed it with a kiss, turned, and went on to the next guest with the same question.

During dinner, a superb orchestra led by Johann Strauss, the younger, played from an elevation in the lower part of the immense dining hall.[14] Coffee was served after dinner in the drawing room and Lucy, seating herself on a green velvet sofa, put her feet on an immense silk cushion after the Russian fashion. Pince Altenberg and Duke de Osuna, misspelled "de Suda" in Lucy's letter, hung over her attentively. While Lucy listened to their well-intentioned English, she imagined how she would describe the scene to her sister.

"I will spread out the folds of my dress, that your dear eyes may observe it. White silk, two skirts, each trimmed with alternate puffs of white tulle and lemon colored silk, striped irregularly with bands of black velvet; the corsage is low long points behind and before, laced in the back with small cord. There is a Grecian of tulle on the corsage in front and back.[15] But in the meantime, Lord Wellansdale and the English Attache have joined our group and as we are becoming rather merry for court etiquette, it is well that the carriage of the American Minister is announced; for at this I arise, and, walking to the center of the room make a profound curtsey, (old style) to the floor—am taken into the possession of two aids of ceremonies, and put into the carriage."[16]

After a drive through the grounds, Lucy and Francis returned to their rooms to rest until it was time to dress for the ball. Lucinda fastened her mistress into the hooped ball gown of white moiré antique with lace trimmings, the lace looped up on one side with white Lilies of the Valley. Lucy recounted the events of the evening as Lucinda brushed and dressed her mistress's hair, looped the heavy titian braids low over her ears and crowned all with a wreath of Lilies of the Valley.[17]

Francis appeared in her dressing room, smiling and quite handsome in the requisite dress for diplomats of a royal blue court suit, white pantaloons, and silver sword tucked in a wide scarlet cummerbund. A gold medal with red, white, and blue ribbons hung over the white satin ribbon drawn diagonally across his chest. They ascended the grand staircase leading to the ballroom and passed by the life-sized golden figures that lined the walls and represented the seasons of the year. Francis whispered in Lucy's ear as they entered the ballroom, "It's the enchanted palace of Aladdin."

Hundreds of candles glowed from crystal chandeliers hanging the length of the immense room. Mirrors lined the walls, creating an illusion of even greater proportions. Diamonds, emeralds, sapphires, and rubies sparkled against bare necks and shoulders made even more beautiful in the soft glow of candle light. Court officers and men of the diplomatic corps, resplendent in formal dress heavy with medals, bowed over extended gloved hands. And the ladies, their hoop skirts swishing provocatively, nodded their jeweled heads and flirted with their fans.

Lucy had dressed to please her husband tonight. She feared her white gown with its modest bertha covering her exposed shoulders, and only flowers in her hair, might be too plain. When the lilting strains of "Tales of Vienna Woods" signaled the first waltz, Francis took her in his arms and whirled her across the highly polished parquet floor. Lucy moved as effortlessly as a wind-blown thistle. Never had she been in such a fairyland of palaces nor danced to such divine music, and she looked with all the wonder and delight of a child on this magnificence.[18] Before they completed the waltz, the sharp high notes of a trumpet signaled the orchestra to stop. Count Folstov moved to the center of the ballroom, clapped his hands, and cried out, "The Emperor."[19] His Majesty, Alexander II, entered through the gilded doors, his mother, the Dowager Empress Alexandra Fedorovna, on his arm.[20] Tall and trim in the white and blue uniform of a military officer, Alexander II smiled on the assembled guests who bowed respectfully as he escorted the beloved Queen Mother to the raised portion of the room reserved for royalty. When it was Lucy's turn to be presented to the Empress, she moved forward and dipped low to the floor in a formal court curtsy. As she did so, everyone heard the Emperor say into his mother's good ear, "Isn't she beautiful."[21]

This spectacular beginning was followed by a whirlwind of social engagements. Francis wrote of their life to Eugenia. "Lucy has been going with much company and at a large Ball, the Emperor singled her out and led her to the stand reserved for the Imperial family, and which is high above the general room for the dancers, and stood they two alone, conversing for near half hour . . . in French . . . then he said she represented a great and beautiful country and etc . . . . It was very marked and not known before to happen to a foreigner, at least lately. Soon afterwards it was perceived, all the courtiers and maids of ceremonies paid Lucy especial attention."[22]

Lucy confided in her letter to Anna Eliza, "The Emperor and Grand Dukes [Constantin and Nicholas, the Tsar's brothers] dance with me now and then but not with any other minister's wife that I know of and of course the other people would court and admire me, if I were the veritable witch of Endor."[23]

Lucy obviously enjoyed the Tsar's undisguised delight in her presence. He was forty, handsome, cultured, and very appreciative of young, beautiful women. His marriage to Marie Alexandrovna had been one of love, but after bearing seven children, the romance faded.[24] Alexander, always susceptible to feminine charms, seemed drawn by Lucy's unpretentiousness and her eyes that were said to "speak love with every glance."[25]

Marie Alexandrovna was aware of Alexander's inclination for sentimental attachments and to mistresses. Lonely, and no doubt unhappy, she turned to religion as a substitute for love and embraced the Russian Orthodox Church. Preoccupied with miracles and divine manifestations, she ignored her husband's attention to Lucy and the gossip and jealousy it created among members of the court.[26] Meanwhile, the Tsar insisted that Lucy speak French and she took more lessons.[27] She also engaged a voice teacher, Monsieur Rubini, who delighted in training her clear true soprano. She learned to love the romantic Italian arias but confessed to Anna Eliza, "I don't think I would ever make much sensation in America with it."[28]

That first summer of new sights and social obligations kept Lucy in a constant state of excitement and wonder. She felt at home with the aristocracy whose manners she likened to those of the Southern planter class of her own background.[29] She accepted the fawning attention of the numerous counts and dukes, yet was not unaware that Russians, as she surmised, excelled in the art of flattery to gain their way into the bedchamber of their desire. She found the Tsar to be a soft, sensitive man with an inclination to quote poetry. He often invited her to sit in the Imperial Box at the Opera and sent his carriage to take her to the theater or ballet. It was impossible not to notice the Tsar's attention to this American woman whose expressive, deep blue eyes were capped by her unusually straight, black eyebrows, creating her most striking facial feature.

Quite aware of the sensation she caused, Lucy had the presence of mind to avoid being put into a compromising position. When she sat in the royal tent, while court musicians played the romantic waltzes from their barge on the Neva, she undoubtedly devoted her attention to the Tsarina and her children. The Empress, grateful for Lucy's unrestrained friendship, found this American woman fascinating, and a genuine friendship developed. In a matter of weeks, and by royal demand, the Pickens entourage moved into the diplomatic quarters on the Quai de la Cour. This placed them in the midst of royalty, between the Great Winter Palace, now the Hermitage Museum, and the residence of Grand Duke Constantin.[30] Lucy grew to love this home called "Landskau" and commemorated it in a poem dedicated to her husband.[31]

In spite of her social success, Lucy claimed that she felt uncomfortable in Russia from the very first time she set foot on its soil. It is quite apparent from her letters that she pined for home's simplicity and endearments. And, regardless of the adulation of the Tsar, she was appalled at the showy expenditures, the blatant flirtations by married persons, and their quite open infidelity. Lucy did not equate this with her own extravagances nor with the harmless coquetry in which she herself indulged. Feeling somewhat betrayed, she became desperately homesick for her family and life's simpler pleasures. She had made her mark at court and now she began to deplore the shallowness and futility of this society.

Furthermore, she was pregnant.

Philemon Holcombe, courtesy
Miss May Margaret Touhey and
Dr. John Touhey

Dorothea Eugenia Hunt
Holcombe, courtesy Davis/
Little Collection

Anna Eliza and Lucy Petway Holcombe, circa 1846-48, courtesy Davis/Little
Collection

Beverly Lafayette Holcombe (left) and unknown man, possibly an older brother, courtesy Davis/Little Collection

Philemon Eugene Holcombe, circa 1856-58, courtesy Miss May Margaret Touhey

Theodore John Hunt Holcombe, circa 1858-60, courtesy Davis/Little Collection

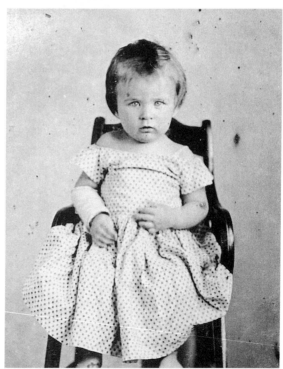

Helen Holcombe, 1841, the Holcombe's adopted daughter, courtesy Davis/ Little Collection

Anna Eliza Holcombe Greer, in her traveling costume, circa 1851, courtesy Davis/Little Collection

Lucy Holcombe, as a Southern belle, circa 1850-58, courtesy Davis/Little
Collection

Francis Wilkinson Pickens, as
Minister to the Royal Court of
Russia, circa 1858–60, courtesy
Davis/Little Collection

Lucy Holcombe Pickens, in her
traveling costume, circa 1858,
courtesy Davis/Little Collection

Tsar Alexandra II of Russia, courtesy Davis/Little Collection

Tsarina Marie Alexandrovna, courtesy Davis/Little Collection

Lucy Holcombe Pickens and daughter, Francis Eugenia Olga Neva "Douschka" Pickens, 1859, in Russia, courtesy Dr. John E. Touhey

Mumka, Russian nurse, with Douschka, 1859, courtesy Davis/Little Collection

Lucinda with Douschka, 1859, in Russia, courtesy Davis/Little Collection

Lucy Holcombe Pickens and stepdaughter Jeannie reviewing troops of the Holcombe Legion, 1861, Leslie Illustrated Newspaper, 22 February 1861

Lucy Holcombe Pickens pictured on $100 Confederate bill

Lucy Holcombe Pickens as a young widow, circa 1870, courtesy Davis/Little Collection

Wyalusing, Marshall, Texas, in winter, circa 1860s–70s, courtesy Dr. John E. Touhey

Lucinda with Lucy's granddaughter, Lucy Francis Dugas, circa 1883, courtesy Davis/Little Collection

Douschka Pickens Dugas with daughter, Adrienne Dorothea Rebecca Dugas, 1887, Davis/Little Collection

The Mount Vernon Ladies' Association 1883 Council with Lucy Holcombe Pickens at far left, courtesy Mount Vernon Ladies' Association

Lucy Holcombe Pickens, circa 1890s, courtesy Davis/Little Collection

Bust of Lucy Holcombe Pickens, Carolinian Library,
Columbus, South Carolina, courtesy Davis/Little Collection

CHAPTER THIRTEEN

1859–1860

"I suspect it will look more like a Moscovite Don Cossack than an honest American child."

Lucy Holcombe Pickens

*T*he November winds from off the Baltic Sea beat against the double windowpanes and chilled the thick walls of the Palace. Daylight hours shortened. The sun did not rise until nine-thirty in the morning and hid its pale face below the horizon by two o'clock in the afternoon. A central furnace brought warmth by a system of flues. Confined to the house as a precautionary measure by her doctor, Lucy spent much time in her sitting room reading and writing. The doctor said that she was "nature's model for child-bearing," and although she suffered intermittently with heartburn and nervousness, her greatest concern was for the child she carried in her womb. She wrote to her sister, "It is so natural for you and Mother to say, 'don't set your heart on a son,' but it is already set, and I could not help feeling sorry, tho' [*sic*] I will thank God for whichever he sends if it is only healthy and well formed in body and mind. I try to feel this, but no human being could imagine my sore disappointment in a girl."[1]

Francis also longed for an heir to carry on the Pickens name. Although he had sired seven children by two previous wives, only five survived to adulthood—all daughters. Now he fussed and waited on Lucy like an old mother and wrapped her in thick red Siberian fox fur against the cold.[2] "The doctors assure me," he wrote to Lucy's family, "that all is exactly right. They have no fears. (Her weakness) will impress on her the necessity of great carefulness and quiet for two weeks after birth."[3]

In the bloom of pregnancy Lucy employed a dressmaker to put gores under the arms of her dresses and lengthen the lace fastenings of the bodice. "My face and neck are full," she confided to Anna Eliza, "and my bosom quite wonderful in size."[4] By mid-February she declined all invitations and was not visible to any but the immediate family.[5]

Outside, the mercury hovered between ten and forty degrees below zero. The broad avenues of St. Petersburg were deserted, but the frozen Neva River teemed with skaters. Francis, bundled against the frigid weather in a coat lined with thick raccoon pelts, joined Grand Duke Constantine for an outing of winter sports. Francis marveled that his royal friend, this great and powerful man in Russia next to the Tsar, was as he wrote to his friend, Milledge Bonham, "as unheated and unaffected in conversations with me as if he were a Southern planter."[6]

Without benefit of sleds but with well-padded trousers, and to the general hilarity of bystanders, Francis and the Duke slid in a sitting position down the popular Ice Mountains constructed like ski slopes. In another area, Laplanders offered rides on rude sledges dragged over the ice by four reindeer.[7] Elsewhere on the river, troikas, thin-bladed sleighs drawn by teams of three horses, tore by at break-neck speed.

Francis, red-faced from the icy blasts, returned from these outings to warm his hands and feet and to detail the sights Lucy could see from her window. He told her of the immense sums bet on the horse races that took place on Sunday evenings. Knowing of Lucy's and her mother's Calvinistic aversion for frivolity on the Lord's Day, he explained, "They keep Sunday evening universally in fetes and dancing. They think it is an evidence of Christian happiness and content and gratitude."[8]

Lucy's time of confinement drew near and the Imperial family expressed great concern. They pointed out the possibility of the babe being switched without the parents' knowledge, as had sometimes occurred in royal births. The Tsar and Tsarina urged Lucy and Francis to move into quarters in the Imperial Palace where all would be under the surveillance of court guards and the birthing attended by witnesses and the royal physician. This arrangement did not suit Lucy but with Southern graciousness, she acquiesced to this royal wish, requesting only that her American physician and Lucinda, her faithful maid and companion, be present.[9] The Empress was satisfied, unaware of the wiles of her American friend.

Family legend, related by granddaughter, and great-granddaughters, has it that nature thwarted plans for a royal delivery. Late on the night of 13 March 1859, Lucy felt the pains of labor. She informed her husband and Francis sent Tom to call the American physician at once. The trusted servant slipped unnoticed through the miles of dark corridors and past the guards. Later, in the privacy of their rooms in the palace, with only her own physician and Lucinda in attendance, Lucy gave birth to a daughter early in the morning on 14 March 1859. Shortly afterwards she sent word to the Empress, assuring her that she would have notified the royal family but did not because of the untimely hour. Empress Marie Alexandrovna forgave her and appointed herself the privilege of acting as godmother.

As further evidence of royal forgiveness, the palace guns saluted the birth and the Imperial band played in celebration of the event. The christening took place in the palace with all the pomp and ceremony that would be given to a child of royalty. As the officiating priest conferred the names, Francis Eugenia, the Empress stepped forward and added two more, Olga and Neva.[10] Turning to the mother and child she threw her arms around both and kissed them affectionately. The urbane and affectionate Emperor bestowed his blessing on Lucy and her daughter with gifts of diamonds. Each month thereafter, he sent Lucy a large diamond for her child. Later, he commissioned the court artist to execute a full-length painting in oils of this most admired wife of the American Minister. A copy was made and presented to Lucy and Francis on leaving Russia, along with a portrait of the Tsar in court regalia. The latter portrait is in the possession of Lucy's great-granddaughter. The portrait of Lucy was believed to have been plundered by Sherman's troops when the Union army marched through Columbia, South Carolina, in 1865. However, evidence has come to light that a Mr. E. A. Richard of New York purchased this portrait from Lucy's granddaughter in 1903 for the sum of one hundred dollars.[11] So far, efforts to locate this portrait have been futile.

The unprecedented attention of the royal couple to Lucy and her child gave rise to much speculation as to the child's father. It was rumored that Tsar Alexander had more than an infatuation with this American beauty. Perhaps, but Lucy did not meet Alexander until mid-July of 1858 and it is not known if the birth of her child was other than full term. Nevertheless, the gossips would not be stilled and Anna Eliza, in a letter of congratulation to Lucy, innocently added, "Your babe must have been born prematurely."[12]

Motherhood put a damper on social activities and, although Lucy fully intended to nurse her child, she felt obliged to engage "Mumka," a handsome Russian girl, to serve as wet-nurse. It was Mumka who gave Lucy's daughter the name "Douschka," the Russian equivalent of "Little Darling."[13] It is the name little Francis Eugenia Olga Neva Pickens would be called the rest of her life. Lucy thought her babe to be a child of singular sweetness and grace with a happy disposition that made up for any imperfections one might imagine. She quickly forgot her disappointment in not producing a son.

A month after Douschka's birth, Anna wrote of their mother's continued cough. A worried Lucy determined to take her child and Mumka and leave for home immediately. Francis advised her to wait.

Lucy begged on her knees but to no avail. She applied to the Tsar for help in obtaining a passport for Mumka but the same day a letter arrived from Mr. Dunlap with the welcome news that her mother had lost her cough and gained strength.[14] Although temporarily appeased, Lucy continued to talk of returning home to Texas. Francis patiently explained his concern that the present unpleasantness between France and Austria and the political turmoil in Europe might prevent her from returning or keep him from traveling to her. But Lucy, with single-minded stubbornness, would not listen.

To keep peace in the family, Francis promised she could travel to Rome in mid-September where she could take a house for the winter and devote herself to music, French and writing. He added further inducements such as having her bust sculpted in marble, cameos fashioned, and her full-length portrait painted. To top it all, Francis said he would pay Theodore's expenses to come to Rome and stay with her.[15] Not completely satisfied with these arrangements, Lucy substituted her Mother's presence for brother Theodore. She then wrote to her mother's friend, Mrs. Lane of Memphis, and urged her and her two daughters to accompany Eugenia to Italy. The ocean voyage from New York to Liverpool would cost $125 she said, and the same amount to go overland from Liverpool to Rome, where they could live very handsomely for $350 a month. Lucy claimed that she knew much of living in Rome from Miss Lander, the Boston sculptor who, with her sister, Mrs. Pierce, spent the summers in Rome.[16]

Surely Lucy realized that Francis also wanted to go home. Politician that he was, he longed to be in the midst of the political turmoil taking place at home between the Unionists and Dis-unionists, but was obligated to fulfill his term of duty in Russia. Frustrated beyond belief, it is no wonder that he was upset with Lucy, who thought only in terms of home and mother. "A husband and a child," she wrote to Anna Eliza, "though sacred are neither so strong or dear as binds me to her."[17]

This closeness of daughter to mother and sister to sister was not unusual in the nineteenth century South where kinship was paramount. Women had greater interaction with family members. Sisters became each other's best friends and confidantes and Lucy, finding marriage to an older, pedantic man less than idyllic, told Anna Eliza that there were unpleasant things connected with her married life which greatly annoyed her. And yet she confessed that she could never bear to tell of disagreeable things, let alone to write about them. She admitted to her sister that her husband was really an excellent man, but added, "Even the best of men are selfish and incapable of sacrifice even for the person they love best on earth."[18]

In spite of her charms, her beauty and intelligence, all of which she used to the utmost, Lucy's rebellion was overruled. Her husband's word was law. Although Lucy had earlier vowed never to condescend to any man, she may have reasoned that it would serve her best to acquiesce to Francis's wishes. He had promised to live in Texas, buy property for her there, and help her father, and that meant a great deal to Lucy.[19]

More pressing matters now demanded her attention. Francis wanted his daughter, Jeannie, age thirteen, to be enrolled in a girls' private school in Germany. Lucy saw an opportunity for escape. Leaving Douschka in the care of Lucinda, Mumka, and Francis, Lucy and her young stepdaughter set off 1 October 1859. John E. Bacon, who resigned his position as secretary to the U. S. Minister when he married Pickens's daughter, Rebecca, accompanied them.[20] They sailed to Stettin then went overland to Berlin where they rested two days before making the seventeen-hour trip by rail to Frankfurt. Mr. Dyer, an acquaintance in Frankfurt, recommended the Grosszer Hirschgraben Boarding School.[21] Lucy enrolled Jeannie and after staying to be certain her stepdaughter was comfortable, returned to Russia fully believing that now Francis would let her go home. He owed it to her, she reasoned, for taking care of his two daughters. Lucy had found the elder of the two, Rebecca Simkins Pickens, to be difficult. It is quite possible that Rebecca resented having a stepmother her own age. As Lucy said in her letter to Anna Eliza, "I fear Rebecca's marriage will be an unhappy one, and I did what I could to prevent it, but she is no loss to me. I don't want to give you a wrong impression, for that is the misery of writing, you must explain so. I did everything for her, and bore her exaction's etc with as much patience as possible and therefore we parted <u>good</u> friends, and she actually did thank me for 'all my goodness,' but a more uncongenial companion I never had."[22]

On the other hand, Jeannie, a loving, warm, and generous child, grateful for companionship and a mother's love, confided to Lucy, "I don't care for any one much but you, Mama, and Papa and baby."[23]

Lucy returned, but Francis would not hear of her sailing to America during the stormy months of winter. The risk of sailing was too great; the Consul informed him of 250 wrecks on the North Sea. Lucy declared that she had no fear and would go anyway. Once again a timely letter arrived from home. Her mother was aghast that Lucy had gone to Germany without her baby. Chastised by both mother and husband, Lucy fumed and stormed. The sparks flew as she vented her fury in a letter to Anna Eliza.

"If Col. Pickens had said, 'I see the bitterness of death is in your heart, take your child and go to your Mother . . . Go rather than suffer such agony'. . . If he had done this, I would have felt bound to him forever and could never have done enough to repay him. I think in my gratitude (nothing touches me like generosity) I would even have consented to live at Edgewood in the midst of all the children, grandchildren and relations of No. 1 and No. 2 etc.[24] But he did not and therefore I owe him nothing."

With undoubtedly a stamp of her foot, Lucy added, "Col. Pickens is only a husband, not a mother."[25]

CHAPTER FOURTEEN

1860

"There is nothing real about European society but its hollowness."

Lucy Holcombe Pickens

$\int$ ick with longing for home and feeling trapped in Russia, Lucy prayed that God would show her what was her duty. Not waiting for divine manifestation, she made up her mind on a Saturday in early December 1859 to leave in the coming week and take Tom with her. That Sunday night Francis became seriously ill. Two doctors attended him while he remained in danger. Frightened by his pallor and weakness, Lucy's anxiety heightened—no word from home and now a seriously ill husband. Finally, on the eighth day of his illness, Francis was able to sit up, but for three long, weary weeks, Lucy continued to pray and worry.

"Never, never," she wrote her sister, "judge harshly of me for you cannot see or understand my situation. I have many faults and sins but I have none to answer for in regard to constant love and devotion to my home and, above all, I have no one even to speak to of all I feel. Do not think I complain of my lot. No, I will be a very happy one if I am spared to return with my husband and child to my mother and home."[1]

While Francis recuperated, Lucy resumed her regimen of reading, writing, and study. She arose at eight and took breakfast with her daughter. Afterwards she studied her French and practiced her voice lesson. At eleven she made coffee for her husband's breakfast and read the French paper to him. Weeks later, when he was able to leave for the office, she went for a drive with her baby or paid and received visits until six o'clock, when they dined.[2] A comparative peace settled over the household. The pleasure Francis took in their daughter and his trustful worship of Lucy compensated for his irritating paternalism. With peace at the family hearth, he likened Lucy to the mythical water sprite, "Undine," who attained a soul after she married a mortal and bore a child. No doubt Lucy smiled to herself for it was the kind and fatherly Rev. Henry Shultz at the Moravian Seminary who first called her by that name.

When this homey regimen began to pale, Lucy turned to shopping. Always generous and thoughtful, she delighted in choosing gifts—slippers for her father, Theodore, Philemon, and Elkanah; boots, gloves, and clothing for her nieces; and nephews and fashionable articles for her mother, sisters Helen, Anna Eliza, and friends. To these boxes of gifts Lucinda added trinkets of ribbons and pictures which she called "trumpery" for some of the slaves, Anna's children, and Helen.

Lucy's love and affection for her family are shown in the letter she wrote to her brother, Theodore, pretending it was from his niece, Douschka.

> My darling Uncle Fee—
>
> My Lulu has just received your pictures and I immediately began screaming for it, and will not let any one take it from me. You may think it strange but it is true. I suppose I knew you by instinct for Lulu and Cindy are constantly telling me of you and saying you would kiss me to death and etc. I dare

say you hardly realize that you have a little Russian niece, but I hope as dearly as you love my precious cousins, there is still a small corner of your heart in which I may nestle.

It seems strange to Lulu to see me with dark hair and (as Cindy says real hazelnut eyes), but she says as I am not a Holcombe, but only a Pickens, it is not so important, and hopes however that you will not be so careless of consequences. I now sit up at the table in my little chair every day, and begin to take a half cup of tea. I am very good-natured and lively, and if you were to hear me laugh sometimes, you would declare it was my own dear grand-papa himself, to whom you must give a heartfull of love from his little granddaughter. I long to be tossed about in his arms like my Bev and Daughtie and Guy and to see Charlie and Earnest and all the wonderful people that I am sung to sleep about almost every night by Lulu or Cindy.

I resemble my cousin Bev in two things, my sprightly manners and unobtrusive nose, and I really think you will love me when you know me, tho' to tell you the truth Uncle Fee I am barely alluded to in the letters my Lulu received from home. But my Mother loves you so tenderly and sincerely that I hope you will love me for her sake.

I have got on my short dresses now, and the first sun-shine that comes (you know it is a very rare article here) we are going to have my picture taken with Cindy, so you may see how I have grown. I hope you have received the likeness sent you of Lulu and myself, but I am much prettier than that now, but my Lulu looks miserable and is grieving herself to death about my precious Ma. I beg of you my dearest Uncle to write to her for it would be a great pleasure and comfort to us both. Kiss my own sweet ma and grand-pa and my Annie, and Helen, and little cousin, and Uncle and Aunt Phil and other little cousins, and don't forget my love to my dear Mr. Dunlap and Mrs. Marshall, Wilson and Ewell. Dearest Uncle Theodore. I am now and ever your own loving little niece.

E. D. H. Pickens

    P. S. My love to the servants especially Aunt Viney and Uncle Neelus [Ned],and Bee and Caroline.[3]

    Gradually Lucy, who derived stimulation from the society of others, returned to the social whirl of the court. Dressed in her red fox furs, adding a cape of sable against the subzero temperature of a Russian winter, she called on her aristocratic friends. In the evenings she went to levees, formal receptions, and attended the Opera every Monday night. Seldom did she miss a court ball, where the Emperor danced with her. When she felt she was beginning to look yellow and haggard like the Russian ladies, she refused invitations for a few days or went to St. Isaac's to hear the singing.[4] Frequently sought by the royal courtiers, Lucy turned her attention to one in particular, possibly to stem the gossip pairing her with the Tsar. She found in the Duke de Osuna of Spain an agreeable and ardent companion. This dashingly handsome and witty bachelor was reputed to be the wealthiest man in all of Europe. Although they were careful to be circumspect, the attention of the Duke to this fascinating American woman did not go unnoticed. Other courtiers chided the Duke for focusing his attention on one woman and not entering into affairs with others.

    Lucy became disgusted with the sharp-tongued aristocracy, with their numerous liaisons and infidelities, and their jealousy and petty grievances. Most of all, she felt the emptiness of European society, in particular, the lack of deference paid to a woman for her wit and intelligence. "If you advance an idea," she wrote to Anna, "you are looked at with a kind of well-bred disgust. You are valued for what you wear, and by the rank you have at court. There is nothing real in European society but its hollowness. I have received great kindness myself, but it does not blind me to the real state of people and society. If I were to live the life of every woman I know here in society, I would be a prey to self-reproach. I make an honest effort to improve, or rather not to lose what little energy and cultivation I have."[5]

    Ten years after Lucy made her mark in Russian court society, Count Leo Tolstoy, who denounced Russian society for its decadence, published his celebrated novel, *Anna Karenina*. In this novel Tolstoy describes a typical social gathering of the Russian aristocracy. One of the characters might easily be recognized as Lucy.

> The party settled itself, divided into two groups: one round the samovar near the hostess, the other at the opposite end of the drawing-room, round the handsome wife of an Ambassador, in black velvet, with sharply defined straight black eyebrows. In both groups conversation wavered, as it always does, for the first few minutes, broken up by meetings, greetings, offers of tea, and as it were, feeling about for something to rest upon. "She's exceptionally good as an actress; one can see she's studied Kaulbach," said a diplomatic attache in the group round the ambassador's wife. "Did you notice how she fell down?"
>
> "Do tell me something amusing but not spiteful," said the ambassador's wife, a great proficient in the art of that elegant conversation called by the English, small-talk. She addressed the attaché, who was at a loss now what to begin upon.[6]

Lucy's distress at the pettiness and lack of morals exhibited in Russian court society did not, however, keep her at home. On Good Friday, bundled against the cold wind in their furs, Lucy and Francis attended services at the English church. Both were fascinated with the differences between the Protestant, Catholic, and Orthodox doctrines, and both were faithful observers of human behavior. Lucy noted that on Good Friday the Russians ate nothing, but went out and embraced and forgave all their enemies in memory of the divine words from the cross, "Father forgive them." [7]

After the Good Friday service, Lucy and Francis drove along Nevsky Boulevard to look at the beautiful gifts displayed in the many shop windows. "For the Russians make presents at Easter just as we do at Christmas." Lucy wrote to Anna Eliza, "Indeed it is by far the greatest fete in the Church. The eggs prepared for Easter are so lovely. They are made of every variety of material from sugar, wood, wax, china, glass, gold, silver, and etc. The shops are full of eggs, natural ones of every color (so pretty, hard boiled and bought to eat.) The poorest Mujick gives each of his friends a gay colored egg on Easter saying with a joyful kiss 'Christ is Risen.' It is said that ten millions of eggs are consumed in Petersburg every Easter. Do you know why the egg is so sacred at this time? They affect to see in it a symbol of the resurrection, the Embryo or new being which will one day burst the shell and fly."[8]

Returning to their apartments, Lucy hastened to fling off her furs and embrace her child, smothering her with kisses. Holding out a furry toy lamb she asked, "Say coo sheep, my precious." Douschka laughed, clutched the toy in her chubby fingers and answered, "Baa," burying her face in the nosegay of fresh violets pinned to her mother's fur cape.[9] Lucinda beamed at the child whom she considered "her baby" and Lucy quoted her in the letter to Anna Eliza as saying, "Bless your pretty soul! Won't you love your Mumsie's flowers."[10]

Lucinda, situated as she was without the companionship of other Black women, may have felt a special closeness to her mistress and her baby. A relationship was established that would put Lucinda in an awkward position—a slave, but a valued servant and surrogate mother to Douschka.

For the celebration of Easter, Lucy and Francis went to the Russian Orthodox Church arriving there shortly before eleven on Saturday night. At the crowded church a guard recognized the official badge of the American Minister and, jostling people out of the way, led them forward to a space where they could stand near the central altar. Masses of people surrounded them praying, bowing and even prostrating themselves regardless of the danger of being trampled. The odors of incense and hundreds of bodies packed within the confines of the church caused Francis to feel faint. Not fully recuperated from his illness, he held onto Lucy and supported himself against the pillars. At the stroke of midnight, the darkened church came ablaze with light from hundreds of candles. Bells rang out and the booming of cannons could be heard in the distance. What had been dark, mumbling commotion turned into a frenzy of joyful sound. "Christ is risen," the priests shouted and the crowd shouted back, "He is indeed, Alleluia." The choir, hidden somewhere behind the pillars, burst forth with Mendelssohn's "Christ Has Arisen" and the priests came down and kissed everyone who could get near. People embraced one another, kissing, and crying with happiness.[11]

Francis and Lucy, overwhelmed by witnessing this renewal of faith, pushed through the crowd to the fresh air of the street. At the heavy wooden doors they stopped in amazement. Great mounds of bread, containers of milk and butter, and trays of poultry and meat filled the porticos and spilled into the street. Smiling peasants stood by, waiting for the priest to bless the food denied to them during the seven long weeks of the Lenten fast.[12]

To cap the celebration of Easter, a grand ball was held at the Winter Palace on Monday. Francis, his dark blue coat fastened with bright blue buttons shaped as eagles, a sash of red and white spanning his chest and the ceremonial sword at his waist, escorted Lucy to what he hoped would be one of the last grand balls they would have to attend. Lucy may have felt otherwise and dressed carefully in one of her new gowns from Paris. The pale amber silk, overlaid with crepe and embroidered with a profusion of sweet peas and purple pansies, showed off her bosom and slender figure to perfection. She confided in a letter to her sister, "The Emperor did me the honor to dance with me."[13]

By now, Lucy's parents had become reconciled to her marriage and accepted Francis. They felt much indebted for his thoughtful and affectionate letters and praised him for his kindness to their darling Lucy.[14] Still weak and feeling "poorly" from his illness, Francis wrote to Eugenia and asked for delicacies from home, thinking they would make him feel so much better. He specifically asked for mayhaw jelly, corn meal, sweet potatoes, dried beef, dried apples and peaches, Garrett's snuff, and fig brushes as "the baby might have croup."[15]

Francis wanted, as much as Lucy, to return home for fear he might miss out on shaping the government of his beloved South Carolina but he felt committed to finish his tenure as Minister. He did correspond with his political friends and through them knew that affairs between the North and the South were alarming. Disturbed by the news of John Brown's raid on Harpers Ferry, in October of 1859, he feared its consequences would drive the conservatives into the camp of the ultras.[16] The disquiet among the abolitionists in the North and the secessionists in the South disturbed Francis, who openly stated that the States must remain united to be a power in the world.[17] Conditions in the South worsened. Crops failed because of the drought. Francis feared he was losing money and his hundreds of slaves on three different plantations needed his attention. The Tsar, interested in the problem of slavery in America, discussed this issue with Francis, comparing it with serfdom in his own country. In just a year Tsar Alexander II would free the serfs and inadvertently hasten his own downfall and subsequent death by Russian activists.

As Francis's tenure in Russia drew to a close, both he and Lucy were appalled at the personal expense entailed over and above his government stipend. Lucy worried that Francis might not have enough money left to buy land in Texas or to help her father as he had promised. Nor might she have enough money for the purchases she wished to make before going home. She regarded all time and money spent in Russia as wasted except for the experience she gained and information she acquired.[18] Faced with the need to entertain as required by her husband's position, Lucy, for probably the first time in her life, practiced economy. Expressing outrage that Baron Gevers spent a thousand rubles for his dinner party, she told her mother that when it was over the guests only remarked, "It was very good but the fish was abominable."[19]

Determined not to try and impress by huge expenditures for the seven and eight course dinners, Lucy planned to do it her way. Francis marveled at his dear wife although he may have seen through her reasoning. Lucy instructed her Russian servants to prepare dishes familiar to the American South. Her European guests were delighted with the innovation. It is said that when Tsar Alexander called, Lucy treated him to fig preserves and hot biscuits. The kind and smitten Emperor reciprocated with gifts of precious jewels. Francis could find no fault.

CHAPTER FIFTEEN

1860

"I find myself going up the hill to Wyalusing."

Lucy Holcombe Pickens

*T*he warm air of June 1860 melted the thick ice on the Neva and swarms of carpenters, plasterers, and painters began repairing the damage caused by the sub-zero temperatures of the Russian winter. Little Eugenia fussed with a cold and teething, and the American doctor thought she might benefit from a more moderate climate. An alarmed Francis urged Lucy to take their child abroad to one of the health-giving Spas.[1] Lucy needed no urging. Her bags packed, she gathered her small retinue—fifteen-month old Eugenia, Lucinda, and a young German nursemaid from Hamburg, Miss Fanny Langdon. By mid-July they were on their way across the Baltic Sea.

"I was seasick and suffered death almost," Lucy wrote to her sister. "Just imagine yourself more hopelessly sick than you ever saw mother, and [a] screaming feverish child in your arms day and night."[2] She worried because her daughter had not been baptized in a Protestant church and determined to have this done in England before crossing the Atlantic.[3]

After taking Jeannie from school in Frankfurt, the group headed for Wiesbaden and a German Spa. Leaving the train at Wiesbaden, they took a carriage up the mountain to the Spa at Schawlbach. The day was hot and a fretful Eugenia cried to be walked rather than ride in the stifling, swaying carriage. Lucy and Lucinda trudged up the mountainside with the squirming child in their arms. When they reached the resort and their rooms at Hotel Duke de Nassau, Lucy felt very unwell with a pain in her side that she attributed to the long, hard walk. The regimen of health improvement she found even more exacting and described her stay at the Spa to her mother.

A German watering place is very different from our springs, because people come here really to take the waters and take care of themselves. They dress plainly and walk a great deal. Yesterday I went with a party to see the ruins of the castle of Adolphseer which was built between two mountains for a favorite mistress of the Grand Duke of Nassau long years ago. As it is reached only by a little path winding over the mountain, we were obliged to take donkeys to ride for they are used entirely in mountain excursions, as they are so steady and sure-footed. They are scarcely larger than big rabbits and have a saddle on (like your old Spanish saddle I remember as a child) covered with a red cloth and [there is] a little boy to lead each one . . . We left at 5 o'clock and trotted about half an hour around the mountain and arrived at Adolphseer just as the sun was going down. After looking over the ruins which were no great things. We had tea and jogged home by moonlight. It was rather a failure in regard to the . . . but was very beautiful. The lovely harvest fields, distant view of the Rhine, with the soft evening sun falling on all . . . I think more and more of my dear home and the sweet joy of seeing you all. I wonder if things will seem strange and changed to me and if the garden and rooms will look like they used to![4]

Lucy's schedule began at six o'clock each morning with an hour's walk before breakfast and a rest under the trees until eleven o'clock. In the afternoon, she lay in the mineral baths and let the steamy water cover her body with tiny bubbles for a half-hour; then Lucinda rubbed her with towels that looked and felt as though steel dust had been spread over them. This regimen made her feel better and after a rest and writing letters, she dined at six, walked again in the evening, and at eight o'clock took tea then went to bed by nine.[5] She seemed dismayed that the other guests spent little time socializing for Lucy enjoyed conversation.

Three weeks of this regimen proved restful, yet Lucy worried constantly about the pain in her side and grew very thin and pale.[6] She considered stopping in Heidelburg for a consultation with a Dr. Cazinoni for assurance that the pain did not foretell something dangerous for, she wrote to her sister, "I have never been normal since Eugenia's birth."[7] On 19 August she received a letter from her sister and answered immediately.

"I was so glad to have a sight of your dear hand but the contents gave me much pain. You cannot tell me anything. I know all you endure with an aching hopeless heart & I shed more tears for you than I would for myself. God willing I will ere long be with you & there is indeed so much comfort in such sympathy as we feel for each other— but there are some things I must say to you. I think you are wrong to go on having children & I would let him spend the pittance he has as soon as possible & then he would feel his true position . . . We have taken passage in the Adriatic to sail 24th of October & will, God permitting, reach N.Y. the 6th or 7th of November. I hope and pray my dear mother will meet me in New York."[8]

Lucy's longing for home and mother was all too apparent and she closed her letter with this touching sentence, "How well I remember everything. I see us all sitting on the gallery after supper having a good talk. I try to feel patient but I find myself going up the hill to Wyalusing."[9]

While Lucy wrote, Lucinda screamed the following message to be included in her letter to Anna Eliza, "Tell Miss Anna I don't know why she don't expect to find 'tuger ting' beautiful. She is the prettiest child I ever saw anyhow, tell Miss Anna I say just wait. I bound Miss'll think her pretty and smart too. Miss Anna'll love her too, her way, but she never was no hand about kissin and goin on over her own children."[10]

For two months Lucy toured the Continent and visited with friends while Francis waited for his replacement and saw to the crating of their belongings, a major undertaking considering their collection of exquisite furnishings and the numerous valuable gifts from court admirers. Disturbing news arrived from home of severe drought, crop failures, and the armyworm ravaging the vegetation. But the happy prospect of home kept Lucy from being too concerned about crop failures unless it would interfere with the purchases she wanted to make before leaving Europe. Thoroughly impractical, she reasoned that her husband, whom she often referred to as "Col. P.," would give her the very last cent of his ability.[11]

Francis did give her carte blanche for expenditures in search of health but it is doubtful he realized that his generous wife intended to surprise her friends with Paris gowns. She asked her mother to send exact measurements for herself and friends and purchased Paris gowns of green and white tulle, lilac moiré, antique pink silk with small pink and white flounces, and a blue pompadour silk. She also made room in her luggage for the cowslips, daisy roots, broom, violet, and heather seeds for her mother and sister and the unusual vegetable seeds for her father.[12]

By mid-September, John Appleton, the new Minister, arrived. Francis relinquished his post and made a hasty tour of Warsaw's antiquities before gathering his family and crossing to Southampton, England, to board ship for America.[13]

With passage booked for 26 October1860, they boarded the *Adriatic* a ship of the Collins Line. This steamship had the distinction of carrying a calcium light, one of the first searchlights ever sent to sea.[14] Once aboard, Francis and Lucy enjoyed the freedom of conversing with shipboard acquaintances without the restraint of diplomatic policy. Conversations centered on the coming presidential election in America, the contest between the Republican, Abraham Lincoln, and the Democrat, John C. Breckenridge of Kentucky.

Lucy and Francis were cognizant of the current political situation through letters from friends and newspapers. Francis had earlier mentioned to President Buchanan that the nomination of a Northerner would split the Democratic party. With an undisguised hint he added, "The way to avoid danger is to elect a Southerner who has the nerve to do what is right for the country."[15] Although the nominees had been named, Francis never gave up hope for himself and let it be known that he was ready "at the first tap of the drum . . . for my home and country."[16] Perhaps he looked to historical precedent to bolster his dreams. Both Buchanan and Lewis Cass had won the Democratic nomination after serving abroad and Francis, with a young, intelligent, and charming wife by his side, was doubly confident of success.[17] Both he and Lucy knew that only another high office would do after the magnificence and prestige of the Russian court.

Eleven days after leaving England, the *Adriatic* steamed into the New York docks. Medical examinations and customs over, Lucy, her children, and servants debarked. Francis stayed behind fuming and fussing until the steward located their missing cases. He joined his family later at the hotel. It is not known if Lucy's mother was there as planned.[18] If this was so, one can imagine the tears of joy shed at their reunion.

The next morning, 7 November 1860, telegraph wires hummed with the electrifying news that the Northern abolitionists had helped to push Lincoln into office. Intense excitement gripped the nation. Prior to the election, the Southern states had blustered and talked of disunion if Lincoln, the "Black Republican," were elected. Governor William H. Gist cautioned his South Carolina legislature to remain in session until the final results of the election were known before taking whatever measures deemed necessary.[19] Francis Pickens, although at this time not in favor of secession for all, agreed that for his home state it might be the better action rather than see South Carolina being dragged into the "mire of submission."

With her husband's future in the balance, Lucy faced making a decision. For three homesick years she had yearned to return to her family in Texas. Now, talk of secession and the threat of war provided the catalyst that overshadowed this overwhelming desire. With no hesitation Lucy chose to go instead to South Carolina and support her husband, but first they would stop in Washington to report to President Buchanan.

The city of Washington, sometimes referred to as "a city of magnificent distances," had been ambitiously laid out over an extensive area.[20] Vast sums had been spent on public buildings, many of which in 1860 were in various stages of completion. These imposing Federal buildings of Greek Revival style lined the avenues leading to the Capitol. One exception in architecture was the huge, red-stone Gothic edifice of the Smithsonian Institution. During the Buchanan administration the city gradually became worthy of its position as representative of all America. The achievement would be of little comfort to the President in the trying days to come.

Buchanan had entered the White House at age sixty-four as one of the oldest and presumably the best qualified statesman to serve as President. He had brought Minnesota, Oregon, and Kansas into the Union, raising the number of states to thirty-three. A handsome bachelor of courtly manners who enjoyed society, Buchanan was known to favor the Southern contingent. But, with the increasing hostility between the Unionists and the Southern political activists, he found himself at the center of a political maelstrom. Reluctant to commit to any definite action, Buchanan did nothing and hoped the problem would go away until the next administration could take care of it.

Early in November 1860, a delegation from South Carolina had called to discuss the president's plans for the unfinished forts in Charleston harbor. Buchanan did not enjoy being caught in the middle of a turbulent situation and tabled the decisions for the new administration. When questioned about the troubles between the North and South, he answered a reporter for the *New York Journal of Commerce* on 7 July 1860, "It is easier to mix oil and water than expect the sections to unite."

Nevertheless, the President was anxious to discuss the situation with his friend, Francis W. Pickens, who had earlier assured him,

"There is one at least who will never forget to remember you with sincere regard & under profound feelings of deep obligation."[21] It is doubtful that either Pickens or the President realized how strained those feelings would become. As soon as Pickens arrived, his fellow South Carolinian, William Henry Trescott, Assistant Secretary of State, briefed him on how the political breezes blew.[22] When Trescott intimated that their State would be seeking a new governor, Pickens's political blood must have flowed faster.

Within a few days, Francis and Lucy received an invitation to dinner at the White House. Senator Jefferson Davis and his wife, Varina, and Senator and Mrs. Louis Wigfall would be there, but the election of Lincoln and the fervor over secession, as well as slavery, had caused several Southern legislators to resign and head home. The Wigfalls had been former neighbors of the Holcombes in Marshall. The caustic Louis and Francis were bitter political rivals and Lucy had once quarreled with Charlotte Wigfall. Although reconciled there remained bitterness between them.[23]

Wearing formal attire, Lucy and Francis arrived at the White House and entered the Blue Room referred to as the parlor by President Buchanan. Harriet Lane, the President's niece, his official hostess, stood apart with several of her lady friends. All held bouquets of camellias or roses and, although Miss Lane never shook hands with guests, she condescended to nod elegantly to those whom she knew. A strikingly handsome woman, Miss Lane preferred wearing gowns that accentuated her lovely shoulders. Lucy no doubt agreed with Mrs. Clement Clay who proclaimed Miss Lane "a poet's ideal of an English dairymaid . . . fed upon blush roses and the milk of her charges."[24]

Introductions over, the Marine band struck up "Hail to the Chief," signaling time for the President to lead the way into the dining room with the lady of his choice.[25] The long dining table featured the mirrored gilt plateau centerpiece first introduced in Monroe's administration. Running almost the length of the table it held figures, and vases filled with fresh flowers from the President's green house.

The conversation was strained this night. Some discussion of current events transpired for Mrs. Wigfall remarked later that "Pickens was all against secession when he was in Washington."[26] With dinner over, the ladies retired to an adjacent room used as a ladies' parlor. The gentlemen remained in the large dining room with chamber pots and screens brought out after the ladies had left. Half an hour later they joined the ladies in the Red Room.[27] While the men enjoyed cigars and whiskey, the ladies inspected the conservatory, recently built onto the west wing of the building. President Buchanan prized this innovative arboretum, heated by gas and filled with azaleas, roses, camellias, tropical trees, and plants. Promptly at ten o'clock, the President bade goodnight and retired to his office, leaving his niece to tend to his guests.

Competent and at ease, Harriet Lane held court. She had recently entertained Prince Edward of England, and before that eight delegates from Japan. Lucy may have felt up-staged as she observed quietly and perhaps with some jealousy. However, better things loomed on the horizon and undoubtedly she hoped as fervently as Francis that they would fall into their proper place.

A few days later Francis met with President Buchanan. In view of their long-term friendship, Francis readily complied with the President's request that he hasten home to South Carolina and try to hold off secession until Buchanan left office.[28] The Pickens's arrival at Edgewood on 20 November was noted by the *Edgefield Advertiser*. The paper expressed the wish that Mrs. Pickens "may find in her new associations simple charms to compensate for the loss of her beloved Texas home."

Lucy took up the reins as mistress of Edgewood and Francis lost no time in getting into the political arena by addressing a large meeting at Edgefield. He spoke long and eloquently, enumerating the wrongs perpetrated on the South and advocating secession as the indisputable right of a sovereign people. Remembering his promise to the President, he urged that secession should not take effect until the inauguration of the "hostile incoming government."[29] This was not what the hot-headed South Carolinians wanted to hear. Politically perceptive, Francis Pickens adroitly changed his tune. Forgetting his promise to the President, Pickens, with spell-binding rhetoric, declared, "If I know the pulse of South Carolina—if I know the pulse of Southern men, the great heart of the South is beating steadily to the march of Southern Independence—Independence now and forever, rather than bear in peace the ignominious bondage whose shadow is already insultingly thrown over our path."[30]

The audience stamped and shouted approval. Pickens scored again 30 November with an address to the General Assembly. "I come as a son to lay my head upon the bosom of my mother [Mother Carolina]," he cried out, "to hear her heart beat-beat with glorious and noble accents worthy of her past and glorious future . . . " His promise to Buchanan forgotten along with his loyalty to the Union, he concluded by saying, "I would be willing to appeal to the God of battles—if need be, cover the state with ruin, conflagration and blood rather than submit."[31]

The audience went wild. Emotions flowed with sentimentality for "Mother Carolina." Francis had played his hand cleverly. One can only guess how much influence Lucy brought to bear on his decisions but it is inevitable that she backed him in his bid for independence of the Southern states. The timing was perfect. Francis Pickens catapulted his State into secession and South Carolinians felt they'd found a champion in Pickens as an elder statesman. Had he not served his state honorably for three decades? He was mentioned to succeed William Gist as governor. Francis demurred, saying that to put his name on the ballot would not be fair to the men nominated prior to his return from abroad.[32] This modest response appealed to many and worked to his advantage. It was an approach typical of Lucy and may have been her suggestion. Now the idealistic South Carolinians, aided by their newspapers, took on the battle for secession and the gubernatorial race—a race between Robert Barnwell Rhett, Benjamin J. Johnson, and Francis W. Pickens who was added to the ballot in spite of his demurral.

Lucy, cognizant of the political scene, refrained from publicly voicing opinions, but in all probability it was she who suggested that handsome son-in-law Mathew Calbraith Butler manage her husband's campaign. It was a wise move. Butler kept Pickens in the race until he emerged victorious on the seventh ballot with eighty-three votes to Johnson's sixty-seven. Francis Wilkinson Pickens took the oath of office at the State Capitol in Columbia on Monday, 17 December 1860, swearing undivided allegiance to South Carolina.[33]

Immediately afterwards, Francis and Lucy left for Charleston to avoid the small pox epidemic then raging in the city of Columbia.

Three days later, Francis, in his bright blue diplomatic uniform, addressed Charlestonians from the balcony of St. Andrews Hall, announcing that the Ordinance of Secession had been unanimously passed. The crowd shouted and cheered and, in a wild frenzy of enthusiasm, stripped the palmetto trees of their fronds, waved them in the air and stuck them in hats. The proud flag of South Carolina, its white palmetto tree centered on a royal blue field, waved above all. South Carolinians signified their independence by pinning cockades of blue ribbon on lapels and bonnets. The excitement was intense. For a short, happy time Francis enjoyed popularity.[34] As for Lucy, she was admired and envied, presenting a delicious target for the gossips.

CHAPTER SIXTEEN

1861

"I am where duty & honor demand me."

Lucy Holcombe Pickens

Governor Pickens settled his family into a luxurious suite of apartments at the Charleston Hotel, and Lucy initiated her new role with dignity. Friends noticed the change. No longer the chatty, frivolous young belle they had known at the Springs, her graceful movements and soft musical voice communicated a tone of gentility and intellect. People, particularly men, continued to be drawn by her femininity and warmth of feeling. More memorable perhaps was Lucy's ability to listen, gracing the speaker with a sense of importance. Placed in an elevated position as wife of the Governor, Lucy, with her keenness of mind, would certainly be aware of her contemporary and social rival, the popular and witty diarist, Mary Boykin Chesnut.

These two women were both consummate flirts, their egos bolstered by the adoration of men. The astute and perceptive Mary Chesnut made many references to Lucy in her diary conceding that she was clever and intelligent, but pronouncing her to be flighty, silly, an audacious flirt, and full of false airs.[1] But Lucy, outwardly impervious to malicious gossip, refused to be a non-entity and continued to stay in the limelight.

The Chesnut's rented house in Columbia stood not far from the house Lucy and Francis occupied when they returned to the capital city, and Lucy's daily excursions did not go unnoticed. Taking her place in the landau,[2] always dressed in the latest fashion, a flower peeping from under her bonnet, she drove about the coastal city. Sometimes Lucy's mother and child accompanied her but more often several male admirers would be in attendance. As the Landau approached the Battery with its magnificent homes and view of the harbor Lucy, in a manner befitting a royal personage, nodded to acquaintances. It is no wonder that the public dubbed her the "Empress" and women, particularly South Carolinians by birth, began to resent this lovely interloper with her jewels, Paris gowns, and Russian sables.[3]

In spite of this facade of regal indifference, Lucy must have realized the problems facing her husband. Francis continually worried that little South Carolina had overstepped its bounds and feared that the North would not bow to the demands of one state. Belatedly, he had misgivings about secession, but it was too late. He had broken his promise to his friend, President Buchanan, and hastened the catastrophe that was to come. Within six weeks' time, Mississippi, Florida, Alabama, Louisiana, Georgia, and Texas joined South Carolina in secession. Francis wrote to Jefferson Davis, who had not yet relinquished his position as senator from Mississippi, stating the need for a Commander-in-Chief of the Southern states and listing the requisites for such a position, "A high-toned gentleman of exemplary purity & firmness of character with full & thorough statesmanship & no demagoguery."[4]

Lucy may have hoped that Francis would fill that role. When this was not to be, disappointment did not dampen her ardor for the "Cause." Larger issues than self-aggrandizement were at stake and she bent her attention to helping her husband. As governor of the first state to secede, now referred to as the "Palmetto Republic,"[5] Francis assumed powers bordering on those of a president. He appointed ambassadors, formed a cabinet, saw to an Army and Navy for defense, and performed myriad duties in the name of the Independent State of South Carolina. Lucy acted as his amanuensis until a proper secretary could take care of the necessary correspondence. Those in authority came to her for news and advice and Lucy never faltered in her allegiance to the Southern States.[6]

The first serious problem that faced Governor Pickens concerned the defense of Charleston, South Carolina's most important harbor. The city was virtually defenseless, threatened by the presence of Union soldiers stationed at Fort Moultrie on Sullivans Island, Castle Pinckney in the harbor, the United States Arsenal in town, and the Federal revenue cutter, the *Aiken*, moored nearby. Added to this, the ominous sight of the large, unfinished Fort Sumter stood guard at the entrance to the harbor. Fearing that the United States might open fire on Charleston, Governor Pickens demanded that President Buchanan recall the Union soldiers and turn the forts over to the citizens of South Carolina.[7] The demand came as a shock to the president, who replied to his fair weather friend, "I have, therefore, never been more astonished in my life than to learn from you that unless Fort Sumter be delivered into your hands you cannot be answerable for the consequences."[8]

Fortunately, William Trescott, acting the calm negotiator, learned of the rash demand and urged Governor Pickens to withdraw his letter.[9] Francis Pickens realized that he had not only made his first serious blunder as Governor but had destroyed Buchanan's trust. The President, on his part, gladly tabled the request as something to be tended to by the incoming President, Abraham Lincoln.

Despite his blunder, Francis felt that his primary objective would be to gain control of these forts and the arsenal with its supply of guns and ammunition. He worried about strategy and ordered two boats to cruise the channel between Moultrie and Sumter. Pickens feared, and rightly so, that Major Robert Anderson might move his forces from the vulnerable Fort Moultrie to the strategically located

Fort Sumter standing alone at the mouth of the harbor approximately three miles from the city.[10] But the Governor with his worries was out-maneuvered by the season. It was December and Charlestonians were more concerned with preparations for Christmas; they refused to worry over any threat the Federals might pose to their city.

Oblivious of impending catastrophe, throngs of shoppers crowded King Street. Children pressed their noses against the shop windows to ogle the dolls, toy drums, tin soldiers, and sweets displayed tempt-ingly. Fat geese and wild turkeys hung above the stalls of the open-air market. Mounds of fresh oysters, casks of fine imported Madeira and other wines—all that one might anticipate for Christmas dinner—tempted the eye and the palate. Unmoved by this holiday atmosphere, Francis urged Lucy to cancel their Christmas reception. Lucy refused, claiming that a display of rejoicing befitted the state's new indepen-dence. Furthermore, an orchestra had been engaged and the chef at the Hotel Charleston had laid in supplies for a sumptuous banquet. Lucy had her way. The reception was held on schedule. Caught up in the holiday spirit, many important Charlestonians attended this first big party tendered by the Governor and his Lady. The next day a startling sight added to the headaches of the over-indulgers—the Stars and Stripes waved from the ramparts of Fort Sumter. Mary Chesnut wrote in her diary, "Fort Sumter seized by the Yankee garrison. Pickens, our governor, sleeping serenely."[11]

A few days later, Captain Coste, a known secessionist in com-mand of the Federal revenue cutter, *Aiken*, beached his ship, dis-missed his second-in-command, and turned the vessel over to the Independent State of South Carolina.[12] Charlestonians cheered the audacity of Coste but the overall situation worsened. Governor Pickens conferred with his Cabinet and sent commissioners to Wash-ington to demand the removal of troops from the forts in Charles-ton Harbor.[13] The governor pushed the impending confrontation further by ordering South Carolina troops to occupy the Federal property of a small battery named Castle Pinckney facing the har-bor. "This was armed aggression at the governor's command, the first overt act of war to come."[14]

Lucy realized the seriousness of the affair. She sent her mother, who had either met her in New York upon their return from Russia, or had perhaps come since to South Carolina for a visit, to Marshall, Texas. Lucy also sent Douschka along.

On the first day of the New Year, Lucy wrote to her father—

> My dearest Father—
>
> The New Years has opened darkly on our unhappy land— Last Dispatches state Floyd, Thompson, Thomas have re- signed—President has gone over <u>entirely</u> to the North—The Harriet Lane left Norfolk last night with 250 men & heavily armed, for Charleston—I believe they will fire into her & then may God help us for Christ's sake—for we are very illy [*sic*] prepared for war—But it is not a contest for victory, but the sword drawn by this brave little state is a solemn & heroic protest against wrong, & in vindication of our natural rights— They say the mails will now be stopped but you must feel dear father that I am where duty & honor demand me, and what- ever dangers surround me, I will be with God's help, true to my name & blood . . . I am thankful my only dear & precious child is safe with you. God bless her & you all dearest Father is the prayer of your loving & devoted daughter.[15]

Once again Governor Pickens tried to coerce Major Anderson into returning his forces to Fort Moultrie and again Anderson re- fused. Acutely aware of Charleston's vulnerability, Pickens moved to erect coastal defenses and ordered cannon. South Carolinians con- sidered his actions justified, believing the honor of the South was at stake. Bristling at the thought of loss of liberty and curtailment of their rights, men rushed to volunteer for armed duty. They swaggered in tall boots, swords dangling from wide sashes of yellow worn by the cavalry, for many of the "sons of Mother Carolina" rode and rode well. Women cheered them on, none more enthusiastically than Lucy. To fight for one's country was the epitome of the patriotism and valor she had been raised to honor and, in this case, patriotism was to the South.

Volunteers from the interior of South Carolina hastened to Charleston. The Richland Rifle Company, the Richardson Guards, the Washington Light Infantry, the Darlington Guards, and the Rhett Guards were only a few of the many volunteer companies that paraded the streets of Charleston early in 1861. They would soon occupy Fort Moultrie, the battery at Castle Pinckney, and seize Charleston's U. S. Arsenal. Beyond the city, the batteries on Morris and James Islands bristled with hurriedly placed fortifications. Governor Pickens sent his slaves to dig harbor defenses and declared that any attempt to send U. S. troops to reinforce the forts would be regarded as an act of hostility.[16]

On the morning of 9 January 1861, Citadel cadets posted on Morris Island watched through their gun sights as the Federal side-wheeled steamer, *Star of the West*, approached Charleston Harbor. This Federal ship had left New York, 5 January1861, with supplies and reinforcements for Fort Sumter. The cadet's commander, Major Stevens, gave the order to fire a warning shot to fall short of the bow. The steamer, its stars and stripes clearly seen, continued on its course. Three more shots were fired. The last shot grazed the side of the ship. The ship did not respond nor did Major Anderson at Fort Sumter come to the ship's defense. Puzzled by the lack of action on the part of the federally held Fort, Captain McGowan, commander of the *Star of the West*, turned his ship about and set out to sea. Charlestonians were ecstatic but Governor Pickens worried that this impudence on the part of South Carolina would have disastrous results.

Now, more than ever, Governor Pickens knew that his state would need help. Lucy may have given him the idea of enlisting the aid of their friend, Tsar Alexander II of Russia, and Francis hastened to write to Baron Stoekle, the Russian Minister to the United States.[17] He listed the fortifications for defense of South Carolina and the number of troops at his command. He also mentioned to the Baron that the South would be happy to supply Russia with cotton in return for imports from Russia. Then Francis had a brilliant idea based on the known antipathy of Russia toward Great Britain. He wrote, "Great Britain may assume to recover her sovereignity [*sic*] upon the principle that she acknowledge the government of the United States consisting of thirteen states . . . If so, I confidently look to the able & patriotic cabinet at St. Petersburg to take the earliest stand against this assumption."[18]

Apparently neither Francis nor Lucy realized that Tsar Alexander II would hardly aid the slave-holding states of the Confederacy when he actively advocated freeing the serfs in Russia. Neither of them seemed to equate the chattel system of serfdom with the human bondage of slavery that they were defending in their own country. Two years later the Russian fleet did dock in New York harbor. Northern supporters feted the Russian officers and sailors, yet Russia never gave any material help to the Union. Perhaps Lucy and Francis considered this act by their friend, Tsar Alexander II, as Russia's threat of power to the Union.

During this period of unrest, Lucy kept up appearances and encouraged the populace. She rode out to review the troops accompanied by her stepdaughter, Jeannie, an attractive young girl of fifteen. Lucy presented her usual striking appearance by wearing a black hat with a red ostrich feather, a sable fur piece thrown about her shoulders and a muff to protect her from the February chill. Journalists noted the occasion as, "A bright flash in the monotonous routine of a soldier's life . . . The Governor's wife and daughter, Mrs. and Miss Pickens came to Sullivan's Island Fort Moultrie, on a bright and genial afternoon. In special honor of them the whole body of troops garrisoning the Fort were passed in review . . . the young soldiers of the Palmetto State were highly flattered by the presence of the beautiful and distinguished ladies. It was a pleasant incident, and one to be long remembered."[19]

All did not appear as rosy in the governor's cabinet and Pickens took it upon himself to order seven heavy mortars and two Dahlgren guns for the defense of the harbor. Charlestonians took this news lightly for they knew the command at Fort Sumter could not hold out much longer on short rations. They began to enjoy their cat-and-mouse game. Also, it was February and Race Week. Talk turned from Fort Sumter to horses and betting and this so-called "carnival of the

State" occupied their full attention. For one week everyone shared in this popular festival, from the Blacks who sat unmolested on the fence rails, to the Governor and the ladies in the grandstand.[20] Carriage after carriage rolled up to the Washington Race Course just beyond the city. Ladies in bonnets and fanciful array alighted. Lucy was not to be left out. Conspicuous in the stands, she watched with Francis and ex-Governor Gist.[21]

Dances and supper parties followed the races. Lucy, now less worried about the danger of conflict and doubly anxious to be with her family in Texas, left at the end of Race Week for Marshall. Francis remained in Charleston and worried when Lucy did not answer his letters. Lonely and jealous, he blamed her negligence on being too happy with beaux and spoke of himself as, "Your poor, solitary, heartbroken lover in Charleston." He sent kisses, and excused past misdemeanors as the result of being overwhelmed with official duties. "Forgive me," Francis entreated Lucy, "I was not myself and I believe it is my destiny to be disliked by all who know me well."[22]

CHAPTER SEVENTEEN

1861

"It was grand—it was awful."
Clara Victoria Dargan

he stagecoach rolled into Marshall and turned up Burleson Street, trailed by boys looking for excitement. The coach's leather curtains pulled aside and two eager faces peered through the narrow opening, anxious for sight of the dear ones they had not seen in three years. Lucinda's hands shook as she brushed the dust from her mistress's heavy cape while the coachman urged his team up the hill to Wyalusing. At the first blast of the coach horn, Uncle Ned came running to grab the halter of the lead team. Anna Eliza ran down the steps, her two young ones stumbling and clinging to her skirt. Douschka, in her dear grandfather's arms, brother Philemon, so tall and grave, with his wife, Emma, and Lucy's own sweet mother—all hurried to greet their beloved daughter and the faithful Lucinda.

All were there but brother Theodore, who promised to arrive soon from San Jacinto. Ned, Auntie Viney, Celah, Beatrice, Ernest, a grown-up little Charlie, and other servants gathered around. One might guess that Lucy hugged them all, tears streaming down her face.

News traveled fast and by evening a constant stream of visitors climbed the hill to greet the prodigal daughter. Mr. Loughrey wrote in the next issue of his paper, "Guests were agreeably surprised to find Lucy the same as of yore; time and absence had worked no perceptible change in her appearance or manners."[1]

The visit was all too short. By the second week in March 1861, Lucy and her mother left for Montgomery, Alabama, the new capital of the Confederacy. Eugenia visited Holcombe cousins and returned to Wyalusing without Lucy and Douschka, who had brought "light and warmth to their sad hearts" while in Marshall.[2] Lucy remained in Montgomery and visited the imposing Capitol building that sat high above the center of town and called on the newly chosen president of the Confederacy, Jefferson Davis. She found him to be handsome, tall, and slightly built, but with no smile to grace his thin lips. Gallant and soldierly, President Davis greeted the wife of the Governor of South Carolina with politeness and banalities, inquiring of the discomfort of her trip and the health of her husband. Perhaps Lucy visited the new President of the Confederacy on official business at the urging of her husband. She made no comment of any conversation they may have had. The following day, 17 March 1861, President Davis wrote to Governor Pickens, "I had the pleasure of seeing your good Lady here yesterday & hope before this reaches you that she will have arrived safely at home."[3]

Lucy, Douschka, and Lucinda boarded the train for the last part of their journey home to South Carolina. Rain and cinders blew in the partially opened windows as the engine jolted along the narrow track at no more than twenty miles an hour. After what seemed an eternity of discomfort, the crowded train stopped for refueling. Passengers got off to stretch their legs, breathe fresh air and purchase refreshment. Lucy, trailed by Lucinda and Douschka, found a seat at a small table set hastily on the station platform. All too soon the stationmaster blew his whistle for boarding. Lucy, seeing that many passengers were still waiting to be served, called the porter to her side. "Please tell your conductor to wait a few minutes. Mrs. Pickens has not finished her coffee."[4] With grumbling but smiling obeisance, the conductor complied.

After three days of excruciating discomfort, struggling to find a comfortable position on the train's hard-backed benches, they arrived at Charleston. A pale, weak Francis met them at the Depot with a bouquet of delicate pink roses. When Douschka hugged his legs and called him "Papoushka", the affectionate Russian term for "father", he instantly forgot his complaints and recent illness, relieved to have his beloved wife and daughter home. Lucy wrote of their homecoming to her mother, assuring her that Douschka had not contracted scarlet fever. She added that her own pain in her back and side had diminished but she would continue to take the bitters and rest a great deal.[5]

Lucy sought relief from various doctors for her pain and tried home remedies to improve the digestion and dipping snuff to calm the nerves. When the pain became too severe, she resorted to laudanum, the favored analgesic of the nineteenth century. Many doctors prescribed a form of hydrotherapy in the treatment of pain. Some preferred the less effective and sometimes disastrous treatment of catharsis and/or bleeding. Still others ignored ladies' complaints of pain, thinking it a form of self-induced birth control.

It is not known what may have caused Lucy's pain in her side and back but, no matter how severe, her complaint was overshadowed by the excitement prevalent in Charleston at the end of March. The city teemed with activity as wagons rumbled into town laden with supplies and artillery. Volunteers from the up-country districts crowded the streets, marching in ragged formation down Meeting Street to the Customhouse and parading in front of the offices of the *Charleston Mercury*. Zouaves in short jackets, colorful red vests and sashes, their ballooning pantaloons caught into white leggings, swaggered and bowed to ladies in silks and veiled bonnets adorned with the familiar blue cockades. Carriages carried ladies to Morris Island and Castle Pinckney. A few ladies gained permission to visit Union-held Fort Sumter and their friends among the Union soldiers. An atmosphere of excited anticipation gripped the city and Governor Pickens continued to lay in supplies of arms and ammunition.

Francis truly hoped that the South would be given its rights and possessions without bloodshed but, he added, "if not, blood must flow."[6] He voiced his fears at the executive meetings which Lucy and her step-daughter, Jeannie, faithfully attended. The two sat in the gallery with blue cockades pinned to their bonnets.[7] Afternoons, Lucy paid duty calls on persons of importance and held her own "at homes." Evenings found her at receptions or at the theater, often in the company of her husband's private secretary, Franklin Moses, or the debonair William Porcher Miles, who made it known that he enjoyed being with an intelligent woman.

Although respected as the wife of the Governor, it is highly possible that South Carolinians treated Lucy with cordiality but with little warmth of friendship. They considered her an outsider. Nevertheless, with head held high, and apparently unruffled by gossip, Lucy conducted herself with dignity and elegance. People referred to her as "Lady Lucy" and sometimes as "Madame Governor." Older women admired and, in the case of Emily Haynes, a respected poet and author, affectionately praised this young woman who had not only become the wife of her nephew and step-mother to his children but had shown untold kindness to others.[8]

As a creative and literary woman, Lucy gravitated to those of like interests. Dr. Gibbes, an ornithologist, writer, and editor of the Columbia papers, the *Daily South Carolinian* and the *Weekly Banner*, made himself Lucy's knight errant and called her his "Fleur de Luce."[9] Dr. Gibbes served as surgeon general of South Carolina during the war. His attention to Lucy caused considerable gossip but gossip attached itself to Lucy no matter whom she favored. To some, the Governor's wife appeared aloof and cold. Considering her vulnerable position, this may have been a front to protect her privacy. She was besieged with requests from people seeking positions, commissions, and appointments and sometimes found it necessary to send word that she was indisposed.

While Lucy played at diplomacy, her husband sat on a powder keg ready to ignite. Tensions mounted and Charlestonians clamored for action. Francis heard that some volunteers were threatening to fire into Fort Sumter in spite of their officers' orders. Alarmed, he requested Adjutant General Evans to notify his officers that "such an act of insubordination would have consequences too monstrous to contemplate."[10] Frustrated at Major Anderson's insistence on remaining at Fort Sumter, and with little or no instructions from President Davis, Francis Pickens felt the fate of the Confederacy rested on his shoulders. A politician at heart, he vacillated between wanting the conflict to disappear peaceably and the desire to appease his fellow Carolinians who cried for action. Goaded by Lucy's fervor, blinded by a sense of patriotism to the South, and man's right to defend his principles, he no doubt felt relief when President Davis sent General Pierre Gustav Toutant Beauregard to command the troops defending Charleston and the coast.[11]

General Beauregard arrived in March and approved the defenses, inadequate as they were, but he was not going to tolerate cajoling Major Robert Anderson into leaving Fort Sumter. In April of 1861, he gave Anderson the ultimatum of an affirmative answer or face the guns of Charleston. On receiving a negative reply, Beauregard conferred with General Leroy Pope Walker, Secretary of War for the Confederacy, and sent a warning notice to Major Anderson, "Unless [Major Anderson's] command left Fort Sumter within an allotted time, firing would commence at daybreak." The Major refused to leave. At dawn, 12 April 1861, Colonel James Chesnut gave the order to fire.[12] Captain George S. James lit the fuse that sent the first shell "screaming from the Battery on James Island into the pale amber sky. The shell arched its way to Sumter and burst directly above the fort."[13] It was the first shot fired in the war.[14] Jolted from sleep, the people of Charleston hurried to the Battery, eyes riveted toward the gray hulk at the mouth of the harbor. Roadways were blocked with carriages and horsemen. Men and boys jumped from pavement to sea wall to avoid the risk of being trampled by horses. Others crowded onto the high galleries or climbed to the roof tops, field glasses pressed to their eyes. Shelling continued from the Confederate batteries, but no response came from Sumter. Even the flag did not go up until the sun rose. It was explained later that Major Anderson waited until breakfast was over. At seven o'clock the flag was raised and the guns of Sumter boomed.

Clara Victoria Dargan, a writer who later became Lucy's friend, watched from the Battery with her sister, Liz, and described the scene, "In the faint morning light with the red sun struggling to rise through the heavy bad-coloured clouds, the flash and report of mortars and canon [*sic*] with now and then a huge shell bursting just above the fort . . . it was grand—it was awful!"[15]

At the first sound of battle Clara and Liz had rushed to the Battery and found it lined with ladies and gentlemen. Not much was said as they strained to make out the fort through opera glasses. Some women fainted from the suspense and fear. It was rumored that the U. S. steamers, the *Harriet Lane*, the *Baltic* and the *Nashville* waited at the bar at the entrance to the harbor, loaded with reinforcements.[16] It was falsely reported that Confederate steamers had intercepted these Yankee ships and left them in a sinking condition. Charlestonians had reason to cheer when they recognized the immense and cumbersome Confederate Floating Battery anchored at the tip of Sullivan's Island and heard the booming of its guns.

After an hour of heavy bombardment, rain fell but no one ran for shelter. Spectators huddled in the downpour, transfixed by the noise and sight of battle. "The anxiety was awful," wrote Mrs. St. Julien Ravenel, "and as the hours passed a silent, mute dread took possession, all keyed too high for audible emotion. At four p.m. word came no one was hurt. Some women burst into tears, some fainted."[17]

The firing continued until dark and resumed at daybreak. On this second day, when Fort Sumter finally surrendered, the bells of St. Michaels Church played "Hail Columbia" and "Dixie" but there was little cheering. Charlestonians worried that the vessels of war, still visible beyond the bar, would attempt to come in at high tide and bombard the city. It was a false rumor. They learned later that the *Baltic* transported the surrendered command to New York and the other ships presumably headed to Fort Pickens, Florida.

Governor Pickens and Lucy may have observed the battle from

the second or third story gallery of one of the fine, stately homes facing the harbor. It has been erroneously reported that General Beauregard held Douschka in his arms and handed her the match to light the fuse that fired the first shell. This is not only incorrect but ludicrous. Douschka, two years of age, loved and petted by her family, would hardly be placed in such a dangerous position or even be out at four-thirty in the morning. And, at the time of the firing, General Beauregard was waiting in his headquarters for Colonel Chesnut to report.[18]

CHAPTER EIGHTEEN

1861

"Submissiveness is not my role . . ."
Lucy Holcombe Pickens

The flag of the Confederacy waved above the battered walls of Fort Sumter, beside it the flag of South Carolina. Charlestonians exulted. But the cheering turned to anxiety when the news reached Charleston that President Lincoln had called up 75,000 men to defend the Union. The nation now faced the stern realities of war. This spurred the holdout state of Virginia to secede, the eighth state to enter the Confederacy.

In mid-April of 1861, volunteer troops from South Carolina marched off to Virginia, the Hampton Legion among the first to leave. They took the train cars part of the way, but for most of the several hundred miles they tramped through mud, swamps, and forests. Spirits soared with hope and bravado while lusty voices kept cadence to the tune of "Dixie Land," and homemade flutes and harmonicas came out of knapsacks to fill the air with "Katy Darlin'" and "Lorena." Late in the month these troops tramped into Richmond, tired and foot-sore.

An immense crowd welcomed this South Carolina contingent with bands and treated them like heroes. Lt. Colonel A. P. Aldrich, the troops quartermaster, wrote to Lucy and mentioned his concern that Virginia was not prepared for defense. Deficient in arms, powder and caps, it also did not appear to have a leader. He worried whether all talk and no preparation made for an effective campaign. Aldrich added the interesting personal observation, "General Lee, one of the finest looking men I have seen, is in command of the Virginia forces. He seems to be in earnest, as does General Johnson [*sic*][1] . . . but, to speak frankly, I have not much confidence in either for prompt & efficient action. They have both been instructed as army officers, & in my opinion they know no more about State Rights—state sovereignity [*sic*] than your man Tom."[2]

Lucy showed the letter to her husband. Fearing the worst, Francis drew up a will dated 4 May 1861. He bequeathed to "my beloved wife" his numerous properties in the state of Mississippi. He also wanted Lucy to have all of his Edgewood property of 3,500 acres with household effects and named specific slaves and their families whose ownership would go to her—if she wished.[3]

By mid-May Lucy left for Mobile, Alabama, to visit Holcombe relatives and quite possibly Fleming Gardner, who let it be known that he was receiving mail at Jacksonville, Alabama.[4] Whether Lucy's trip included official business for Francis and the Confederacy is not known. Francis missed her and was distraught when he learned that Lucy posed as his sister-in-law when away from him.[5] It is unclear just why Lucy chose this masquerade, for she prided herself on being truthful. In view of her vulnerable position as wife of the governor of the first state to secede, one might think that she had legitimate reason to pose as someone else. Francis, hurt and not understanding, scolded, questioned, and poured out his love in a letter, "Oh! how can you keep one so loving and tender as I in doubt—I love you wildly—madly—kindly—I dote on you, I have to desert my duty. I can stand it no longer. In haste but your devoted lover."[6]

Lucy returned to South Carolina and contributed nobly to the Cause. It is not known if she, like many Confederate women, sewed shirts and trousers for the soldiers, stuffed cartridges, rolled bandages, and knitted woolens, but she did contribute in her own regal fashion. She sold some of the jewels given her by Tsar Alexander II and other admirers, contributing the money realized from the sale to help out-fit troops for the Confederate army. In recognition of Lucy's generos-ity, Colonel P. F. Stevens, commander of The Citadel in Charleston, called on the Governor and his Lady to offer his services to the State. They received him in the drawing room and the Governor immedi-ately commissioned Colonel Stevens to raise a legion consisting of infantry, artillery, and cavalry.[7] When the question of name was broached, Colonel Stevens turned to Lucy and with a courtly bow replied, "We will call it the Holcombe Legion, Madame." Lucy smiled. Francis seemed gratified and the legion bore that name in honor of Lucy Holcombe Pickens.[8]

Recruitment for the Holcombe Legion continued throughout the summer of 1861. Volunteers came from Newberry, Barnwell, Spartanburg, Anderson, Abbeville, and Atwell counties. When their ranks were filled, the recruits marched to Adams Run, twenty-five miles south of Charleston, to be presented to their benefactress. Lucy, always wanting to look her best, chose a black velvet riding costume and a large black hat turned up on one side with a long white plume as its only ornament. Mounted side-saddle, she focused her attention on the soldiers passing in review.[9] All eyes turned to her as she pre-sented the large eight-by-five foot flag of blue silk with heavy gold bullion fringe, said to have been made from one of her ball gowns.[10] The center of the flag bore a palmetto tree in white and apparently, from Lucy's speech, a single star that represented the "Lone Star" of Texas. Above these, in crescent form, was the name "Lucy Holcombe" and underneath the word "Legion."

The commander introduced Mrs. Pickens and the men listened as she praised their gallantry, their valor and devotion to the Confed-eracy. Lucy explained the positioning of the Palmetto and the Lone Star on the flag. "These two devises [*sic*]," she said, "share the devo-tion of my own heart." She reminded them that several South Caro-linians were among those brave men who fought at the Alamo in

Texas, their action typified in the motto inscribed on the banner, "It is for the brave to die but not surrender."

In the sentimental Victorian manner, Lucy's speech praised, cheered, and inspired. She urged the men and boys to fight with honor and valor, and, if need be, with reckless bravado, ending her speech with a stanza from Lord Macaulay's "Horatio at the Bridge."

> Death comes but once to all,
> Then how can man die better,
> Than facing fearful odds,
> For the ashes of his fathers
> And the temples of his Gods? [11]

Cheers resounded and officers offered their arms to escort Lucy about the camp. She made the most of this excursion, looking into the tents, wanting to know how the men slept and what they ate. She tasted the cooks' cornbread and beef, and thoroughly charmed every soldier with her smiles and interest. Seven companies marched to the station to see her off with an infantry salute. "God bless her, we all loved her," commented Pvt. Dock Owens in an interview many years later.[12]

The Holcombe Legion participated in battles in Virginia and North Carolina and later went to the relief of Vicksburg. It returned to Virginia and spent nine months in the trenches around Petersburg. After the Battle of the Crater the Legion surrendered, being then only about 300 strong. Nothing was left of their battle flag but the leather sheaf in which it was carried. This meaningful relic was saved by the Legion's fifteen-year-old color sergeant.[13]

It may be surprising that Lucy, in her extreme fervor for the Confederacy, continued friendship with those of strong Unionist sentiments. Ellen Middleton, the wife of a Union sympathizer, was her close friend. Ellen, an Englishwoman, was married to Henry Middleton, a South Carolinia writer and traveler. His brother, John Izard Middleton, owned large plantations in Beaufort and Georgetown districts.[14] Another friend was Jane Petigru, wife of the avowed Unionist and Charleston lawyer, James Louis Petigru. Petigru's views on nullification and secession were well known, but he retained the respect of his opponents.[15] Jane was not above asking favors for her son, Daniel. "For obvious reasons," Jane Petigru wrote to Lucy, "I can not ask Mr. Davis [President Jefferson Davis] for anything for my son, but he (Mr. Petigru) suggested, that I write you, my friend, Mrs. Pickens, and get her to induce the Governor to write and ask a place for Daniel, so here I am begging this favor again . . . If [you] can by any means get him an appointment [in the Confederate forces] however low except in the common ranks I know he would be glad of [it], and I would consider it an act of kindness toward me all the rest of my life."[16]

Apparently Lucy did not comply with her friend's wishes. Perhaps she took offense when Mr. Petigru openly declared South Carolina as, "Too small to be a republic, too large to be an insane asylum."[17] Other influential men in Charleston and Columbia, known for their Union sympathies and as defenders of free speech, were Benjamin F. Perry, George S. Bryan, and Judge John Belton O'Neall. All three openly condemned the war, yet no hand was lifted to turn them aside from any public praise or honor. As Mrs. Chesnut said, "We know they are honest. They have a right to their opinion."[18]

For the remainder of 1861, Lucy spent more time traveling and visiting than with her husband. Douschka and Lucinda accompanied her and probably her new friend, Floride Cunningham, a cultured and highly literate young woman from Charleston. They may have gone to the mountain resorts as was the custom in South Carolina during the fever infested summer months. While she was gone, Francis, wanting some cologne, rummaged in her wardrobe and made a startling discovery. A box, tucked under lingerie, contained letters that Francis claimed fell out by accident. The letters addressed Lucy as "My sweet darling Lady-Bird." Stunned and hurt, Francis read on, "Your match was made from calculations of the head not the feelings of the heart, for your youthful and tender heart was lavished on your first and only love."

Francis may not have known that it was Lucy's old beau and fiancé, Fleming Gardner, who called her "Lady-Bird." Francis rummaged more and found the hair of the gentleman writer tenderly kept in letters while his own letters were scarcely opened and no remembrance in them.[19]

Hurt and anger turned to jealous rage as Francis went through the letters until he found one written 3 April 1858—then his fury turned to squashy sentimentality. The letter, addressed to him, was written by Lucy. "Written," he said, "in language that no human being would use without an absorbing, & mad passion." Mollified, he sent the letter to her to keep for their darling child. Then Francis performed a little blackmail. He spoke first of their love when, as he put it, "We first leaped into each others' embrace." Begging forgiveness he childishly flaunted his faults. Francis reminded Lucy that she had promised him a bright and noble boy on her return. He believed the hand of Providence had guided him to find the letters and he stated, "I am to meet you my bride, is it not so?"[20]

It was quite obvious that Francis wanted a son to carry on the Pickens name. Lucy had other plans. She was young—still in her twenties—and married to an old man who doted on her in a paternalistic, dogmatic, stubborn, opinionated way. No doubt she was faithful to her husband. Lucy, who openly confessed to loving admiration, would never make concessions against her will to any man, let alone her husband. She had borne him a child. That was enough. Now she intended to have a good time. In an earlier letter to her mother, she said of a friend who was again pregnant, "[She] should be ashamed to be like a rabbit. I am for more genteel ways."[21]

In the mid-nineteenth century "genteel ways" seldom proved to be successful birth controls. Women tried to control child bearing by extended nursing, observing the "safe period", withdrawal called "truncated practice", abstinence, and sometimes abortifacient patent medicines advertised as "not to be taken by those in the family way."[22] Others tried douches concocted in a number of ways from alum, vinegar, carbolic acid, rose leaves, or just plain water. Later in the century diaphragms called vaginal shields were used and, still later, condoms could be had from "first-class druggists." One woman, although revolted by this idea, remarked, "One must face anything rather than the inevitable result of Nature's methods."[23]

The most frequently used method of birth control was the head-
ache or complaint of sickness and pain. Lucy favored the latter and
in her charming way managed to put off Francis's amorous advances.
Her frequent trips also took her out of harm's way. Traditional in her
loyalty to husband, and reluctant to infringe on the accepted mascu-
line spheres of political activity, Lucy maintained her autonomy by
refusing to devote her life to motherhood. "Submissiveness is not my
role," she stated, "but certain platitudes on certain occasions are
among the innocent deceits of the sex."[24]

CHAPTER NINETEEN

1861–1863

"The only comfort in all this misery is a little good talk now and then."

Lucy Holcombe Pickens

The fall of Sumter, followed by the Confederates' victory at Manassas in July, 1861, raised the fighting spirit of the South's soldiers. The Confederate Legislature selected the motto, *Deo Vindice*, (defended by God).[1] Bulletins arrived daily, citing the Union forces as panic stricken and fleeing in terror. The South felt justified in separation from the Union and looked on itself as God's chosen people. Encouraged with this first flush of victory, the Confederacy tended to overlook the shortage of shoes, uniforms, arms, and ammunition that plagued its army. The Union blockade of Southern ports prohibited supplies being brought in by ship and, with lack of appreciable industry and commerce in the agricultural South, the situation worsened. Daring Confederate blockade runners sometimes succeeded in getting safely past the Union blockade but this was not enough and blame was heaped on Governor Pickens. The hapless governor provided a scapegoat for every shortage, disaster, and defeat. He was even blamed for the fire caused by lightning that destroyed much of Charleston in the last days of that fateful year of 1861.

With his abundant political savvy, Francis continued to juggle what he thought best and what he thought the people wanted. No one was pleased. A crowning blow came in January of 1862, when the state convention selected a council of four men to act as a control to his actions. Lieutenant Governor W. W. Harlee, former United States Senator Colonel James Chesnut, state Attorney General Isaac Hayne, and former Governor William H. Gist would now pass judgement before the governor could act.[2] Pickens was furious. It was obvious from the start that Chesnut and Hayne would thwart his every move. Lucy was indignant and bitter against the convention for questioning government decisions, many of which she may have influenced. Anonymous letters rebuking the governor's detractors appeared in the *Mercury*. Mrs. Chesnut said that Franklin Moses Jr. wrote them. He denied and said that Lucy was the author. Mrs. Chesnut, vacillating between scorn and admiration for Lucy and Francis, likened the council to a "bundle of sticks and crutches for old Pickens." But she added, "He will outwit them all yet, with the aid of the lovely Lucy, who is a host in herself."[3]

In a rare moment of compassion or possibly curiosity, Mary Chesnut paid Lucy a call on the cold, wet day of 9 January 1862. "We flattered each other," Mrs. Chesnut wrote in her diary, "as far as that sort of thing can be done. She is young, lovely, clever—and old Pick's third wife. She cannot fail to hate us. Mr. C. put as [a] sort of watch and ward over her husband."[4] As educated and intelligent women, these two might have been friendly rivals under different circumstances. Both were conversant in French and read German and, aside from their intellectual qualities, both loved admiration and were experts in the art of flirtation. Men were attracted to them. Mary Chesnut, nearing forty and never considered a beauty, drew her admirers by her wit, conversation, lively personality, and appreciation of fine foods.

Lucy had matured from the impulsive, self-centered, ambitious belle of earlier years to a woman of direction. She possessed an appreciation of her physical attraction but was wise enough not to rely on it. Instead, she used intellect and charm to mold men to her liking, commanding them with her femininity. Mary Chesnut, on the other hand, coveted men's adulation and received it with clever repartee believing that she could take their place if need be. Kind and thoughtful, she lamented the horrors of war and its waste of manhood whereas Lucy Pickens, ever the idealist, thought it man's privilege to die for his country and championed patriotism.

Many men in executive positions in the Confederacy noted Lucy's qualities. As wife of the Governor of South Carolina, she was in a position to meet those in authority. Mr. Christopher G. Memminger, Confederate Secretary of the Treasury, considered himself a friend of the Governor and his wife. When Duncan Blanton, a handsome lawyer and able engraver, established a printing office in Columbia,[5] Secretary Memminger gave his approval to have Lucy's image engraved on the 2 June 1862, issue of the Confederate States of America one-dollar bill.[6] The bill shows in the center, a side-wheel steam sailing ship in mid ocean giving chase to a sailing vessel. A female figure of Liberty appears in the upper left corner. In the lower right corner, an oval portrait of Mrs. Pickens, wife of the Governor of South Carolina. No identity is given on the bill but it was immediately accepted to be a portrait of Lucy Holcombe Pickens. In this portrait Lucy is pictured as wearing a large hat turned up on one side with a long white plume. She wore a similar hat when reviewing the troops known as the Holcombe Legion.[7]

Lucy definitely had a feather in her cap. By the end of 1862, her face, in a different pose also appeared on one-hundred-dollar bills. This engraving, executed by Keating & Ball Engravers in Columbia, South Carolina, was thought by early authors and historians to be that of Mrs. Jefferson Davis, wife of the President of the Confederacy.[8] Their assumption was proved false in 1917 by the extensive research of Mr. H. D. Allen, a reputed numismatist.[9]

Allen claimed that the portrait was that of Lucy Holcombe Pickens, wife of the Governor of South Carolina. After interviewing numerous friends and relatives of both Mrs. Davis and Mrs. Pickens and obtaining sworn affidavits of their statements, Allen also declared that the portrait on the Confederate States of America one-hundred-dollar bills of 2 December 1862, 6 April 1863, and 17 February 1864 to be that of Lucy Holcombe Pickens.[10] Sworn statements follow—

Mrs. Stoess, the sister of Mrs. Davis, says, "I have no hesitation in saying that the picture is intended to represent Mrs. Pickens. The features and head dressing are like Mrs. Pickens and totally unlike Mrs. Davis." Mrs. Stoess goes on to say, "I can only repeat that it is not Mrs. Davis, and I cannot understand how anyone knowing her could think so. She never wore her hair in that style, nor dressed like the picture. I never heard that Mrs. Davis was on any of the notes, but did have an impression that she objected to having herself on Confederate money, though I never heard why."

Mrs. N. W. Trump of Columbia, South Carolina, worked in the Treasury Department during the war said, "How on earth did the statement get out that the portrait was Mrs. Davis? No one here ever heard such a thing. There is no doubt of the picture on the $100 bills being Mrs. Lucy Holcombe Pickens, wife of Governor Pickens."

Frederick Hill Meserve of New York City says, "The vignette could not have been made from a sitting or drawing of Mrs. Davis who was probably in Richmond when the bill was engraved at Columbia."

Mr. S. McGowan Simkins who knew Mrs. Pickens for at least twenty years swore that he knew the likeness on the one-hundred-dollar bill to be a genuine likeness of Mrs. Lucy Holcombe Pickens, as her facial expressions are very clear-cut, with the classic beauty of a Greek goddess. Simkins goes on to say that he heard Mrs. Lucy Holcombe Pickens acknowledge that it was her picture.

Lucy F. P. Dugas, granddaughter of Lucy Holcombe Pickens, declares the likeness to be that of her grandmother who admitted to her that it was indeed her portrait.

Mr. A. S. Tompkins, a lawyer and resident of Edgefield, South Carolina, visited Lucy Holcombe Pickens at Edgewood from 1876 to her death in 1899. He stated that Mrs. Pickens had a very clear-cut, beautiful, and distinct set of facial features and he is positive that the picture of a woman on the one-hundred-dollar Confederate bill is her likeness. Tompkins claims to be able to gather a great many affidavits to this effect.

Evidence in favor of the portrait being that of Lucy Holcombe Pickens is further bolstered by the lack of any mention in biographies of Mrs. Davis that she was the subject for the portrait; nor is any mention made in the *Jefferson Davis Papers*.[11] Moreover, Mary Chesnut, a close friend of Mrs. Davis, makes no reference in her *Civil War Diary* to the portrait on the one-hundred dollar Confederate Treasury Notes. As mentioned before, Keating and Ball, the engravers of this note, were located in Columbia, South Carolina, whereas Mrs. Davis was in Richmond, Virginia.

It must be remembered that Mr. Allen collected his evidence and affidavits in the period between 1917-1919. Since that time, historians and authors have accepted his evidence as positive that the portrait is that of Lucy Holcombe Pickens and it is so listed in all books on Confederate currency.[12] Mr. Arlie Slabaugh, historian, concedes in 1961, that Allen "is undoubtedly correct." Mr. Slabaugh then offers his personal opinion, "Mrs. Pickens was apparently used as the model, the wreath being added to indicate she was intended to represent something more, the 'Women of the South.'"[13]

In view of this evidence it is fair to say that Lucy Holcombe Pickens was the only woman of her time to be pictured on Confederate currency. Journalists began to refer to Lucy as the "Queen of the Confederacy." Numerous articles giving her this accolade appeared in newspapers from Charleston and Columbia, South Carolina, to Memphis, Tennessee, Dallas and Marshall, Texas. This is also noted in John B. Edmund's book, *Francis W. Pickens and the Politics of Destruction*. It is not surprising that no mention of this coup is found in Varina Davis' *Memoirs*. The fact that Lucy never mentions it in letters may be because she was not pleased with the somewhat unflattering engraving.

Lucy and Francis left Charleston and came back to the state capital in Columbia after the small pox epidemic of late 1861 had abated. They rented a house on Hampton Street and Lucy entered into the social life of the city and wartime activities with her usual enthusiasm. Along with many other women of the Confederacy, it is quite possible that the governor's wife helped to care for the sick and wounded. Fleming Gardner, in a letter to Lucy, noted, "I believe you are never so happy as when you actively nurse."[14]

These ladies not only boosted morale but organized benefit parties, teas, and receptions to raise money for the hospitals, and the families of the wounded soldiers. At these affairs Lucy dressed her servants in livery in the Russian manner, served tea from a Samovar and made certain that the champagne flowed. Of special note was her reception in late summer, 1862, for the wounded General Wade Hampton.[15] On this occasion, Mary Chesnut complained that Lucy overplayed her part when she greeted the handsome General.

"This is the way to greet great heroes," Lucy said, her blue eyes sparkling. She removed the General's crutch and put his arm on her shoulder. General Hampton, ever the gallant, never took his eyes from his hostess.[16]

Lucy continued with her playful banter when she approached Mary McDuffie Hampton, the General's wife. "I think Wade Hampton the handsomest man in the world except the Tsar, Emperor of Russia."

"Do you?" replied Mrs. Hampton. "I don't."

"Oh," said Lucy, "don't be modest. I own that I think Governor Pickens very handsome."

"Do you?" said Mary, more surprised than ever. "I don't."[17]

Women did concede that Lucy was a charming hostess and her parties great successes, yet they were quick to find fault when Dr. R. W. Gibbes proposed that South Carolina's new gunboat be named the *Lucy Holcombe.* His proposal was overruled.[18] Lucy had to be content with her name emblazoned on two large Columbiads mounted by the Confederate battery opposite Fort Pickens, Florida. The 1863 issue of the *Texas Republican* quipped, "If the Lucy Holcombe looks half as winning as her namesake, Fort Pickens will be surrendered without delay."[19]

Every move of the Governor's lady was noted and criticized. On her frequent trips to Charleston, Beaufort, and to various plantations,

Lucy drove about with officers in the family's open carriage. When asked why she should indulge herself and friends in this show of frivolous ostentation when soldiers were doing without simple comforts, she calmly replied, "Why not? General Washington attended the assembly balls and wanted everything done that could be done to amuse his soldiers and comfort and refresh them [and] give them new strength for the fray, when they came home for a short visit."[20]

Not everyone accepted Lucy's actions as fitting for a governor's wife. A scathing letter with no date was mailed to Lucy from Augusta, Georgia, and signed "Bucket." The writer rebuked her, "for marrying an, old bald-headed fellow old enough to be your grandfather" and added, "Shakespeare denominated your case one of 'legal prostitution,' . . . yet, with this glaring fact constantly brought to your mind by his presence, you have the unblushing hardihood to exhibit yourself to the public gaze seemingly unconscious of your degradation. This is not to be wondered at, for we always see the most noted whores most fond of exhibiting themselves and when they do so, generally bedecking their persons with the finest feathers and other trunkery [*sic*]. No more at present Lucy from Bucket."

On the reverse side of this letter, the writer invokes Lucy to see oneself as others see one.[21] The identity of "Bucket" is not known. The writing is bold like a man's handwriting. From the content, one might think it is from a rejected suitor, yet it may well have been the ranting of a jealous woman. One wonders if Lucy kept this letter as a reminder to guard her conduct or if she knew the identity of the writer and anticipated the possibility of blackmail.

While Lucy fed the gossip mill, cheered the soldiers, aided in the war effort, and bolstered the governor's image, other Southern women, including her sister, Anna Eliza, had more direct contact with the battlefield. Anna Eliza, with seven year-old daughter, Markoleta, had followed Colonel Elkanah Greer to the battlefront. Anna Eliza wrote to her parents from Van Buren, Arkansas, 2 March 1862, "My dear Father and Mother, Colonel Greer has been gone three weeks today. I have not heard from him for four or five days. There has been so many unreliable telegrams that General McCulloch [22] will not permit any dispatches to be sent except official communications . . . Fayetteville which is occupied by the Federals is only one days ride from Van Buren. Our army is on the other side of Boston Mountain. I think our regiment is in pursuit but have not been able to hear for several days."[23]

Anna had not long to wait. On 4 March 1862, Colonel Elkanah Greer, commanding the 3rd Texas Cavalry, joined with Brigadier General McCulloch's and Major General Earl Van Dorn's combined forces of 16,000 men and headed into Missouri intent on capturing Union held St. Louis. Three days later the Union Army, under the command of Brigadier General Samuel R. Curtis, met the Confederate Army. A confused and fierce battle followed at Pea Ridge near Elkhorn Tavern in Arkansas. For two days the Confederates held out. General McCulloch and General James McQueen McIntosh[24] were killed and the armies badly scattered.

Communications failed to reach Colonel Greer in time for him to make use of McCulloch's scattered forces. Chroniclers say, "The Battle of Pea Ridge was an oddly fragmented engagement that lasted two days and extended across several miles of varied terrain." The battle was said to be "a scene of inexorable confusion."[25]

After the Confederate defeat at Pea Ridge, Elkanah and his troops headed Southeast, expecting to take part in the battle to be fought at Corinth, Mississippi. Fearing the worst, Elkanah sent a letter to Anna with a memorandum of money owed to him "in case I should be killed." Elkanah suffered a painful wound at the Battle of Pea Ridge and also received his commission as brigadier general. Anna waited for him at Memphis and by August her mother was begging her to exert herself and come home.

"Passengers come every stage & meet with no trouble or detention," Eugenia wrote. "You have only to start . . . You know if you wait for everything to be ready & someone else to start you, you will die there. My best love to Gen Greer, Markolita [*sic*] and yourself from your ever loving and anxious Mother. Bring some white rather coarse crochet cotton & a bottle Garrets snuff."[26]

Anna Eliza did come home and waited there for Elkanah who

accepted the post of Conscription Bureau chief for the Trans-Mississippi Department with offices in Wyalusing, the family home.[27] Meanwhile, Lucy, far from the hardships of battle, kept in the limelight. After performing her duties as "Madam Governor," she sought the advice of doctors for the chronic pain in her side and made numerous trips ostensibly to visit relatives or friends. Her frequent absences from home did not please her mother. "The time you are now spending away from Columbia," she wrote, "might have done your body as much good spent at home here [Marshall, Texas] as anywhere else. That is if you could have made up your mind to stand it. You will never get well living the life you do now."[28]

For all Lucy's seemingly frivolous ways, she was deeply concerned about the war. A friend of many in command, she kept apprised of the Southern army's moves as much as possible.[29] Suffering defeat after defeat, the Confederacy continued to rally in spite of the crushing blow afflicted at the Battle of Shiloh and the fall of New Orleans, both in April of 1862. From battle-scarred returning soldiers she learned that federal troops occupied her birthplace, La Grange, Tennessee, and neighboring Holly Springs, Mississippi. Skirmishes had been fought around La Grange. Confederate General Earl Van Doren destroyed General Ulysses S. Grant's supply base at Holly Springs, Mississippi, and took one-thousand Union prisoners during the winter of 1862. This action forced General Grant to postpone his advance on Vicksburg. General Benjamin A. Grierson, U. S. Cavalry, retaliated by tearing up three different railroads in the area of La Grange and successfully kept the Confederate army from transporting supplies.[30] General Grant, it was said, occupied Dr. Pulliam's home, Hancock Hall, in La Grange, and the village's Immanuel Church served as a hospital for Union soldiers.[31] Lucy must have wondered if her old home, Ingleside, survived the Yankee invasion. Present owners have noted initials of soldiers from an Iowa unit scratched in the plaster walls of this house.

At the end of 1862, Francis's tenure as governor ended and Lucy did not look forward to returning to the quiet solitude of Edgewood. She would miss the social life of Columbia and the power and intrigue associated with her husband's office. More upsetting was the uncertainty of the whereabouts of her brothers. She learned that Theodore was in west Texas helping to put a stop to the raids on settlers by the Comanche Indians and had not been heard from. Younger brother, Philly, riding with a cavalry unit, might have been captured, and Elkanah and cousin Beverly were somewhere in the thick of battle. She held not least among her concerns the fate of relatives and friends remaining in Tennessee. Her mask of bravado faltered. She began to personally experience the uncertainty, worry, and despair wrought by war. In an attempt to make light of oppressing news, she remarked to her friend, Ellen Middleton, "Ah, but the only comfort in all this misery is a little good talk now and then."[32]

CHAPTER TWENTY

1863–1865

"A volcano under that exterior of stillness and glitter."
Clara Victoria Dargan

The administration of Francis Wilkinson Pickens as governor of South Carolina ended 31 December 1862. At the forefront of politics since the age of twenty, he had thrived on the arguments and decision-making of government. Having reached the age of fifty-nine, tired and ill, he longed to return to the quiet solitude of his beloved Edgewood. It is doubtful that Lucy shared this longing. She'd miss the society and cultural aspects of Charleston and Columbia and her stellar position as the Governor's wife and, although she used discretion, her influence in governmental matters was known and respected. Now, to avoid oblivion and boredom, she knew that all activity and entertainment must originate with her. She began by transforming Edgewood into a home of elegant distinction.

As a kindness to Jeannie, her favorite stepdaughter, Lucy placed the portrait of the child's mother, Marion Antionette Dearing, the second Mrs. Pickens, above the mantle in the young girl's bedroom.[1]

The Tsar's portrait in oils hung in the sitting room and even in the dimmed light one could not help but admire the handsome figure. Clara Victoria Dargan described Edgewood and its interior as she saw it on a visit in March 1863, as a "beautiful spot. Long rambling building, large grounds with an extensive prospect of tangled shrubbery. Indoors taste reigns with elegance. In the sitting room where we were shown a pleasant fire, several lounging chairs, and fresh flowers in antique vases . . . In the billiard room, an opened armoire displayed Francis's court costume, a coat of royal purple velvet with gold embroidery and white silk pantaloons. Holcombe and Pickens family portraits sat amongst photographs of men and women in court dress. And, in the large dining room, gleaming silver service and colorful Bohemian glass sparkled under the huge candle-lit chandelier."[2]

Edgewood reflected elegance and comfort, from the wide verandah with its rocking chairs and joggle-board, a type of seesaw often seen on the porches of Southern homes, to the orange trees growing in the conservatory. Knowing her fondness for flowers, Francis urged Lucy to plant some of her mother's favorite rose bushes, "Souvenir de Malmaison" and "Baron Prevost." Iron statuary stood here and there in the garden beds, and privacy and romance beckoned from the maze of hedges. Beyond, paths lined with the fragrant sweet olive trees led to the fishpond, the stables, and the slave quarters. Other large plantations spread out around Edgewood's three thousand acres. Central to them was the town of Edgefield with its county courthouse, shops, churches, and comfortable homes. The owners of the plantations and the townspeople worked and played equally hard, keeping their problems hushed behind parlor doors, and Lucy dreaded being confined to the boundaries of this close and selective society.

Lucy had never allowed herself to be constrained by society's rules nor did she fit the unfair image of passive simplicity so many nineteenth century writers gave of Southern women. Rather, Lucy exercised her inquisitive, educated mind to her advantage, feeling at ease in the most learned circles. In Charleston and Columbia, she had taken pleasure in women's literary societies. The members, Southern women of education and privilege, read and discussed French literature in fluent French. On the lighter side they read the popular novels, *St. Elmo* and *Macaria*, written by their contemporary, Mary Ann Jane Evans [pseudonym George Eliot], as well as those of the scandalous George Sand[3] and the novels of Bulwer-Lytton. And, they entertained strong opinions about politics and government, territories monopolized by men.

Knowing full well that it would be considered scandalous for her to take a vocal part in politics when in Edgefield, Lucy voiced her opinions in anonymous letters to the editors of local newspapers and through Francis. Separated by circumstance from her more intellectual friends, she looked about for someone with whom to converse on an equal basis and discovered Clara Victoria Dargan.

Miss Dargan, young, attractive, and educated, came from a respectable South Carolina family. She sought employment as a governess, a profession many young women embraced before marriage. The Arthur Simkins family engaged her to teach their three young children.[4] Through her Simkins relations, Lucy learned that Clara was a published writer and an accomplished musician, talents that might qualify her as a friend. On a cold day in early February Clara wrote in her diary, "Mrs. P. and her confrere Miss Floride Cunningham called on me. Mrs. P. wore her full suit of Russian sable furs and a superb velvet cloak. She is rather affected I think and very vain of having been Mrs. Governor—people still call her the Empress. She spoke of Russia—and has offered to send me Sir Edward Holmes late work called "A Strange Story."[5]

Ten days later Clara and Mrs. Simkins repaid Lucy's call but found that she suffered from some illness and was confined to her room. Floride, Lucy's "confrere," welcomed them. In a short while the former governor appeared and, with his usual stiff formality, invited Clara to see the improvements in the garden. When they entered the little greenhouse built especially for Lucy, ex-governor Pickens presented Clara with a bunch of violets, then escorted her to the house for tea. The thoroughly charmed Clara lingered over her tea while Miss Cunningham told of the Pickens's stay in Russia, of the valuable gifts showered on them by the nobility, and the Tsar's attention to Lucy.

That evening Clara wrote in her diary, "Poor Mrs. P., in spite of the idolatry lavished upon her, in spite of beauty, wealth, talent (for they say she is talented) & all that could make one happy, is destined for an early grave. She grows thin & pines away every day."[6]

When Lucy learned that Clara was to play the organ at Trinity Episcopal Church, she insisted that her new friend practice on the melodeon at Edgewood. Clara accepted and the pompous Colonel Simkins, his wife, oldest son, and three of his daughters and their governess, bundled into the carriage to make the trip. Rains had turned the road into a quagmire of ruts. Coming too fast around the last curve, the horses skidded, the carriage swerved toward the stone steps of the veranda, and tilted at a precarious angle. Colonel Simkins toppled from his high seat beside the driver and landed in the mud. Screams of alarm turned to laughter as the doughty Colonel picked himself up and the family trooped up the steps onto the porch. Francis met them at the door. "Why, What is this?" he exclaimed in his nervous, high-pitched voice, "God Bless my soul! Arthur, what is the matter?"[7] Lucy appeared, the slightest breath of surprise on her face, and Douschka peeped, wide-eyed with impish delight, from behind her mother's silk skirt.

Clara marveled at how delicate Lucy appeared, dressed in mauve pink with pink hyacinths in her golden-brown hair. The young governess watched with admiration and awe as Lucy manipulated the large Russian samovar and poured tea into delicate china cups. Flowers filled the rooms with a faint, sweet aroma and when Clara admired one, Lucy took it from its vase. "I want you to have this," she insisted and pinned it to her new friend's blouse. "You must promise me that you'll come soon again and spend the night. I want you to know Edgewood."[8] Rising gracefully, she took Clara's hands and led her to the melodeon, and together they entertained with songs.

The young and talented Clara proved a welcome companion for Lucy. Most Friday evenings the two sang for Francis and guests. Saturdays, Clara brought her sister, Liz, or one of her pupils with her and spent the night. After church on Sunday, Lucy and Clara walked through the gardens. Lucy leaned over to pick several buds and put them in Clara's hair.[9] "It is such a comfort to have someone to talk to—to pour out one's whole heart," she said quietly, and taking her new friend's arm they followed the winding path through the maze of boxwood until they reached a garden bench near the fish pond. Sunset's glow dappled the water and fish darted from under water lilies and rose to the surface with a faint bubbling sound. Lucy took out a gold and enamel locket and slowly opened it. "This is the Duke de Osuna, a Spaniard. He's dressed in his court costume."

Clara recognized the man as one whose numerous photographs she had seen throughout the house. "He is a bachelor," Lucy continued, "and the greatest catch in Europe with a palace in every capital and inestimable wealth. He used to tell those who wondered at his celibacy that he was waiting for 'His excellency Monsieur Pickens to go to Heaven.'" Lucy laughed. "I suppose he was attracted to me because of my unheard-of faithfulness to my husband for it seems women and men are little better than heathen in that respect."[10] Clara detected a wistful note in her hostess's voice. "Oh, what an exciting time it must have been."

Lucy sighed and looked away. Clara waited quietly for her hostess to continue. With a bright smile, Lucy turned and, clasping Clara's hands, began to tell of her experiences at court, of her laurels, her adventures, her friends abroad and her marriage. Lucy mentioned that she had loved once and well, and Clara, wanting to know more, asked if the character, Mabel Royal, in Lucy's novel, *The Free Flag of Cuba*, was not patterned after herself. "The description and character of Mabel suits you exactly!"

"My dear Miss Dargan," Lucy replied, "you truly know Mabel."[11]

Clara went to Edgewood quite often, taking along one or two of her Simkin pupils to play with Douschka while she and Lucy visited. Mutual interests drew the two friends into an intimate friendship. Clara sensed that Edgewood, with all its in-laws and relatives of earlier marriages, was proving claustrophobic, particularly when Lucy said that she felt her older stepdaughters did not like her. "Her feelings are intense," Clara wrote in her diary, "a volcano under that exterior of stillness and glitter."[12] On the next visit Clara found her hostess had taken to her bed with an unexplained illness.

"Oh when I am sick I can bear no one near me but those I love very much," Lucy confided. "How I long for you to sit by me and talk and give me my medicine. It would be such a comfort to me. You must remember your promise to come live with us when Douschka is older."[13]

In June of 1863, the reality of war broke the serenity of Edgewood. Lucy's stepson-in-law, the handsome and gallant Colonel Mathew Calbraith Butler, was wounded in the Battle at Brandy Station, Virginia. His serious injury necessitated the amputation of his leg. Francis left at once for Richmond with his daughter, Maria, Mathew's wife. The trip was beset with problems. The military guard refused to let Francis back on the train at Rocky Mount, North Carolina. Francis knew no one there who could identify him and didn't know what to do. Presently a stranger walked up and said, "I know you, Governor, and will vouch for your passport."[14]

"But for this I would have been stopped," Francis wrote to Lucy. "Such is the change of circumstances! My name was the passport for thousands two years ago & now so humble that this stranger, a detective, has to vouch for my good character! . . . As soon as I hear from Col. B [Butler] I will telegraph you & I hope to return immediately . . . The armies are on the move this day[15], & a general fight is expected tomorrow or next day. So I may be in the midst or near . . . Kiss my precious little one for me 100 times & a thousand on your own sweet bosom—Kiss Jennie [Jeannie] . . . I am glad I came & saw things myself. I may be able to know the future better."[16]

Lucy and Clara prayed for Colonel Butler and for Francis's safe return. They held benefit evenings where Lucy displayed her court costumes. The venture added much needed money to the fund for wounded soldiers and their families.[17] But worry was ever prevalent that loved ones might be wounded, taken prisoner, or worse.

News traveled slowly and accounted for many inaccuracies in reporting the outcome of battles. On the Mississippi, General Ulysses S. Grant and his federal forces kept Vicksburg under siege while in the East, General Lee and his command fought valiantly at Gettysburg. Late in July of 1863, word came from Lucy's cousin, Brigadier General Beverly H. Robertson, assuring her that the Gettysburg campaign was not a failure. They had procured quite a number of horses, cattle and supplies, but the Confederacy lost nearly 27,000 men in the three-day battle.[18] Lucy also learned that the Holcombe Legion had fared badly at Vicksburg. The list of dead, wounded, or missing climbed to fearful proportions. Daily the tolling church bells signaled the funeral processions—the riderless horse, the empty boots hanging from the saddle, the black-veiled widow and mother, the fatherless children. Worried and fearing the worst, Lucy, as did many other women, sought solace in religion. Bible readings were of great comfort as was the shared agony of worry. Religion, as delivered from the pulpit, offered Southerners a basis for strength and confidence and gave consolation that hardships and losses were only way stations on the road to a grander victory.

Lucy attended Trinity Episcopal Church in Edgefield, where the words of the rector and the music that she loved gave her courage and temporarily chased away the gloom of war. But it was not to last. On a bleak November day in 1864, Lucy's beloved father, Beverly Lafayette Holcombe, died at Wyalusing. She hastened to make the sad and difficult trip to comfort her poor mother. Francis, fearing that Union forces might detain her, waited impatiently at Edgewood for letters informing him that she had reached Marshall safely.

The Union forces were now in control of transportation across the Mississippi and citizens could not venture up that great river and cross into Texas without the required pass. With this proximity of the enemy, Francis fully expected South Carolina to be attacked from the mountains to the west as well as from the sea to the east. Scared, depressed, and ill, he spent much of his time writing letters to President Davis, Governor Milledge Bonham, of South Carolina, and his old political friends and foes. He had long since lost faith in the leadership of the Confederacy. Early in 1865, word reached him that the Yankees were advancing toward South Carolina. When he learned that South Carolina's Governor-elect, Andrew G. Magrath, had fled Columbia, as had many of the more outspoken Carolinians, Francis feared for his family, his property, and for his own safety.[19]

CHAPTER TWENTY-ONE

1865–1869

"Out of the dead, cold ashes, life again."

John Bannister Tabb

*E*arly in February of 1865, Union soldiers left Augusta, Georgia and headed to Columbia, South Carolina. Their route took them close to Edgefield and talk ran high of plundering the ex-governor's plantation. It was rumored that Francis had vanished into the dim unknown of the interior.[2] He may have gone to his sister's plantation in Alabama. It is not known if Lucy went with him. She may have been in Marshall or, with characteristic self-assurance, she may have stayed at Edgewood.

Confederate Major General Daniel Harvey Hill learned of the Union's advance toward Edgefield and sent word from Augusta to Major N. W. Smith, chief inspector of field transportation. "Place 1,000 or 1,500 men on the Edgefield plank road, about 10 miles from the city, to guard approach in that direction."[3] General Wade Hampton and his cavalry unit were posted to guard the roads leading to the neighboring plantations. Hampton, considering the Union's force, urged Major General Joseph Wheeler, CSA, to move his troops at once to Columbia. This mass movement of Wheeler's troops toward the Congaree River and Columbia did not go unnoticed by the Yankees. Union officers immediately ordered their troops to turn off the road leading to Edgefield and proceed post-haste to Columbia.[4] No doubt there was grumbling among those Yankee soldiers who had looked forward to plundering the home of the ex-governor.

On 16 February 1865, General William Tecumseh Sherman's army shelled Columbia mercilessly. The Confederate forces, though badly out-numbered and out-maneuvered, met the attack with brave but ineffective resistance. A day later, the city fell to the Union. By eleven o'clock that morning, the colors of the 13th Iowa were flying over the Capitol building.[5] Union soldiers tore through the city with triumphant abandon. They set many buildings on fire after plundering the interiors. Nothing was sacred. The unfinished State House was emptied of its contents including papers, letters, and mementos belonging to Lucy and to Francis. Much was lost to greed or to flames. Soldiers and stragglers, drunk and disorderly, destroyed or stole whatever met their fancy.

Burned-out buildings left families without shelter. Evidence of Union destruction was everywhere as the Yankee forces combed a path nearly thirty miles wide through South Carolina. Miraculously, the sprawling plantation of Edgewood escaped. Its remoteness perhaps assured its salvation. Other plantation owners were not as fortunate. In many cases homes were pillaged, supplies and stores depleted and the owners' wealth disappeared along with their slaves. The Union army headed northward trailed by hundreds of jubilant slaves.[6]

The news of General Robert E. Lee's surrender to General Ulysses S. Grant at Appomattox, in April of 1865, provoked varied feelings of relief, bitterness, and exhaustion. The long, hard struggle had ended. Now the South faced a bleak and uncertain future. Discouraged and sick, the Southern soldier made his way home to face a different and very difficult future. Many would find their homes destroyed and families marked by illness and starvation. The South, depleted of its manpower and slave work force, lay in ruin.

At first, the Reconstruction measures as set forth by President Andrew Johnson in 1865, followed Lincoln's lenient policy toward the South.[7] Johnson appointed provisional governors to the Southern states of Mississippi, Georgia, Alabama, Texas, and the Carolinas. Judge Benjamin F. Perry would serve as provisional governor of South Carolina.[8]

The slave was now a free man who worked by contract, was entitled to wages and, in some cases, was supplied with food, housing, and promised a share of the crop. Many Southerners, finding their age-old positions reversed, would not accept these conditions and, most certainly, many balked at any suggestion of suffrage for the Black man. The freed slave, however, anticipated "a better time coming" and the division of land—the proverbial "forty acres and a mule."[9] When this did not happen some refused to work and were thrown in jail by the Federal authorities. Disorder and violence flourished and offenses to both Black and White were "so varied and so numerous as to defy classification"[10] and all under the ruse of self-defense.

In the "up-country" of South Carolina the large plantations, such as Edgewood, lacked the slave-power that had kept them in operation. Lucy was not unfamiliar with the duties of a plantation mistress. Food was not a problem. Edgewood's farm yielded enough to supply family, servants, friends, and those in need. It continued as a working plantation although under the difficult conditions of Reconstruction.

In Texas, Wyalusing did not fare as well. The grand house had served as headquarters for the Trans-Mississippi Agency of the Confederate Post Office Department during the war.[11] Now taxes, repairs, and lack of cash forced Eugenia and Anna to take in boarders to unravel the tangled web of debts. Back in July of 1865, Lucy, with Douschka, had gone to Marshall to be of help to her mother and sister. She had found a distraught Anna saddled with four small children and worried that her husband would go away with the Confederate General Joseph Shelby.

The feisty Shelby had appeared at Wyalusing urging other discouraged Confederate veterans to seek refuge with him in Mexico. Francis advised Elkanah to abandon the idea of going to Bogota or

Mexico and reminded him that a foreigner never has sympathy in a foreign land. "We have to accept our condition for the present," he counseled and wrote to Lucy, "I shall be most happy for your dear sister to live so near in Augusta if it suits her, and I only wish I could offer her any substantial aid, but I am far too poor for that . . . But [to] our precious dear mother say to her I will always give her a home, as long as I can be able to plough a corn patch." Then he reminds Lucy, "I have no son to work & to help me or I might be independent."[12]

While Lucy and Douschka were gone, Francis became increasingly melancholy and spilled out his loneliness, love, and sentimentality in a letter to his six year-old daughter. "Wednesday 1865—My sweet beloved darling—I write to let you know how Papouschka has been suffering to see you . . . I am all alone by myself and at night I dream of my dear child & feel for her and she is not in the bed . . . Indy [a pet dog or cat] has been looking for baby . . . The flowers are looking for you too—Bring us some good fish for our pond. Your affectionate & devoted—F. W. Pickens."[13]

Late in May of 1865, one month after the surrender at Appomattox, President Andrew Johnson issued a proclamation extending amnesty to Confederates who would take an oath to support the Constitution and the Union. Francis was quick to take the oath and besieged the provisional governor, Benjamin F. Perry, to influence President Johnson to grant his pardon.[14] Governor Perry thought Pickens would not qualify for pardon as he was worth over $20,000. Francis objected and wrote to Lucy who was visiting in Marshall, Texas, with her mother and sister, saying, "I know I am not worth it, except in your jewelry, if it be I am equal owner of that. I know I own my wife and that she is worth over one million in hard money, but then the gove[rnment] will not value hers that high."[15]

Lucy hurried home. She went to Columbia and prevailed upon Governor Perry to send a long telegram to President Johnson on behalf of her husband. The Governor complied but said he could draw no fire from the President.[16] Francis, the former "fire-eater" senator and governor who had fueled the catastrophe by urging his state to secede, feared more than ever that he would be imprisoned along with Jefferson Davis and other officials of the Confederacy. Added to these worries, a severe drought threatened the crops, his contracts were not honored, men refused to plant and harvest his cotton, and creditors hounded him like a pack of hungry wolves. "There can be no peace for me," he told Lucy.[17]

While Francis fumed and worried, Lucy quietly sold many pieces of her jewelry and other gifts from the Tsar and various royal admirers. She knew that in many, but not all Southern states, women in the nineteenth century had no legal recourse or control over their own money after marriage but jewelry was a tangible asset she could control. With the gradual sale of these valuables Lucy managed to save Edgewood and keep up appearances. The house servants, Caroline the cook, Uncle Harper, Wallace, and Alfred, chose to stay and work for their board and a small stipend. Lucinda, Lucy's intelligent and literate maid, preferred to remain close to the mistress who had taught her to read and write, speak French and Russian, and whose only child she had raised from birth. Lucy was Lucinda's "family." But Tom, the manservant who had traveled with Lucy and Francis to Russia, headed north. The majority of the Edgewood field hands and their families remained and worked as sharecroppers. But the integration of these former slaves into American life, particularly in the Southern states, was a principal and troubling issue of Reconstruction.

Meanwhile, Lucy, beset with everyday problems, bored with domesticity, and depressed by the rising tolls of the dead, wounded, and missing, took comfort in her correspondence. She answered Miss Anne Pamela Cunningham's request that she accept the position of Vice-Regent for the state of South Carolina in the Mount Vernon Ladies Association. The offer flattered and tempted Lucy. She could serve a patriotic cause while associating with a group of ladies intellectually inclined, socially correct, and affluent. She knew that Miss Cunningham, a semi-invalid, had succeeded in raising funds to purchase the home of the nation's first president from his great-grand-nephew, John Augustine Washington, Jr. In the belief that women could best preserve this historic home for the enjoyment of the nation, Miss Cunningham instituted the Mount Vernon Ladies Association wherein ladies from each state would be appointed to serve as vice-regents.[18] Lucy penned her acceptance, for what could be more patriotic than to serve this worthy cause?

From her desk at Edgewood Lucy could look out over the gardens and the big magnolia with its sweet smelling blossoms. It was a pleasant, homey sight yet she would find it difficult to block from her mind the haunting scene of men returning, maimed, sick, and discouraged. She had sent these men off with cheers and high hopes to defend their country. Now they returned to nothing. Their homes had been destroyed, crops burned, livestock killed or stolen, fences and sheds torn up for firewood. The scene was constant yet Lucy was not overwhelmed with remorse. She believed in the South and its Cause, however vainglorious that might be, and now she dipped her pen in the inkbottle and wrote to her friend, Clara Victoria Dargan.

Edgewood, 2nd June 1866
Dear Clara,

I prize your kind letters sincerely . . . For a woman I am uncommonly fixed in my fences & if I should not see or hear of you for ten years or longer, I would then meet you with the same interest & affection which marked our parting. Feel this always. How much has happened since then! It is scarce a year since we've surrendered unto chains. The past with its high endeavor, its noble aspiration, its grand heroism is dead . . . a gloom dark & bitter indeed to all who love our desolate & helpless land—The shadow of the cross is over every heart & home & the dreary clanking of our chains comes shudderingly [sic] on every breeze. I will not dwell on this theme which is always, ever & ever, wailing through my heart. The inevitable must be endured, & God reigns over all—

I received your last yesterday & will write myself to the gentleman at once—I can shake off my painful insolence to do a service to one who so truly merits my interest. I hope you will obtain the situation for I earnestly sympathise [sic] in your noble endeavor to live an earnest & useful life—I cannot tell you how your compliment (in the first letter) to Mabel touched me—I dare say you can imagine for you know how fond one is of these brain children, however pale & "fade" they may be—I assure you Mabel would feel very vain to sit for your heroine—[19] I am so strong & well—in fact, quite fat—I am, since the desertion of Bess & illness of our dear & faithful old housekeeper, Aunt Betty, a victim of keys, bad dinners, & great, alas very great uncomfortableness—I do so dislike practical duties but am ashamed & grimace at the truth of the confession—

I wish so very much you could come to me for a little while [I] will likely be gone for a short visit to my friends in Va about the 15th of July—I should be so glad to have you at Edgewood in the meantime—Write me—I enclose a $300 New Orleans bill—Please send it to the magazine (you don't give the name) in which your story is appearing & beg them to send it (beginning with the first number) to Gov. Pickens, Edgefield Dist. S. Ca.—

The gov[ernor] joins my lovely star-eyed "Grand Duchess" in love to you—I am faithfully & truly yr. Friend—L. H. Pickens [20]

Finally Congress, in an attempt to undermine presidential leniency and secure control of Reconstruction, passed the Reconstruction Act in 1867. "This act provided for the establishment of five military districts in the remaining ten Southern States." [21] Further acts also sought to protect Blacks by enacting the Fourteenth Amendment giving equal rights to them, but political unrest continued in South Carolina.

In the spring of 1867, an unexpected ray of sunshine broke through the gloom at the Pickens home. A crated gift arrived at Edgewood for ex-governor Pickens. It was sent free of rail charges by the New York Mutual Insurance Company. At the beginning of the war this same crate had arrived by ship from Italy and because of hostilities could not be forwarded to its destination in the South. The

New York Mutual Insurance Company held itself responsible. A representative of the company opened the crate and saw within a bust of purest Parian statue stone. Much taken by the beauty of the model, Lucy Holcombe Pickens, the Northern insurance company paid the storage charges and kept it until the end of the war before sending it to its rightful owner.[22] This same bust of Lucy is displayed alongside one of Francis in the Caroliniana Library of the University of South Carolina at Columbia.

Francis continued to worry and fume, plagued by memories of the horrible destruction he had condoned. He feared that he was under surveillance. His letters were opened and the Provost Marshal would not honor his contracts with laborers. A new overseer, a White man, was sent to Edgewood and the Blacks refused to work. Furthermore, Francis's cotton was stolen or confiscated and what money he was able to retain proved worthless. He sold or lost to taxes his plantations in Mississippi and Alabama. Only Edgewood remained, saved by the sale of Lucy's jewels and valuables.

Gradually conditions under Reconstruction improved. The great migration of North into South stimulated the economy. Northern industrialists and investors recognized an opportunity to develop this new frontier. They brought money and equipment for industry and breathed new life into a ravaged land. Along with them came the ne'er do wells who embraced Reconstruction for their own benefit and profit. These people were tagged with the name, "carpet-baggers," referring to their single piece of luggage containing all their possessions. The term was soon applied indiscriminately to many Northerners in the South during Reconstruction. Southerners, who sided with the radical Republican government for self aggrandizement and greed, were called "scalawags."

Francis, failing in health, became more and more depressed not only by the post-war situation in the South but by his mounting debts. Much has been said and written that Lucy's expenditures and extravagance put Francis in debt. As a very thoughtful and generous woman, Lucy bought expensive gifts and gowns for not only herself but for her mother, sisters, and her friends. Possibly she believed

Francis to be wealthier than he admitted and took him at his word when he urged her to "buy linens to last a lifetime" and "to spare no expense in search of health." Her extravagance and immodest displays of affluence caused many to gossip about this young, third wife of one of South Carolina's foremost citizens. Then too, Lucy's haughty attitude may have caused people to forget her better qualities—loyalty to her husband, kindness to those in need, and determination to help the Confederacy and save Edgewood. None of this had been easy for her and since the death of her father, tragedy followed tragedy in what seemed a never-ending cycle.

Jeannie, Lucy's dearest stepdaughter, had fallen in love but Lucy and Francis opposed the match. They preferred that she marry a young general of their choice. When the man whom they chose for their eighteen-year-old daughter was killed at the Battle of Gettysburg, Jeannie was free to marry Edward Mitchell Whaley of Charleston.[23] After five months of wedded bliss, Jeannie, barely nineteen, died. Lucy confessed to her friend, Clara, "I can truly say, next to my husband & my little one, she was dearest my heart & my loss is bitter beyond any words to express . . . The Gov[ernor] is much broken in spirit & for the week past has been very unwell—The whole of our State is almost in a state of destitution. We are able to live comfortably still, having the supplies of the Plantation but are greatly reduced & entirely without means. Unless there is a successful crop this year, God only knows what will become of us as a people." [24]

One year later, broken in spirit and health, Francis borrowed a thousand dollars to take his wife and child to the Virginia springs to seek health.[25] They boarded the train, accompanied by the faithful Lucinda and probably Wallace, Francis's valet. For two months the invigorating air and health-giving mineral baths benefited Francis, while Lucy and Douschka cantered over the rolling hills and chatted with guests. They returned in October of 1868, rested and refreshed. Riding home through town, Douschka might have noticed the large yellow and red placards advertising the circus and the "World's only female bareback rider."[26] The young girl hurried to greet her pets while her parents rested and presently Lucy and Francis heard a fa-

miliar nickering and the clop clop of a pony's hooves. Douschka, bare
feet balanced on her pony's bare back, stood upright, snapped Dixie's
reins and started off. The child knew no fear. A skilled equestrienne
like her mother, she laughed and waved, her brown pigtails slapping
against her back.

Francis took Douschka to the circus, hoping the child would not
imitate other performers. Instead, she only begged for a monkey but
soon this adored pet developed a habit of terrorizing servants and
visitors alike by jumping on their heads and pulling their hair.
Douschka, spoiled and petted, was a constant source of pride and
delight to her parents and could do no wrong. Yet this joy could not
dispel the worry and fear that continued to plague Francis.

The ex-governor continued to look for the pardon that never came
and sat for hours under his favorite Magnolia tree muttering griev-
ances and worrying that he would be imprisoned. Exasperated by her
husband's depression, smarting under the lasting humiliation of the
defeat of the Confederacy, and bored with the quiet, bucolic life of
Edgewood, Lucy determined to raise their spirits. What would be
better than to give a party for their friends on the very day they were
expected to show obeisance to the newly elected Reconstruction
Governor, Robert Kingston Scott. She traded some of her precious
bibelots for party fare and invited friends and neighbors to a sumptuous dinner party.

Details of this party were related in a book written by an Edgefield
resident who knew Lucy and her family. Family members also tell of
the exciting and terrorizing incident that occurred the night of the
party. Lucy, arrayed in an old but elegant ball gown, diamonds sparkling at her throat, greeted her guests as they arrived. Servants, at-
tired in the livery that Lucy favored, kept the champagne glasses filled.
Just as dinner was announced, a loud shouting commotion came from
the gardens. The guests and Lucy hurried to the verandah to see
what caused this noisy interruption. Lucy walked calmly to the head
of the porch steps, her diamonds sparkling in the candlelight. Behind her stood her own liveried servants in gold braid, the maids in
their blue and white dresses and high turbans. Guests crowded around

and stared at the shouting black faces massing in the gardens below. Someone suggested shooting into the mob but was hastily quieted. As Lucy watched, the Freedmen and stragglers trampled her rose bushes, swung their clubs at the tame deer and chased the peacocks. Satisfied that they had wrecked the gardens and terrorized the guests, they melted into the darkness. A guest, admiring Lucy's cool daring, remarked, "Ah, you were like Marie Antoinette."

Lucy laughed. "They would not have hurt me. The soufflé may be ruined but we can always eat cake," and led the way into the dining room.[27]

How much of this episode is fact or fabrication is debatable. The incident makes a good story and possibly reflects the way Lucy would react in a similar situation. However, while Blacks sought equality as human beings, they manifested no desire to involve themselves in social relations of Whites as individuals or as groups.[28] And, more to the point, there is no evidence of outward dissension at Edgewood during Reconstruction years.

Christmas that same year, Francis Pickens lay dangerously ill of inflammation of the lungs.[29] Toward the middle of January he knew that he was breathing his last and called his faithful servants to his room. Alfred, Uncle Harper, Wallace, and others quietly entered the darkened room and stood by the foot of the bed, hats in hand and eyes averted to hide their tears. "My faithful servants," Francis spoke in a voice barely audible and motioned them closer. Struggling to continue, he asked them to look after their mistress as faithfully as they had taken care of him. Lucy knelt by his bed, his cold hands in hers as he breathed his last. Francis Wilkinson Pickens, once the dynamic political force behind South Carolina's government, died 25 January 1869, unpardoned, a man without a country.

Faithful to their master's instructions the men, heads bared in respect, lifted his coffin and carried it from Trinity Church to nearby Willowbrook, Edgefield's town cemetery. Lucy, her face heavily veiled, followed on the arm of her brother, Theodore. Surely Lucy, the force behind her adoring husband, knew that his death signaled the end of an era just as surely as the war had ended a period of fame and fortune and her place in the spotlight of the Confederacy. Francis had worshiped her, overlooking her faults and catering to her whims. In return she had provided him with a sense of worth and esteem that kept him in the forefront of politics. They had respected each other's talents and overlooked their shortcomings. Lucy had felt safe with this man old enough to be her father. Although often impatient with his paternalistic attitude, his stubbornness, and pragmatic ideas, she had possessed the grace to withhold criticism publicly. Now, a widow at age thirty-seven, her future depended on the manner in which she handled herself and the estate—and Lucy became her mother.

CHAPTER TWENTY-TWO

1869–1875

"Rouse yourself from the sweet sad dream and face the battle of life."
Ellen Middleton

Tears blur Lucy's letter to her mother—"Come back. I can not stand another night or day . . . I feel an insane instinct to flee to the uttermost parts of the earth yet I know I can never flee from the awful void & dreary pain & desolation in my breast & in my miserable life . . . Aunt Charlotte [one of the house servants] has come in to say she must have her winter frock—checked homespun please get it 9 yds. Your most miserable daughter. Lucy H. Pickens."[1]

Eugenia made the long journey from Texas to comfort her daughter and granddaughter, Douschka, the affectionate, winsome ten year-old. The child proved their salvation. Like her mother at that age, Douschka preferred her pets and the outdoors to society. Mornings found her making the rounds of the farm with her mother, seeing to the needs of the servants and the care of the animals. With the diminution of help, it would not be unusual to see the two of them dressed plainly, directing the treatment of a horse for worms or walking one with colic.[2] Practical when it came to the preservation of self and property, Lucy certainly preferred these duties to those of housekeeping.

With heavy heart she addressed myriad and seemingly insurmountable financial problems brought on by Reconstruction. The settlement of the estate she expressed as, "Three long miserable years dragged through the courts [by] Baxter & Carrol [lawyers]."[3]

Lucy's step-son-in-law, General Mathew Calbraith Butler, advised her to rent Edgewood and go away for a year, but Lucy refused and told him, "I will never, with God's help, shirk my duty or betray the sacred trust reposed in me by the noblest & best of men, my kindest & dearest Husband."[4]

Her close friend, Ellen Middleton, wisely predicted, "I do not think you will succumb under this blow, though it will no doubt cost you many a sharp struggle to rouse yourself from the 'sweet sad dream' and face the battle of life."[5]

Edgewood, no longer the dull, quiet place that Lucy had initially resented, now housed the homeless, the wounded, and the disconsolate. Major Samuel Kirkland, a wounded veteran of the Confederacy came for tea and stayed for life. Cousin Beverly Robertson made Edgewood headquarters while he squired the eligible belles of the neighborhood and continued to profess his love for his cousin. It was not long before Fleming Gardner, the disappointed suitor, returned to his "Lady Bird." Near and distant cousins, friends, and acquaintances arrived, assured of Lucy's company and hospitality. Suitors, old and new, spiced their lives with flirtations but with no matrimonial success. Everyone found a welcome at Edgewood and Lucy generously supplied food and perhaps financial help. Anna's children came for visits of several years' duration, and occasionally brother Philemon galloped up the winding road to renew family ties. Theodore moved in to assist his sister but, from his habitual prone position on the sofa, he avoided work as much as possible.[6] Thee had never labored in "The Lord's vineyard" as his mother wished, although it was said he consumed much of the vineyard's yield. Handsome, debonair, and lazy, Thee's greatest contribution to the household proved to be his good humor, his tender love, and the connection to home ties that he provided for Lucy whom he called, "Little Darling of our Sainted Mother" or sometimes the "Woman of Hapsburg."[7]

During the Autumn following Francis's funeral, Lucy visited her friends, the Middletons, at their summer home near Asheville, North Carolina. From there she resumed her correspondence with Clara Victoria Dargan. As she sat by the window and looked out over the mountains resplendent with fall foliage, she once again expressed her wish that Clara could come live with her.[8] But it was not to be. Eugenia's health, Anna's strained situation with finances and pregnancies, worried Lucy. Then too, her own health was fragile yet she was "now able to take long walks without more than passing fatigue, & eat and drink like an honest mortal."[9] In her next letter to Clara she wrote, "I am now but a slave to free Negros [*sic*] & lawyers & factors—Life with me, no longer means happiness but duty—I hope some day to be [free] from the care that just depresses me & to welcome you to Edgewood. I am scarce able even to send you this scrawl— I suffer toujours with my chest."[10]

It is not known what caused Lucy's physical ailments. Her mother mentioned, in a letter written in 1846 to Herr Shultz at the Moravian Seminary, that Lucy suffered from a weak back. This may have developed into an arthritic condition. On the other hand her physical problems may have been brought on by depression. An unreconstructed Southerner, Lucy could not fully reconcile herself to the fall of the Confederacy nor to the demise of slavery no matter how kindly she felt toward her own former slaves. Without further knowledge one cannot chance an educated guess as to the cause of Lucy's maladies.

The situation was no better for her mother. Eugenia returned to Marshall in 1870 and faced insurmountable financial problems. With Anna's help she opened Wyalusing to boarders but this meager income added little to ease the situation. Desperate, Eugenia sold various parcels of land to save her home.[11] Soon Wyalusing sat on a dwindling eight acres, all that remained of the vast acreage Beverly had amassed. The worry and stress coupled with her concern for her children proved too much. Eugenia Dorothea Vaughan Hunt Holcombe, the mother who had guided her family with moral strength, religious faith, and unfailing love, died 17 February 1873, age sixty-two years. Lucy expressed her feeling poetically, "The cord of tender love that bound us together tho' loosed from earth, still exists as a golden chain to draw me upwards to her & to add a new delight, even joy to Paradise."[12]

Anna Eliza struggled to keep the family home and land intact. The Holcombe's farm at Fern Lake had been sold and the mortgage on Wyalusing was due. A Mr. Poland of Marshall offered two thousand dollars for Waylusing. Insulted by the offer, Anna retorted, "I can do without it, and I will let it rot down before I will place such a low value on Ma's old home."[13] Theodore and Philemon failed to respond to Anna's pleas and Lucy, preoccupied with her own struggle to keep Edgewood, could not help. Anna, left to bear the brunt of the distressing problem, must have felt completely deserted. When a note on the property came due 1 January 1874, there was no money to pay it. Wyalusing, the beautiful home so proudly built in 1848 by Beverly Lafayette Holcombe, was sold at auction in May of 1874.[14] In 1880, Wyalusing was purchased by former slaves of Harrison County and occupied as Bishop College for Negroes until 1950. The beautiful, historically significant, antebellum home stood vacant until demolished in 1961.[15] A low income housing development has taken its place.

These trying times did not end for Anna, yet she understood that "Sis Lucy" had her own worries and problems in keeping Edgewood. She sent her daughters, Markoleta and Anna Theodore, on long visits to their Aunt Lucy. Anna kept them apprised of town doings in her chatty letters, and sometimes enclosed a bit of spending money. She urged them to husband the money and make good use of it. Although she didn't grudge the sending of it, Anna wanted her daughters to know how difficult it was for her to spare it, yet she knew her girls would have many incidental expenses.[16]

Lucy's situation had its similarities but on a larger scale. Although the farm continued to supply them with food they were dependent on the yield of the cotton crop for cash. Months passed between harvests with no money for wages or taxes. Lucy began to sell parcels of property to pay the freedmen's wages and buy seed. Various pieces of furniture, silver, and valuable gifts from admirers found their way into the hands of Yankee dealers. Bit by bit her wealth, the diamonds and jewelry bestowed on her by the Tsar and nobility of the Russian court, paid for the maintenance of the plantation and provided cash for friends in need and loans to Philemon and Theodore.

Francis had foreseen financial difficulties under the new Republican rule and willed a tract of land on the Saluda River to be sold, if necessary, to finance his daughter's education and "raise her in a pious and lady-like manner."[17] Lucy enrolled Douschka in the fashionable St. Mary's Hall, Raleigh, North Carolina, and sent the faithful and redoubtable Lucinda, affectionately called "Mamee," to watch over her mistress. It was November and Lucy, feeling sad and lonely, expressed her melancholy in poetry. She offered her poems to the eminent South Carolina poet, Paul Hayne. He thought she dwelt too much on mournful thoughts, yet showed a fine knowledge of the classics.[18]

The Civil War made many White women of all classes into authors. Writing provided not only a release from the daily trials but gave to women a significant understanding of themselves and of others. Using writing as an escape, Lucy turned to fiction. She began a novel set in Charleston at the beginning of the great conflict. The characters are drawn from those whom she knew best—her mother, her sister, a composite of various suitors, and herself; writing is as much self-creation as self description. This unfinished novel is written in flowery Victorian prose and tends to sound quaint and overly sentimental. The theme is undying patriotism to "Mother Carolina."

The protagonist, "Madelyn," on the day of her marriage, implores her father to make certain that her husband is called to join his regiment. When her surprised father reminds her that the bridegroom arrived only yesterday from a hard frontier journey and married today, Madelyn, beautiful, vain, and charming, explains, "It is because I love him that I wish him to be foremost where our noblest will be found—under the Palmetto flag. Nothing should make him for one moment forget his holiest right. The right to defend the soil & honor of Carolina."[19]

Lucy never wrote more than three chapters of this novel. She began others. The most notable is the autobiographical tale of two young girls returning home from boarding school in Pennsylvania. In all her manuscripts as well as her letters, Lucy mentions the presence of God in her life and cites high-minded sentiments of patriotism and glory. One is also struck by her concern for the welfare of others, including slaves.[20] She advises various medical treatments that might be outlawed today, such as arsenic tablets for a clear complexion and general well-being. In other letters she promotes acid-phosphate for health, laudanum for pain, hot baths, massage, and quinine for fever. Along with advice Lucy often enclosed in her letters tokens of endearment such as a sprig of sweet olive or ambrosia,[21] "from the gardens of our grandmother's day" or "the tender violets you love."

As the years began to take their toll, the mistress of Edgewood spent much of each day lying on the sofa in her husband's library. The pain in her side worsened. She relied on laudanum for relief and, inevitably, her beauty faded. Her thoughts and hope dwelt on her sixteen-year old daughter away at school. The faithful Lucinda wrote to her from St. Mary's Hall, April 14, 1875.

> Dearest Miss Lucy:
> I was so glad to get your letter on Monday with the box. I fear that you have been sick now that you acknowledge to be indisposed worse even than you write! The baby was delighted with her dresses. The one you had made fits her very nicely only I think a little short although she says that it is not. . . My eyes are much better, still weak enough, however to require a shade to protect them. Douschka is to play next music night. The piece is "Silvery Waves." You never have said whether you have decided to go to Texas or not altho [*sic*] I have asked you several times . . . Did Miss Rebekah stay with you at Mills House? Please send Mrs. Brodnax's bulbs to her. I wish if you go to

Augusta that you will have my leghorn hat trimmed over. I
thank you so much for the lace tie. It is lovely. I do want to see
you so much (so does your little "witch"). I thank you also for
the money you sent me. Douschka sends so much love to her
dear Mamasha . . . I wish you would take some notice of Mrs.
Brodnax's letter if you have re'd it—Love to all especially Miss
Lu Smith.
Your devotedly attached Lucinda.[22]

A strong bond of mutual dependency existed between Lucy and
Lucinda, a bond that transcended the racial bar and lasted unto death.
As her mistress's maid and companion, Lucinda had traveled abroad.
Her ability to read and write, to speak French and Russian phrases,
and her favored position set her apart from other Blacks. Aloof and
opinionated, carrying herself with regal dignity, Lucinda rose above
most women of her own race, yet she was not accepted as an equal
among Whites in the nineteenth century. Haughty and a legend of
contrariness, this woman born into slavery and now experiencing freedom, ruled from a position of privilege that she never allowed others
to forget. Small wonder that the other servants called her "Duchess"
or that she was fiercely possessive yet devoted to her mistress and
considered Douschka "her child."

CHAPTER TWENTY-THREE

1876–1893

"The Joan of Arc of Carolina"

John Hope Franklin

*D*ouschka returned to Edgewood the summer of 1876, a time of unrest and revolt. Throughout her adolescent years, Douschka witnessed her mother and others loyal to the Confederacy refuse to accept defeat and, like most White Southerners, found it difficult to accept the concept of Blacks and Northerners placed in positions of authority. Unable to adjust to the changed political scene that stripped them of power and angered by the loss of their slaves, Carolinians of the up-country took matters into their own hands. They openly defied and heaped abuse upon those in authority. A contemporary source related, "Negroes are shot dead or wounded. Nobody is convicted because no adequate testimony is found or the magistrates don't prosecute."[1]

Many freed slaves believed that the lands of their former owners would be divided amongst them. For the most part Republican agents supported this belief and tried to act fairly. South Carolina voted to break up and sell to Blacks small lots from an acreage of 80,000 but this never came to fruition. It is no wonder that the freed slave faced confusion laced with bitterness and anger as he now worked the same land as a "share-cropper."

In Edgefield County, a guerrilla band tried to compel the freed slaves to remain with their former masters.[2] In retaliation, the Radical Republicans blocked the Southern Democrats from the polls at election time by intimidation and physical force. Angry and humiliated, South Carolinians planned secretly to vote for the candidates of their choice. They met in bands of white-hooded Ku Kluk Klan and spread terrorism in the up-country of South Carolina until finally suppressed by martial law in 1871.[3]

Although forbidden to gather in large groups or to possess weapons, these South Carolinians met under the guise of "Recreational Clubs" at Edgewood and other plantations. In secrecy they collected weapons and ammunition, adopted a uniform of red shirts and rode about the countryside at night terrorizing the radical Republican rulers. These activists considered themselves to be on a religious crusade for deliverance or, as they saw it, the redemption of a prostrate state.[4] It was said that the Rebels were not whipped only overpowered.

In 1876 Governor Daniel H. Chamberlain came up for re-election as Governor of South Carolina. His opposition proved to be Wade Hampton's Red Shirts who, 600 strong, took over a political meeting and heaped abuse upon carpetbaggers and scalawags. They denounced the governor as one who had come to prey upon Southerners and steal from them their substance. The war heroes Martin Gary and Mathew C. Butler are credited with instigating this group of "Red Shirts" and Douschka is said to have led their most famous wild ride. Articles, newspapers, and an historical novel mention a ride of the Red Shirts as taking place on election day, November, 1876.[5] That dramatic incident would undoubtedly have had Lucy's blessing.

Douschka, mounted on her horse, Bonnibell, a red cape draped about her shoulders and red plume dangling from her Garibaldi cap, moved to the front of a company of Red Shirts on horseback. At a given signal the young girl stood in her stirrups, gave the Rebel yell and galloped her mount through the town with the Red Shirts thundering behind her. Waving carbines and yelling, they headed to the polling place. The Republican radicals blocking the polls ran in terror before this avenging sea of red. Taken by surprise, the Republican Provost Marshall made a feeble attempt to retaliate with his troops, but Douschka drove them back. With the company of Red-shirts now guarding the polls, the Southern Democrats entered and cast their vote for their candidate, Wade Hampton. He won the election as the first Democratic Governor for South Carolina in over ten years. Douschka Pickens was called "The Joan of Arc of Carolina" for helping to make this possible. This ride of the Red Shirts is said to have heralded the end of Reconstruction pretensions in South Carolina, Florida, and Louisiana, as well as on the national scene.[6]

The past fifteen years with their sorrows and worries had drained Lucy of health and stamina and she no longer felt free to travel. Theodore, knowing her interest in maintaining George Washington's home as a national shrine, urged her to attend the fall meeting of the Mount Vernon Ladies Association as Vice-Regent for South Carolina. With the assurance that the formidable Lucinda would look after Douschka, with Major Kirkland to oversee the servants' care of house and grounds, and Theodore in charge of the planting and rentals, Lucy set off for Mount Vernon. It is probably not a coincidence that this avowed Southern Patriot chose the American Centennial of 1876 to make her debut at the home of America's first President. Her introduction into this high-minded, interesting group of women began a new era for Lucy.

She arrived in Washington toward the end of November and took the steamboat, the *W. W. Corcoran,* to Mount Vernon. The boat left the Seventh Street wharf at ten o'clock sharp. A cold breeze rippled the water and Captain Blake urged the ladies to stay in the cabin for the half-hour trip. The captain enjoyed his position and, when they sighted Mt. Vernon, his crewmen tolled the ship's bell in memory of George Washington, America's First Patriot.[7] The big white frame house on the hillside was impressive even in its unfinished state of restoration. The morning sun shone on the golden weather vane atop the cupola and highlighted the tall pillars stretched across the verandah facing the Potomac River and the Maryland shore.

Twelve ladies attended this 1876 November Council at Mount Vernon. Madame Berghmans, the wealthy wife of the Belgian Minister in Washington, served as Regent replacing the ailing Miss Cunningham.[8] Of the ladies attending, Mrs. Berghmans and Mrs. Eve from Georgia and later Mrs. Sweat from Maine, were among Lucy's close friends. The sleeping accommodations, with three or more ladies sharing a room, might have reminded Lucy of her years at the Moravian Seminary.

Lucy's interest and work as vice-regent continued for twenty-two years attending twice a year with but a few absences. Each vice-regent, and consequently the state they represented, helped to make Mount Vernon a public shrine. Restoration of the small dining room fell to South Carolina and Lucy furnished and decorated the room to fit the period it represented. Serving also as Chairman of the Garden and Greenhouse Committee she helped preserve the valued trees and saw to cuttings and seeds in the restored greenhouse. Lucy delighted in sending plants to Anna Eliza and explained in a letter, "Nothing rare or of value only that they came from Mt. Vernon . . . The ladies are all clever, kind and agreeable and oh! the rest that it has been. The house and grounds are kept up as in Washington's time, and we are served by a butler in dining room and maids in our chambers who are descended from his [George Washington's] body servants."[9]

Anna Eliza may not have appreciated Lucy's enthusiasm. Finances and husband Elkanah's unexplained absences continued to vex Anna. She worried that he would never be able to pay his debts. Like her father, Beverly Holcombe, Elkanah was quick to aid his friends, yet they often failed to repay his generosity.[10] Although Elkanah worked with the railroad and tried farming, the years were not fruitful. Depressed and looking for ways to make money to pay his debts, Elkanah Greer visited his sister in Arkansas in 1877. While there he contracted pneumonia and died. Anna, left with five children and many debts, struggled as best she could finding comfort in her children, her church and her many friends. Early in August, 1881, Anna received a letter from Lucy.

> [Douschka] wrote you of her engagement to Dr. Dugas of Augusta [Georgia]. He is a well born, well bred young physician of talent and ample fortune entirely devoted to her— There is nothing to be said against it tho it is not what I wished—You will be surprised to learn that I expect to sail for England in a few days with Judge Bacon—entirely business— If I succeed, I may hope to see you and yours once more in this life . . . I have lost all my property but E [Edgewood] and that not secure. Thee [Theodore] rents a small place 15 miles away—Is the same, only older and poor health—I want you to know that I love you and your precious children with tender unfailing love, and grieve deeply I am not to help or be near you—I hope for a brighter future—I shall not be absent more than 4 or 6 weeks and will send my address from N.Y., God bless you my darling—with tenderest love to you and all in which my heart delights from your devoted sister – L. H. Pickens[11]

It is supposed that her trip was made with the intention of borrowing money. Lucy had many friends in Europe, not the least of whom was Tsar Alexander II. However, by this time, she must have heard of his assassination in February of 1881. Quite possibly she meant to turn to her old friend, Judah P. Benjamin, for a loan of money. During the war years, Benjamin served as Secretary of State for the Confederacy and had been counted among Lucy's many admirers. He escaped to Great Britain after the war and, maintaining his British citizenship, became a wealthy and successful barrister.[12] Perhaps Lucy felt that England would provide a better market in which to sell her remaining jewels. Whatever her objective, she succeeded and returned to devote full attention to Douschka's wedding 10 October 1881.

Guests came from far and near. Statesmen and their wives, congressmen and senators, relatives and friends, all gathered to witness the brilliant nuptial ceremony of Miss Douschka Pickens and Dr. George Cuvier Dugas. One of Douschka's bridesmaids, her cousin Eugenia Markoleta Petway Greer, later described the event to her own daughter, Miss Anna Holcombe Smith of Marshall. The following description is taken from Miss Smith's memoirs.

To guide the many guests, bonfires of fat pine burned at intervals along the half mile of darkened avenue leading to the house. Faithful Black servants guarded these fires while others stood on each side of the high steps with pine torches to light the way as the guests left the carriages. Uncle Harper, in spotless livery, his white hair and side burns gleaming, opened the doors of the carriages and assured a firm footing into the house where "Mamee" Lucinda, and Mary Johnson, a house-maid, received their wraps.

The glow of hundreds of candles in cut-glass chandeliers shone on antique Bohemian glass vases filled with roses, carnations, chrysanthemums, and Southern smilax. A stringed orchestra played soft music until the notes of Lohengrin's wedding march sounded and the bride appeared on the arm of her venerable uncle, Theodore Holcombe. This brown-eyed and brown-haired girl of twenty-two wore a veil of imported lace, her cap caught in the back with Lilies of the Valley. The white brocaded satin dress was draped with a filmy lace point de venise that had been worn by her mother at the Russian court. She carried a small bouquet of Lilies of the Valley in her white lace mittens. The only jewel worn was a diamond necklace given to her by the Czar Alexander of Russia. [13]

Theodore gave his own account of the match in a letter to Anna Eliza, "Dr. Dugas is I think a fine looking or better than all, a religiously reared and piously inclined man, firm withall [*sic*] and I think will make a good woman of Douschka. God grant it for she was a full rigged ship without ballast or rudder here. You know very well what I mean. Her every wish was her mother's pleasure, every thing irreproachable but extravagantly gay."[14]

After a wedding trip to New York, Douschka and George Dugas settled in Augusta, Georgia. But Douschka could not bear to be away from Edgewood. Unlike her mother, she found social life distasteful and soon moved back to manage the farm for her mother. Her husband joined her on weekends. Lucy and "Mamee" were delighted to have their "baby" home and their pleasure knew no bounds when grandchildren began to arrive.

Lucy continued her sometimes twice-a-year pilgrimages to Mount Vernon, knowing that Edgewood was in good hands. As vice-regent for South Carolina she organized a concert and ball to benefit Mount Vernon's Ladies Association. It was held in Charleston at the Academy of Music and performed on Washington's birthday, 22 February 1884. Although no longer the governor's wife, Lucy possessed an aura of mystery that assured her an audience. Old friends and enemies flocked to the benefit in the name of a good cause—and out of curiosity—and the "Charleston, S. C. and Mount Vernon" benefit proved a success. As another vice-regent remarked in a letter to Lucy, "It is lovely to think that you were personally & officially recognised [*sic*] & made much of for the dear & fine qualities you posess[*sic*]."[15]

The time Lucy spent among the other vice-regents provided a cultural and intellectual ambience that she enjoyed. But her pleasure was shaken when she received word that her beloved sister, Anna Eliza, died 28 July 1887. Lucy, Douschka, and Theodore returned to Marshall where each flower, each shrub, and each duckling in the pond brought fond memories of her sister and of her mother. Lucy wrote—

> Oh sad is the garden of roses
> My Anna no longer I see.
> Here flora all withered reposes
> And mourns o'er her absence with me.[16]

Tired and depressed, Lucy returned to Edgewood and tried to ease the pain of separation from first her father, her husband, her mother, her stepdaughter Jeannie, and now her beloved sister. From habit she turned to Trinity Episcopal Church in Edgefield, where she had been confirmed in 1868. But now the music and ritual that had so appealed to her brought only painful reminders of happier days. She continued to attend for Douschka's sake and for the three grandchildren, Lucy Francis Pickens, Louis Alexander, and Adrienne Dorothea Rebecca Dugas. The children called her "Dan" and once again the wide porches and tall rooms of Edgewood echoed with the sound of their laughter, but it was not to last.

On a hot day in August 1893, tragedy struck. Douschka rode in from Augusta with her three young children and their governess to spend the week with her mother. Lucy marveled at her daughter's vigor and health and thought nothing unusual when Douschka retired early that sultry August evening. But Douschka, the darling of friends and family, died in her sleep at thirty-four years of age. The cause of death was said to be a "type of fever."

Shocked and devastated by her only child's death, Lucy allowed herself a private grief until the funeral. Ashen-faced and leaning heavily on Theodore's arm, she stepped to the head of the white draped casket covered in white flowers and spoke to the assembled guests and servants, "My friends and faithful servants, I have sent for you to do this honor because, I wish to make a public acknowledgment of your faithfulness and devotion through all her sweet life to this, your young mistress. When your master died, you will remember, he sent for you and confided to your faithful care and protection his wife and little child. You have been faithful to that trust. In all the dreadful times of riot and thieving you have stood by us and protected us, and I thank you now in the presence of all these friends for your loyalty and devotion."[17]

Eight servants, their heads bowed in grief, bore the casket to the family burial plot and laid their young mistress beside her father's grave. As the casket was lowered into the ground, Lucy, struggling to control her emotions, raised her veiled head skyward, arms wrapped about her daughter's children, her remaining ties to her beloved Douschka.

CHAPTER TWENTY-FOUR

1894–1899

"We do not forget!"
Lucy Holcombe Pickens

*G*rieving friends and family gathered to comfort Lucy and Douschka's children. Fleming Gardner arrived with love and support for his dear "Lady Bird." And there were Theodore and dear "Mamee" Lucinda to console, for they, too, were heartbroken. Lucy tried to rouse herself from the depths of despair, knowing that with Lucinda's help, she must care for her grandchildren. They needed her and they in turn provided a link with her beloved Douschka. Although she admitted to being "much tied within my gates by grand-children," she kept them constantly in her thoughts, particularly when they visited their father's home in Augusta.[1] About 1895 she wrote the following letter to the eldest grandchild, Lucy, now in her early teens.[2]

> My darling Lucy—
> I sent Dolly's [Adrienne Dorothea Rebecca] clothes—not

that I think she will need all of them as your Papa promised to send her home after a few days visit, but I want her to have a fresh dress every day, even if it is simple & plain she will be at least clean.

You looked so ill—so deadly pale when you left that I have been most wretched. I hope you will take quinine. I send you $100 & beg you to send Joe & get some pt bottles of Claret & take it for it refreshes & strengthens you—I was shocked at seeing you in the hot kitchen looking after your Papa's breakfast when you had a nurse up to that time looking after & giving you your meals.

I send you arsenic. It is very important if nothing else, it will make your complexion fair & beautiful—many society women take "arsenic wafers" solely for their complexion—I will write you tomorrow. Do let me hear from you. I will telephone to know how you stood the journey.

God bless you both—My darling—With love from all to all—Your devoted—Dan.[3]

Lucy attended Trinity Church each Sunday but it afforded little solace. Every glance at Douschka's empty place in the pew beside her brought tears she found difficult to control. The longing for her daughter remained an aching pain in her heart. Trouble with her vision and the pain in her side and back caused Lucy to spend much of her time lying on the sofa dreaming of better days or hobbling about the garden on her cane.[4]

Lucy Holcombe Pickens's life had been full. She held the South to be a Kingdom and gave to it her unquestioned patriotic loyalty. For this she was recognized and lauded, but in the cruel aftermath of war, glory, and recognition for her role in the Confederacy mattered little. Time had swept away her loved ones, her fortune, and her country. She was not alone in her misery. Her one-time rival, Mary Boykin Chesnut, spent the post-war years in poor health, without money or a home, and with an ailing husband. Virginia Clay, wife of ex-senator Clement Clay, tried for years to have her husband released from the Yankee prison where he was held under suspicion of having plotted the death of Abraham Lincoln. Varina Davis, wife of the president of the Confederacy, spent the post war years dependent on the hospitality of friends while she struggled to have her husband pardoned. These women, once pampered and waited upon, experienced a rude awakening of suffering and privation that left them in pain and poor health.

Sick and despairing, Lucy, like her mother, devoted herself to her family and to the memory of those who had gone beyond. Now out of the public eye, her name and achievements slipped from view yet she never faltered in upholding with patriotic fervor her belief in the South. And, with charm and intelligence she had succeeded in her own quest for recognition as a woman, assisted at times by what she termed, "the innocent deceits of the sex."[5]

Now Lucy's thoughts turned to former days and when Mrs. Atha, an old family friend from Marshall, arrived, Lucy welcomed her with tears of joy. Soon the two of them, comfortable in their age, slipped back to the old ways of "chewing hickory bark and locust nuts and indulging in Old Scotch honey-due [*sic*]."[6] With Theodore, the two friends reminisced of happier days in Texas. Occasionally, brother Philemon rode in for a visit and joined the small group in keeping alive fond memories of family. Except to Lucy and perhaps Theodore, Philemon remained an enigma to the family. His great granddaughter, May Margaret Touhey, mentioned his skill with horses, a skill that served him well as a messenger with Parson's Brigade Texas Cavalry.[7] Theodore often spoke of his father's deathbed injunction to take care of Philemon, "Share your last dollar with him my boy, he is the baby, he is deaf, take care of him."[8] Philemon married his childhood friend, Emma Hilliard, when both were in their teens. They had one child, Lucy, and after Emma's death, he married Nannie Baldwin and sired two children. Philemon lived in Marshall until his death in 1917.

Restless and lonely, her waking hours filled with memories of better days, Lucy liked to be driven through town to visit the graves of her daughter and husband. In remembrance of her dear stepdaughter, Jeannie, she had the remains of Jeannie's mother, Marie Antoinette Dearing Pickens, brought from its burial place at Cedar Fields to rest on the other side of her husband in Willowbrook, Edgefield's village cemetery.[9] Holding on to threads of the past, her thoughts returned to the men who had given their lives to the Confederacy, men she had known and loved and sent cheerily on to their fate. Why, she wondered, did Edgefield not have a monument to honor these brave soldiers? She suggested such a memorial to Edgefield's Historical Society. They, in turn, chose Lucy to serve as president of the county's Ladies Memorial Association and of the Abner Perrin Camp of United Confederate Veterans. Once again Lucy tackled a patriotic project and doubled her pleas for a Confederate monument to be erected on Edgefield's courthouse square.

She wrote and circulated a "broadside" titled, "The Patriotic Women of Edgefield County."[10] With eloquent and stirring words, she urged mothers, wives, sisters, friends, and countrywomen to pledge themselves to keep faith with the past, to pay this last debt of love to their honored flag and to the men who guarded its honor with their lives. "We do not forget!" Lucy reminded. "The vacant chair never loses its pathos and pain for us; the dear voice silent in death, still speaks to our constant heart, and the fair young nation drowned to death in the blood of her martyred sons, claims our truest, deepest, our loving tho [*sic*] silent homage."[11]

Lucy worked tirelessly to raise money to commission a marble shaft for Edgefield's town square. She succeeded but it was not until shortly after her death that her dream became a reality.

The years passed, years when Lucy sometimes felt too tired to go beyond her beloved garden. Days were spent on the sofa by the window where she could see the wondrous magnolia tree that held so many memories. When April and November arrived she roused herself to attend meetings of the Mount Vernon Ladies Association but her grief lay heavily on her mind.

A year before her death Lucy wrote a letter to Sally Simkins Butler, Douschka's girlhood friend and once a permanent guest and housekeeper at Edgewood. It is a letter typical of Lucy's thoughtfulness and concern for others.

> My Dear Sally,
>
> I am very sorry to hear your little Francis is sick. I would gladly furnish you milk of which we have abundance, if I could send it to you—but have no one to take it. I send a mite to buy milk for the dear little baby just as our Douschka would do— only she would go to you and help and comfort you with her divine sweetness and goodness.
>
> I can't come now being so weak and downed by the fearful heat. I am much better in health, and refreshed by my trip and the comforts of it of which I will tell you later—but I am a poor frail piece of patchwork holding onto life by my eyelids—for Douschka's children's sake. I know you can't come to me, but if it ever rains, I will try to come to see you.
>
> It is a fearfully gloomy prospect here—all crops dead and dying for want of rain my splendid garden burned up—and flowers famished. I cannot tell you dear dear Sally how I miss more and more than ever my own dear darling Douschka, as I know you do. I cannot, cannot get accustomed to her absence—I miss her love and sympathy and help every moment and it all seems so dreary and weary to me—Yet I must go on and do my duty and pray God to help me. You do not know how awful it is to come home to Edgewood and miss her dear voice and face and know it is forever—God above knows the agony of it. But it must be endured—and I try to be calm under its gnawing pain—and do my best for her children's sake. Lucy Francis is well and happy in Baltimore with Idoline—Dolly and Oui [Louis Alexander Dugas][12] are kept by Dr. Dugas in Augusta but I hope will come last of this week. With love—yr ever aff and devoted—L. H. P.[13]

Lucinda, crushed by the death of the child she had cared for from birth, remained with her former mistress. Although she had married sometime around 1880 Lucinda often stayed overnight at

Edgewood to be with her mistress and in the humid month of August both women became ill.[14] Lucy, whom Fleming Gardner claimed was happiest when nursing, tried to minister to "Mamee" as the former slave had so often done for her, but the effort taxed her own weakened condition.

The morning of 8 August 1899, the sun peeped in through the shutters and gauze curtains drawn against the heat. A maid came with a cooling drink, but her mistress could not be roused. Alarmed, she ran for help but "Mistrus Lucy" was beyond human help. At age sixty-seven years she had died in her sleep, having suffered a cerebral embolism. Three days later, Lucinda, her devoted servant, friend, and companion, joined her mistress in death.[15]

The entire town and community, friends from far and near, White and Black, young and old, came to pay tribute to the memory of this woman who so touched their lives and their hearts. Her pew at Trinity Church was draped in white. The eight older servants, Wesley Bostic, Daniel Thomas, Archie Simpo, Jackson Royal, John Simmons, Sr., Andrew Perry, John Simmons, Jr., and Wallace Morgan, carried their mistress's white draped casket to the family burial plot in Willowbrook cemetery.[16] Theodore and Philemon, Cousin Beverly, Major Kirkland, and Fleming Gardner followed, heads bowed in grief.

In a tribute to Lucy given at Mt. Vernon, Mrs. Sweat, Vice Regent for Massachusetts, read this touching eulogy to her dear friend, Lucy Holcombe Pickens, "The imaginary kingdom, the Confederacy, which to many was only an ill-considered political experiment, was to her a glorious reality, a faith, a religion, and she gave it a loyalty that only strengthened as it became hopeless . . . Her intense sorrow over this lost ideal grew to a passionate pain, as it swept away her friends, her fortune, and, as she expressed it, her country."[17]

Lucy Petway Holcombe Pickens rests at the foot of her husband's and daughter's graves. Beautiful flowers no longer cover her grave but magnificent trees bend over her and every spring the wild violets she loved peek-out between the mossy bricks and in the fall red-tinged leaves cover the breast-stone that bears this inscription—

This stone is erected in memory of a
beautiful and gracious lady of the
old South. She was the wife of Francis
Wilkinson Pickens, the war Governor
of South Carolina from 1860 to 1863.
Beautiful in person, cultured in mind,
patriotic in spirit, she was loved by all
who knew her.

Epilogue

Theodore Holcombe continued to live at Edgewood at the invitation of Lucy's granddaughters. He wrote to his brother, Philemon, saying he had little to do but "superintend with the general charge of the place and things." He rented out the parcel of land that Lucy gave him but regretted that he hadn't the means to develop it. Theodore missed his sister and dreamt very often of her, "always lovely dreams. I feel as if she and Effie [perhaps companion] are my guardian Angels."

In Lucy's will her granddaughters, Lucy Francis Pickens Dugas and Adrienne Dorothea Rebecca Dugas, were named to receive in equal shares, "All and singular my personal property of every kind and description whatsoever—including my diamonds and other jewelry. All my silverware and china plate and paintings and pictures and my library and my household and kitchen furniture and all other species of personal property which I may own at time of my death and all which may be useful for agricultural purposes such as horses and mules, cows and sheep and goats and wagons and harness and agricultural implements of every kind."

Lucy bequeathed to "John Theodore Hunt Holcombe, my faithful brother, land enough for a two-house farm not to exceed seventy acres wherever he designates to cut it off from my realty. To be held and worked for his own use."

The rents, issues and income from her property were to be used for the education of her granddaughters.

The two granddaughters later married and moved away from Edgewood and the beautiful house and grounds lay vacant for a number of years. In the 1920s Miss Eulalie Salley of Aiken, South Carolina, bought the house. According to the *Aiken Standard*, 24 May 1991, Edgewood became known as the Pickens-Salley house. In 1928–29, Mrs. Salley had it taken down, board by board and moved to Gregg

Avenue in Aiken. Sometime after this—in the 1930s—the house was listed on the National Register of Historic Places and known as the "Pickens House." Over the years changes were made to update this house which became the Salley family home for about fifty years.

Mrs. Salley transformed Lucy's bedroom into her guestroom, and soon tales of ghosts began to circulate. Some said that Lucy, recognizable by the lingering fragrance of honeysuckle blossoms and the swishing sound of her silken skirts, awakened them. Others felt a strong presence in the room along with a beguiling fragrance. Legend though it may be, the beautiful and talented Lucy Petway Holcombe Pickens continued to make an impact on peoples' lives, if only in memory.

Some years later, possibly in the 1970s, the Salleys sold this historic home to the Aiken developer, Ronald B. Bolton. Mr. Bolton donated the house to the University of South Carolina at Aiken in 1989. Edgewood, the former home of Governor and Mrs. Pickens, is currently used by the University for its Studies in Southern History program.

The life of Lucy Petway Holcombe Pickens continues to fascinate. In the 1950s a spate of undocumented articles lauded Lucy with such titles as, "Uncrowned Queen of the Confederacy," "Fluer de Lucy," and as the "Texas Girl Pictured on Currency." Research has shown that much of the information given was imagined. Lucy does not need such publicity to be celebrated.

As a romantic young woman, Lucy Petway Holcombe championed filibusters, gained literary recognition, entered the political field, and all the while held her own as a Southern belle. She was not a "woman's rights woman" yet she advocated higher education for women insisting that with intellect a woman could better the conditions in America by taking a rightful place in politics and government.

Later, as Lucy Holcombe Pickens, she used her wit and charm to champion another cause, the Confederacy. Cognizant of the political situation, she became the driving force behind her husband in his role as Governor of South Carolina the first state to secede from the Union. Mary Chesnut noted in her Civil War diary, "He [Governor

Pickens] will outwit them all yet, with the aid of the lovely Lucy, who is a host in herself."[1]

Lucy advanced the cause of the Confederacy holding the South to be a "kingdom" and by 1862, her portrait was chosen to be on Confederate currency, the only woman of her time to be so honored. By this and her generous aid of money to help outfit a Confederate regiment named in her honor, she gained a place in history.

By her extreme patriotism, and in this case patriotism to the Southern Confederacy, Lucy sent men and boys on to war with brave words of valor and high ideals. In the aftermath of war, saddened by its destruction and carnage, Lucy commemorated those who died for her "kingdom."

Despite her faults, for we all have them, Lucy Holcombe Pickens was a woman whose convictions took her beyond the accepted role of women in the nineteenth century. Claiming that "submission is not my role," Lucy raised the hopes of women in a time of patriarchal domination. Ever loyal to her friends and family, she strove to be a credit to her ancestors and faithful to her country, which in this case she deemed to be the Confederacy.

Lucy was aware of her own mental capacity and sought out people of like intelligence, yet she never snubbed those of lesser ability. It is said that her extravagance put her husband in debt. This may be true to some extent but Lucy's lavish spending was not just for self aggrandizement; to the very end she reached out to help others in need and showed by example that women could exert great influence on society. It could be said that Lucy Holcombe Pickens sailed through the turbulent years before, during, and after the War Between the States, with wit and intelligence as her compass, loyalty her ballast.

Appendix A

ON LEAVING VILLA DE LANSKOI
Russia Sept.7ᵗʰ,1859

The sun in all his splendor red
Has sunk away to rest
With clouds of gold and purple heaped
Upon his royal breast.
And twilight with her dreamy eye
Looks out on earth and sea
And consecrates this mystic hour
To thoughtful reverie.
                    2
I gaze upon this lovely scene
These garden walks and flowers
Where I so fondly whiled away
The long long summer hours,
And watched each lovely plant expand
And praised its grace and bloom
And sighed to think its beauty came
    To fade alas! So soon—
                    3
Ah: yes how every shady spot
Brings back some joy I've known
A loving look, a tender smile,
A low persuasive tone.
As by this calm and placid lake
My little one would play
Or wander where the lilies grew
As pure and fair as they—

4

Ah! I had garnered in this home
A wealth of joy and love
And God had daily sent us down
His blessing from above.
For we had health and we had joy
And love so fond and mild
My heart was centered in the two
My husband and my child.

5

For all the dreams of young romance
That filled my girlish heart
Sweet visions of a lovely home
Where I would fondly rest.
Of one fine heart and noble mind
Responsive to my own
Who caring nought for all besides
Would love but me alone.

6

All this I found in this sweet spot
For'er endeared to me
I love each tender blade of grass
Each fragrant flower and tree.
And sadness will steal o'er my heart
And tears will fill the eye
For evening shadows slowly fall
The parting hour is nigh.

7

But when in my own native land
Far distant o'er the sea
I sit beside the quiet hearth
Or join in mirth and glee.
A voice will whisper in my heart
What time can ne'er destroy
A thousand tender memories of
Our happy home Lanskoi.

Written for my husband.

Lucy Petway Holcombe Pickens

Appendix B

PICKENS GENEALOGY

m= married   b = born   d = died

Andrew Pickens
  m Rebecca Calhoun
    1. Ezekiel
    2. Andrew
      m 1. Susannah Wilkinson
        1. Francis Wilkinson, b 1805 d. 1869
          m 1. Eliza Simkins
            1. Susan
              m Lipscom
            2. Andrew
            3. Francis
            4. Maria
              m Butler
            5. Eliza
              m Coles
            6. Rebecca
              m Bacon
        m 2. Marion Antoinette Dearing
          1. Jeannie b. 1848 d. 1866
            m Mitchell Whaley
        m 3 Lucy Petway
          1. Francis Eugenia Olga Neva (Douschka) b. 1859 d. 1893
            m George Cuvier Dugas
              1. Lucy Francis Pickens b. 1882
                m Benjamin R. Tillman, Jr.
                  1. Douschka Pickens Adrienne
                    m Robert Thach
                      1. Douschka
                      2. Lucy Francis Dugas
              2. Louis Alexander b. 1884 d. 1898

3. Andrienne Dorothea Rebecca b. 1886 d. 1953
   m W. W. Sheppard
   1. Lucy Holcombe
      m Bradley
      1. Dorothea
         m Sherrill
   2. W. W. Sheppard, Jr.
   3. Dorothea
      m Jenkins
      1. Adrienne Dugas
         m Austin T. Moore, Jr.
         1. Adrienne Dugas
         2. Alexandria Pickens

2. Susan
   m James H. Calhoun

Appendix C

HOLCOMBE GENEALOGY

m= married   b = born   d = died

William Holcombe b? (came to America in 1600s)
 m ?
  1. James Philemon Holcombe b 1720
    m Ann Walthall b 1721
      1. Philemon Holcombe b 1762 d 1836?
        m Lucy Maria Anderson b 1765 d 1834? (see note)
          1. Thomas Anderson b 1785
          2. Philemon b 1788
          3. Elizabeth Ann b 1789
          4. Sarah Taylor b 1791
          5. Frances A. b 1793
          6. William James b 1798
          7. Lucy Ann b 1800
          8. Martha Maria b 1801
          9. Amanda born 1802?
          10. Beverly Lafayette b 1806 d 1864
            m Dorothea (Eugenia) Vaughn Hunt b 1811
              1. Anna Eliza b 1830 d 1883
                m Elkanah Greer
                  1. Beverly Holcombe b 1852
                  2. Eugenia Markoleta b 1855
                  3. Guy Holcombe b 1858
                  4. Anna Theodore b 1856
                  5. Francis Pickens b 1865
                  6. Clarence Ambler b 1870
              2. Lucy Petway b 1832 d 1899
                m Francis Wilkinson Pickens
                  1. Francis Eugenia Olga Neva (Douschka)
                    b 1858 d 1893
                    m George Cuvier Dugas 1881
              3. John Theodore Hunt b 1834 d 1906
              4. Martha Maria b 1836 d 1839

5. Philemon Eugene b 1838 d 1917
 m 1. Emma Elizabeth Hilliard b 1840 d 1864
  1. Lucy Petway b 1856?
   m George Owen Caven
  2. Philemon Eugene Jr.
  3. J. Hilliard b ? d 1860
 m 2. Louisa Garrett
 m 3. Nannie Amelia Baldwin
  1. Daisy b 1887
   m Touhey
    1. May Margaret b ? d 1998
    2. John Henry
     m Ina Allen Bramlette
      1. John Edward Touhey
  2. Henry Hilliard b 1889
   m Leeta McGimpey
    1. Doris

note
Lucy Maria Anderson genealogy:

Baron von Hardeman [Hardimann] b?
 m ?
  1. John Hardeman b?
   m Henrietta Maria Taylor (daughter of John of Flowandra)
    1. Henrietta Maria Hardeman b?
     m Captain James Clark
      1. Sarah Clark b?
       m Thomas "Gentleman" Anderson
        1. Lucy Maria Anderson b 1765 d 1834
         m Philemon Holcombe

Abbreviations

AEH   Anna Eliza Holcombe
AEHG Anna Eliza Holcombe Greer
EDH   Eugenia Dorothea Holcombe
FWP   Francis Wilkinson Pickens
JTH   John Theodore Holcolmbe
LPH   Lucy Petway Holcombe
LPHP Lucy Petway Holcombe Pickens

D/L-G/H   Davis/Little Collection-Greer/Holcombe Families

SCL-USC   South Caroliniana Library, University of South Carolina at Columbia

SHC-UNC   Southern Historical Collection, University of North Carolina at Chapel Hill

Pickens Papers, Duke University
              Franics W. Pickens Papers, Special Collections, No. M. 2321, Perkins Library, Duke University, Durham, North Carolina

Notes

PREFACE

1. EDH to Reverend Henry Shultz of Moravian Female Seminary, 1846, La Grange, Tennessee. Moravian College Archives.

2. Lucy Holcombe [H. M. Hardimann, pseud.], *The Free Flag of Cuba or the Martyrdom of Lopez*, (New York: Dewitt and Davenport, 1855), 70.

3. Lucy Holcombe Pickens, Collected Writings, Pickens Papers, South Caroliniana Library, University of South Carolina at Columbia, 66.

CHAPTER ONE

1. Holcombe, *Free Flag*, 86.

2. McPherson, Elizabeth Weir, *The Holcombes, Nation Builders* (Washington, D. C.: McPherson, 1947), 312–314.

3. Ibid., 734.

4. Ibid., 736.

5. Ibid.

6. McPherson, *The Holcombes*; Thomas Perkins Abernathy, *From Frontier to Plantation in Tennessee, A Study in Frontier Democracy* (Chapel Hill: University North Carolina Press, 1933), 236–250.

7. Dr. William Henry Holcombe's Autobiography, Pickens-Dugas Papers, No. 1492, Southern Historical Collection at the University of North Carolina; Ada Holcombe Aiken, "What I Remember," Dr. David Wyatt Aiken private collection; McPherson, *The Holcombes*, 736.

8. Incorporated in 1824 La Grange's population grew to 8,000 by 1830 attesting to the large influx of settlers from the South and the East. Dorothy Rich Morton, *Fayette*, Tennessee County History Series, (Memphis, Tennessee: Memphis State University Press, 1989), 13.

9. Eugenia's paternal grandparents, Thomas and Dorothea Vaughan Hunt, emigrated from England and settled in Sussex County, Virginia. Their son, John Hunt, married first Rhoda Petway. One daughter of this union lived to adulthood. Born in 1811, they christened her Dorothea Vaughan but the child was always known as Eugenia, a name she preferred. Greer, Jack, *Leaves From a Family Album-Holcombe and Greer*, (Waco, Texas: Texian Press, 1975), 21.

10. Greer, *Leaves*, 15.

11. Fayette County Tennessee Court Records and Marriage Record Book. The house originally known as Ingleside, is presently called Westover and continues at its original location in La Grange, Tennessee.

12. Greer, *Leaves*, 17.

13. EDH to LPH, Marshall, Texas, 11 June 1852. Pickens-Dugas Papers, No. 1492. SHC-UNC.

14. Lucy Holcombe Pickens, Collected Writings, Pickens Papers, SCL-USC.

15. EDH to JTH, and LPH to JTH, Marshall, Texas. 1851. D/L-G/H.

16. Greer, *Leaves*, 16. Portrait in possession of descendants.

17. Greer, *Leaves*, 18–19.

18. McPherson, *The Holcombes*, 736.

19. Dr. William Henry Holcombe Autobiography, Pickens-Dugas Papers, No. 1492, SHC-UNC. Also private collection, Dr. David Wyatt Aiken, New Orleans, Louisiana.

20. McPherson, *The Holcombes*, 774–775.

21. Fayette County Tennessee Deed Book D, p. 410 and Deed Book H, p. 192. Site confirmed by Mr. Jamie Evans of the Ames-Hobart Foundation, present owners of the property.

22. Greer, *Leaves*, 15. Court records show that Beverly Holcombe bought 735 acres from Samuel Dickens in 1834 and 167 acres from Ephraim Jackson in 1838 making a total of 902 acres.

23. Greer, *Leaves*, 15.

24. Catherine Clinton, *The Plantation Mistress: Woman's World in the Old South,* (New York: Pantheon Books, 1982), 49.

25. An agreement between Mrs. E. D. Holcombe and Eliza Herd, 24 April 1848. D/L-G/H.

26. Greer, *Leaves*, 22.

27. Ibid.

28. Greer, *Leaves*, 20.

29. Ibid.

30. Greer, *Leaves*, 16.

CHAPTER TWO

1. Catherine Clinton, *The Plantation Mistress, Woman's World in the Old South* (New York: Pantheon Books, 1982), 14.

2. Elizabeth Fox-Genovese, *Within the Plantation Household* (Chapel Hill: University of North Carolina Press, 1988), 38.

3. Ibid, 44.

4. Greer, *Leaves*, 21.

5. Ibid., 16.

6. Ibid., 18.

7. Ibid.

8. These books and many others with Eugenia's or Lucy's name, remain with descendants.

9. LPHP to AEHG, La Grange, Tennessee D/L-G/H.

10. Greer, *Leaves*, 18–19.

11. Ibid., 19.

12. Story in an unidentified news clipping found among Holcombe letters; fam-

ily oral history.

13. Harrison County, Texas, census for 1850 lists a female child under ten years of age in the Holcombe household as H. H.

14. Dr. William Henry Holcombe papers, Pickens-Dugas Papers, No. 1492, SHC-UNC.

15. Harrison County, Texas Deed Record Book J (1837), 497.

16. EDH to Beverly Holcombe, La Grange, Tennessee circa 1842. D/L-G/H.

17. Wat Harris letter to Beverly Holcombe, La Grange, Tennessee, 3 November 1842. D/L-G/H.

18. Maria Hawley to EDH, New Albany, Indiana, August 1842. D/L-G/H.

19. Ibid.

20. Greer, *Leaves*, 23–24.

21. Fayette County Deed Record Book 1847–1849 Vol. 2:418.

22. As told to author by present owners of Westover, Mr. and Mrs. Stanley Allen.

23. Receipt, D/L-G/H.

24. Nat Willis letter to AEH, La Grange, Tennessee, 7 April 1850. D/L-G/H.

25. Greer, *Leaves*, 17.

26. Lucy Holcombe Pickens, Collected Writings, Pickens Papers, SCL-USC.

27. Christie Ann Farnham, *The Education of the Southern Belle* (New York: New York University Press, 1994), 3.

28. Ibid, 39.

29. *Historical Sketch of the Moravian Seminary for Young Ladies at Bethlehem, Northampton County, Pennsylvania*. n.p., n.d., 25.

30. Greer, *Leaves*, 18.

31. Ibid., 17.

32. Rebecca Smith Lee, *Mary Austin Holley, A Biography* (Texas: University of Texas Press), 261, n42, 396.

33. Harrison County, Texas, Deed Record Book J, 30 June 1837.

34. Thomas N. Polk to AEH and LPH, Washington City, Texas, 13 December 1845. D/L-G/H.

35. The Bill to admit Texas to the Union was signed by President Polk, 29 December 1845.

CHAPTER THREE

1. Nat Willis letter to AEH and LPH, La Grange, Tennessee, 11 February 1847, D/L-G/H.

2. Mr. Wright's letter to LPH, La Grange, Tennessee, 18 March 1846, D/L-G/H.

3. Joseph Mortimer Levering, *A History of Bethlehem* (Times Publishing Company, 1903.) 631.

4. Ibid.

5. Mrs. Brock is frequently mentioned in family letters.

6. EDH letter to Herr Shultz, La Grange, Tennessee, 10 April 1846. Moravian College Archives.

7. AEH to family, Bethlehem, Pennsylvania, c.1846–48. D/L-G/H.

8. Fourteen of the American Colonies issued their own paper money and currency until 1862 when the Treasury Department of the United States issued the legal-tender notes, generally called "greenbacks." *Selections from the Numismatist,* Paper Money Used In The United States From 1690–1866," D. C. Wismer: Whitman Publishing Co., 1960) 178–179.

9. *Historical Sketch of the Moravian Seminary, Pennsylvania,* n.p., 1850. D/L-G/H.

10. EDH to AEH and LPH, La Grange, Tennessee, 9 May 1846. D/L-G/H.

11. Frederic Klees, *The Pennsylvania Dutch,* (New York: Macmillan Company, 1950). 101–102.

12. Mr. Mathews to AEH and LPH, La Grange, Tennessee, March 1846. D/L-G/H.

13. EDH to Rev. Shultz, La Grange, Tennessee, 10 April 1846. Moravian College Archives.

14. EDH to AEH, La Grange, Tennessee, 1846. D/L-G/H.

15. EDH to LPH, La Grange, Tennessee, April 1846. D/L-G/H.

16. EDH to LPH, La Grange, Tennessee, 26 October 1846. Courtesy of Marcia Thomas, Jefferson, Texas.

17. By "shoes" Anna Eliza probably means the felt slippers worn indoors.

18. AEH to Beverly Holcombe, Bethlehem, Pennsylvania, 25 June 1846. D/L-G/H

19. Henry Clay to EDH, Ashland, Kentucky, 17 August 1846. D/L-G/H.

20. EDH to LPH, La Grange, Tennessee, 9 May and 26 October 1846. D/L-G/H.

21. Greer, *Leaves.* 51. The term, "bluestocking," referred to someone, particularly a woman, in the nineteenth century who was an intellectual.

22. William C. Reichel, *Bethlehem Souvenir* (Lippincott & Company. 1858). 157, 243; EDH letter to Theodore, Marshall, Texas, 10 August 1852. D/L-G/H.

23. This scene and the following quote attributed to "Mabel" the character in Lucy's published novel, *Free Flag,* 80–81, 85. Lucy admitted that "Mabel" was in reality herself. Clara Victoria Dargan, Dargan-MacLean Papers, Duke University.

24. Lucy Holcombe Pickens Collected Writings, Pickens Papers, SCL-USC.

25. Ibid.

26. Dictionary of American History, Revised Edition, (New York: Charles Scribner's Sons, 1976), 323–324; Jaime Suchlicki, *Mexico, From Montezuma to NAFTA, Chiapas and Beyond* (Washington & London: Brassey's, 1996), 70–74; Linda S. Hudson, *Mistress of Manifest Destiny, A Biography of Jane McManus Storm Cazneau, 1807–1878* (Austin: Texas State Historical Association, 2001), 69–93.

27. Ron de Paolo, "First Vespers," *Moravian College Magazine,* 1996, p. 9. Also "Moravian Christmas" *Alumnae Bulletin,* December 1946.

28. EDH to AEH and LPH, La Grange, Tennessee 1846. D/L-G/H.

29. Lucy Holcombe Pickens Collected Writings, Pickens Papers, SCL-USC.

30. Ibid.

31. As told to author by Mrs. Margaret Hutchings of Houston, Texas, a descendant of St. George Lee.

32. Nat Willis to AEH, La Grange, Tennessee 1850. D/L-G/H.

CHAPTER FOUR

1. Newspaper write-up. No date or identification. Holcombe File, Harrison County Historical Museum, Marshall, Texas.

2. Alex Kirkpatrick letter to AEH, Memphis, Tennessee 4 March 1850. D/L-G/H.

3. Robert Dortch letter to LPH, La Grange, Tennessee circa 1850. D/L-G/H.

4. EDH to "My dear Children," La Grange, Tennessee 9 May 1846. D/L-G/H.

5. St. George Lee letter to LPH, Mobile, Alabama, 1850. D/L-G/H.

6. Ibid.

7. Description of "Mabel" (Lucy) in *Free Flag*.

8. The story of the Holcombes crossing Caddo Lake is a family legend as told to author by the late Miss May Margaret Touhey of Marshall, Texas and other descendants; St. George Lee letter to LPH, 6 April 1850, Mobile, Alabama. Pickens-Dugas Papers, No. 1492. SHC-UNC.

9. Many articles erroneously claim Texas as Lucy's birthplace.

10. These family portraits, in possession of descendants, have been restored.

11. These pieces of family furniture are now owned by friends in Jefferson, Texas.

12. From a sketch by Pleasant Vickers, 10 September 1854. Harrison County Historical Museum, Marshall, Texas.

13. United States Bureau of Statistics, 505; *Texas Almanac 1850*. 181.

14. Greer, *Leaves*, 25.

15. Harrison County, Texas Census, 1850.

16. The First Presbyterian Church of Marshall, Texas, observed the 140th anniversary of its founding, by the B. L. Holcombe family and the Rev. N. W. Staples, on 10 May 1990; *The Marshall Messenger*. Microfilm, Marshall Public Library, Marshall, Texas.

17. Greer, *Leaves*, 10–11.

18. Descendants believe that Mr. C. H. Alexander supervised construction.

19. Receipt. D/L-G/H.

20. Wyalusing is also spelled with c, but I have used Lucy's preference of spelling throughout.

21. Thomas Nelson Page, *Social Life in Old Virginia* (New York: Charles Scribner's Sons, 1897), 38–42.

22. Miss Anna Smith papers, circa 1940–50. D/L-G/H.

23. Robert Dortch to LPH, La Grange, Tennessee 1850. D/L-G/H.

24. Lucy Holcombe Pickens Collected Writings, Pickens Papers, SCL-USC.

25. F. M. Kyle letter, Greenwood Depot, Virginia, 17 September 1902, courtesy of Mrs. Margaret Hutchings; *Galveston News*, 28 April 1870.

26. *Harpers New Monthly Magazine* Vol. 19, August 1854, 415; F. M. Kyle letter, Greenwood depot, Virginia, 1902.

27. St. George S. Lee to LPH, Victoria, Texas, c. 1849–1850. D/L-G/H.

CHAPTER FIVE

1. St. George S. Lee to LPH, 9 December 1850. D/L-G/H.

2. Description of wedding by Miss Anna Smith as told to her by her mother, the daughter of Anna Eliza Holcombe Greer. D/L-G/H.

3. Newspaper on microfilm, Marshall Public Library, Marshall, Texas.

4. AEHG to LPH, Holly Spring, Mississippi, 18 March 1851. D/L-G/H.

5. Quoted by Lucy ("Mabel") in *Free Flag*, 70.

6. This incident is referred to in B. H. Robertson letter to LPH, 25 February 1853, undated newspaper article. D/L-G/H.

7. Entries from Eugenia Dorothea Holcombe's diary, October and November 1851. Holcombe Papers, Harrison County Historical Museum, Marshall, Texas.

8. Holcombe Papers, No. 11132, Vol. 1. SHC-UNC.

9. *Biographical & Historical Memoirs of Louisiana* (Chicago: Goodspeed Publishing Company, 1892), Vol. 2:480–482.

10. John Duffy, *Healers A History of American Medicine* (Chicago: Urbana University Illinois Press, 1979), 162.

11. Emanuel Swedenborg claimed to receive special scriptural revelations from God that dealt with the mystery of the spirit world and its inhabitants.

12.William Henry Holcombe, Diary & Notes, MSS Vol.2:1113–2, SHC-UNC.

13. Monmouth was restored and now operates as a bed and breakfast inn.

14. As described in *Free Flag*. Lucy states in the Preface: "It is the object of the succeeding pages to depict the occurrences of those hours of which there can be no record left. My characters are then not all fictitious; some of them have or have had, living originals in the actual world."

15. Lara Gara, *The Presidency of Franklin Pierce* (Kansas: University Press of Kansas, 1991), 149.

16. Alexander DeConde, *A History of American Foreign Policy* (New York: Charles Scribner's Sons, 1963), 220.

17. Anderson C. Quisenberry, *Lopez's Expeditions to Cuba, 1850–1851* (Louisville, Kentucky: John P. Morton & Company, 1906), 68.

18. Ibid.

19. Ishbel Ross, *First Lady of the South, The Life of Mrs. Jefferson Davis* (New York: Harper & Bro., 1958), 59.

20. Lynda Crist and Mary Dix, eds., *The Papers of Jefferson Davis* (Louisiana: Louisiana State University Press, 1983) Vol. 4:59n.

21. Quisenberry, *Lopez.* 68.

22. Lynda Crist and Mary Dix, eds., *The Papers of Jefferson Davis*, Vol. 4:260–261, 272n.

23. Holcombe, *Free Flag*, 86.

24. Quisenberry, *Lopez*, 68–74.

25. Ibid.

26. Description of General Narciso Lopez as written by Lucy in her historical novel, *Free Flag*. Lucy may have dramatized certain aspects of the meeting, typical of the Victorian style of writing.

CHAPTER SIX

1. The Sigur family had two plantations, Cypremort (Dead Cypress) near Franklin, Louisiana, and Old Hickory near Iberville, Louisiana. Information from Sigur descendant, Ms. Norma Mumme Wimbish; letter to *Times Picayune*, 22 August 1916.

2. Quisenberry, *Lopez*, 74.

3. President Millard Fillmore's proclamation of 25 April 1851, United States President Messages and Papers, No. 5:111.

4. Quisenberry, *Lopez*, 77.

5. *Harper's New Monthly Magazine* Vol. 18:692–693, October 1851.

6. Quisenberry, *Lopez*, 89–90. Author has been unable to identify Dr. Lucien Hensley.

7. Ibid., 92–93.

8. DeConde, *A History of American Foreign Policy* (New York: 1963) 221; Quisenberry, *Lopez*, 109.

9. Unsigned letter addressed to the "Colonel" and dated December 1851. Collection M13–Lopez Expedition, Howard Tilton Memorial Library, Tulane University; DeConde, *American Foreign Policy*, 221.

10. Quisenberry, *Lopez*, 116.

11. Lynda Crist and Mary Dix, eds., *The Papers of Jefferson Davis* (Louisiana: Louisiana State University Press, 1983), Vol. 4:261 and 273 n17.

12. "Gerard" to LPH. D/L-G/H.

13. Unidentified newspaper. D/L-G/H. The book is available on microfilm at Rice University, Houston, Texas, The Library of Congress, and several other university archives collections.

14. Charles Spalding Wyley letters to James Henry Rice, 1922 and 1923. Special collections, Duke University. No record has been found of *The White Diamond* by Lucy Holcombe or H. M. Hardimann, her pen name. Perhaps the manuscript was not accepted by a publisher and was destroyed.

15. Wyley letters, Ibid.

16. C. Van Woodward, ed. *Mary Chesnut's Civil War Diary* (New Haven and London: Yale University Press), 143 n9.

CHAPTER SEVEN

1. EDH to JTH, Marshall, Texas, 20 August 1852. D/L-G/H

2. Greer, *Leaves*. 13. Ned Hood's descendants have since dropped the name Hood.

3. LPH to JTH, Marshall, Texas, 26 July 1852. D/L-G/H.

4. C. W. Hunt to JTH, La Grange, Tennessee, 23 March 1853; EDH to JTH, Marshall, Texas 18 February 1853. D/L-G/H.

5. EDH to JTH, Marshall, Texas, 18 February 1853. D/L-G/H.

6. JTH to Philemon Holcombe, Edgefield, South Carolina, 18 November 1906. D/L-G/H.

7. Fleming Gardner to LPH, Marshall, Texas, February 1855. Pickens-Dugas

Papers, No. 1492, SHC-UNC.

8. Charles Spalding Wyely to James Henry Rice, Brunswick, Georgia, 20 January 1923. Special Collection, William Perkins Library, Duke University.

9. A reference to General William Walker, Americas most notorious filibusterer. Walker took over Nicaragua for almost a year. In 1860 he was killed in Honduras.

10. LPH to Fleming Gardner, Marshall, Texas, 1 August 1856. D/L-G/H.

11. *Harper's New Monthly Magazine*, letter to the "Easy Chair" Editor, Vol. 17:556, September 1858.

12. Ibid.

13. LPH to EDH, Point Coupee, Mississippi. 11 January 1857. Pickens-Dugas Papers, No. 1492, SHC-UNC.

14. LPH to Col.Wm. H. Bell, nd. Probably from Marshall, Texas. Pickens Papers, SCL-USC.

15. LPH to JTH, Marshall, Texas. July 1852. D/L-G/H. A check of newspapers on microfilm did not reveal any submissions signed Helene, H. M. Hardimann, or L.P.H.

16. *The New Harpers Monthly Magazine*, Vol. 17:556, September 1858.

17. Lucy Holcombe Pickens Collected Writings, Pickens Papers, SCL-USC.

18. Ibid.,10–11.

19. Jemine lived with the Holcombe family in Marshall. In 1865 she married Morys Haggar, an Englishman employed as overseer by Beverly Holcombe.

20. Harnett T. Kane, *Queen New Orleans* (New York: William Morrow & Company, 1949); Kane, *Plantation Parade* (New York: William Morrow & Company, 1945). Robert C. Reinders, *End of an Era, New Orleans, 1850–1860* (Pelican Publishing Company, 1964); Lyle Saxon, *Fabulous New Orleans* (New York: Century Company, 1928).

21. LPH to EDH, on board steamer at Point Coupee, Mississippi, January 1857. Pickens-Dugas Papers, No. 1492. SHC-UNC.

22. *The Southern Parlor Magazine and Ladies Book* was published twice, in 1857 and 1858.

23. LPH to EDH, January 1857. Point Coupee, Mississippi, Pickens-Dugas Papers, No. 1492, SHC-UNC.

24. Ibid.

25. Ibid.

26. Ibid.

27. Virginia Clay-Copton, *A Belle of the Fifties, Memoirs of Mrs. Clay of Alabama Covering Social and Political Life in Washington and the South, 1853–1866* (New York: Doubleday, Page & Company, 1905), 86.

28. Lucy Holcombe Pickens Collected Writings, 25–27, Pickens Papers, SCL-USC. "Clotilde's" identity is unknown but speculation places her as one of three women of this period who were known for their intellectual, spiritual, and physical qualities: Therese Chalfant Pugh; Madame Le Vert, nee Octavia Walton; and Adelaide Cutts Douglas.

29. Fredrika Bremer, *Homes of the New World: Impressions of America*, translated by Mary Hewitt (London: 1853), Vol. 3:259.

30. Lucy Holcombe Pickens Collected Writings, 27. Pickens Papers, SCL-USC.

31. AEHG letter to LPH, 7 February 1857. Pickens-Dugas Papers, No. 1492, SHC-UNC.

32. James D. Horan, *Confederate Agent, A Discovery in History* (New York: Crown Publishers, 1954) 16–18.

33. *Historical Times Illustrated Encyclopedia of the Civil War*, Patricia L. Faust, Editor (New York: Harper & Row, 1986), 58. Also Horace Greeley, *American Conflict, A History of the Great Rebellion* (Connecticut: O. D. Case & Company, 1864) Vol. 1:350–351.

34. *Historical Times Encyclopedia*, 420.

35. Philip Van Doren Stern, *Prologue to Sumter* "New Orleans Hears That Sumter Has Fallen" by Benson J. Lossing, (Indiana University Press, 1961), 534–535.

36. Greer, *Leaves*, 35–36.

CHAPTER EIGHT

1. William Alexander MacCorkle, *The White Sulphur Springs* (New York: The Neale Publishing Company, 1916).

2. *Charleston Courier,* 15 August 1857. D/L-G/H.

3. Lucinda, a slave given to Eugenia Holcombe by her father's will in 1847. Her position in the Holcombe household was that as house servant and personal maid to the Holcombe women.

4. From the unpublished manuscript of Raven Simkin Graydon as told to her by her mother, Lucy's friend, Sallie Simkin. Courtesy Mr. Augustus Simkin Graydon, Columbia, South Carolina.

5. Francis W. Pickens's obituary and tombstone give 1807 as date of birth yet he is listed as being born in 1806 by the *Dictionary of American Biography*. Other articles have 1805 as Francis W. Pickens's birthdate.

6. FWP to LPH, Sweet Springs, Virginia, 8 August 1857. Pickens Family Papers, Washington & Lee University, Lexington, Virginia.

7. This quotation attributed to Anna Eliza.

8. FWP to LPH, Sweet Springs, Virginia, 18 August 1857. Pickens Family Papers, Special Collections, Leyburn Library, Washington & Lee University, Lexington, Virginia.

9. *Mary Chestnut's Civil War*, 369.

10. FWP to LPH, Edgewood, South Carolina, 8 November 1857. Pickens Papers, Duke University. Lucy's mother had money from her father, John Hunt, but the Holcombe family seemed always to be in hard straits.

11. Pickens Papers, SCL-USC.

12. Memo dated September 10, 1857 and signed F W. Pickens. Pickens Papers, Duke University.

13. FWP to LPH, Edgewood, South Carolina, 2 November 1857. Pickens Papers, Duke University.

14. Ibid.

15. Ibid.

16. Ibid.

17. FWP to LPH, Edgewood, South Carolina, 6 November 1857. Pickens Papers, Duke University.

18. Francis W. Pickens tried three times to be chosen to the United States Senate.

19. President James Buchanan to FWP, Washington, D. C. 26 May 1857. Pickens Papers, SCL-USC.

20. FWP to LPH, Edgewood, South Carolina, 28 November 1857. Pickens Papers, SCL-USC.

21. FWP to Milledge Bonham, St. Petersburg, Russia, 14 October and 31 December 1859. Pickens Papers, SCL-USC.

22. Pickens family album in possession of direct descendants.

23. FWP to LPH, Edgewood, South Carolina, 28 November 1857. Pickens Papers, SCL-USC.

24. LPH to Fleming Gardner, Marshall, Texas. nd. Pickens-Dugas Papers, No. 1492, SHC-UNC.

25. Fleming Gardner to LPH, Dallas, Texas, 2 June 1857. Pickens Papers, SCL-USC.

26. FWP to LPH, Edgewood, South Carolina, 27 January 1858. Pickens Papers, Duke University.

27. Ibid.

28. FWP to LPH, 4 March 1857, Edgewood, South Carolina. Pickens Papers, SCL-USC.

29. The words "A poem from Lucy" are written above the poem, circa 1857. Pickens Papers, SCL-USC.

30. FWP to LPH, 27 January 1858, Edgewood, South Carolina. Pickens Papers, Duke University.

31. FWP to LPH, 28 November 1857, Edgewood, South Carolina. Pickens Papers, SCL-USC.

32. FWP to Beverly Holcombe, 27 February 1858, Edgewood, South Carolina. Pickens Papers, SCL-USC.

33. FWP to LPH, 27 January 1858, Edgewood, South Carolina. Pickens Papers, Duke University.

34. Pickens Papers, SCL-USC.

35. *Texas Republican*, Marshall, Texas, 1 May 1858. Microfilm, Marshall Public Library, Marshall, Texas.

CHAPTER NINE

1. Charley was an orphan whom the Holcombes cared for after his parents, their slaves, died of cholera in 1850.

2. Greer, *Leaves*, 28.

3. *The Texas Republican*, 1 May 1858, Microfilm, Marshall Public Library, Marshall, Texas.

4. Invitation to the reception. D/L-G/H. The Adkins House opened in 1857. It was built of brick fired on site by two slaves.

5. John Hunt's will recorded in Chancery Court Somerville, Tennessee in 1849. Deed Record Vol. 2:421.

6. Way, Fred, ed. *Steamboat Directory.* (Columbua, Ohio: Ohio University Press, 1950.) The *Lucy Holcombe,* a side-wheel packet commanded by Captain William D. Bateman, ran from New Orleans to Shreveport. One year later, in 1859, it burned and sank a mile above Helena, Arkansas.

7. Jeannie Pickens's name is sometimes spelled "Jennie" in various letters.

8. T. C. DeLeon, *Belles, Beaux and Brains of the '60s* (New York: Dillingham Company), 33; Margaret Leech, *Reveille in Washington 1860–1865* (New York: Harper & Brothers, 1941) 20.

9. Virginia Clay-Clopton, *A Belle of the Fifties* (New York: Doubleday, Page & Company, 1905), 93–94.

10. Lucy's reluctance to leave is a family legend and noted as fact in a newspaper article of unknown source. D/L-G/H.

11. Frank C. Bowen, *A Century of Atlantic Travel, 1830–1930* (New York: Little, Brown & Company, 1930), 95.

12. John Malcolm Brinnin, *The Sway of the Grand Salon,* (New York: Delacorte Press, 1971), 933.

CHAPTER TEN

1. FWP to LPH, Edgewood, South Carolina, 27 January 1858. Pickens Papers, Duke University.

2. William McKendres Gwin, originally from Louisiana, served as California's United States Senator during the Buchanan administration.

3. This and the following impressions are found in Lucy's letters to her family. Pickens Papers. SCL-USC and Pickens-Dugas Papers, No. 1492 at SHC-UNC, and D/L-G/H.

4. Robert Blair Campbell, a South Carolinian, served as Consul at London, England 1854–61. He died in London and is buried in a crypt at Kensington Church. *Who Was Who in America,* Historical Vol. 1607–1896, Chicago: Marquis' Who's Who, Inc., 1963, 94.

5. The National Gallery opened in 1838 with the noble intention, as stated in its catalogue, of presenting an exhibition of fine art to the public that might: "improve social behavior, cement bonds between rich and poor and provide a cure for uneasy passions."

6. National Gallery Catalogue, (London: 1970).

7. LPHP to EDH, London, England, June 1858. D/L-G/H.

8. Ibid.

9. Ibid.

10. Ibid.

11. Greer, *Leaves,* 66.

12. FWP to LPH, Edgewood, 8 October 1857, Pickens Papers, Duke University.

13. Greer, *Leaves,* 67.

14. This area described by Lucy is known as the "Bois de Boulogne."

15. Louis Napoleon, nephew of Napoleon Bonaparte, was elected President of the Second Republic of France. In 1851 he seized all power and declared himself Emperor. As Napoleon III he held power over an assembly that thrived on jealousy and intrigue.

16. LPHP to her family, St. Petersburg, Russia. D/L-G/H.

17. FWP to LPHP, St. Petersburg, Russia, August 30, 1860. Pickens Papers, Duke University.

18. LPHP to EDH, Berlin, Prussia, 2 July 1858. D/L-G/H.

19. Bev and Daughtie are the children of Lucy's sister, AEHG.

20. Mr. W. C. Dunlap is a family friend living in Marshall, Texas.

21. LPHP to EDH, Berlin, Prussia, 2 July 1858. D/L-G/H.

CHAPTER ELEVEN

1. LPHP to EDH, Berlin, Prussia, 2 July 1858. D/L-G/H.

2. Thomas Hart Seymour, 1807–1868, served as Governor of Connecticut prior to his appointment as Minister to the Russian Court in 1854. *Dictionary of American Foreign Affairs* (Flanders & Flanders), 775. John E. Bacon, associate editor of the *Edgefield Advertiser* was a widower when he entered the diplomatic service. Orville Vernon Burton, *In My Father's House Are Many Mansions* (Chapel Hill & London: University of North Carolina Press, 1985), 67, 141.

3. LPHP letter, St. Petersburg, Russia, 7 July 1858. D/L-G/H.

4. Ibid.

5. LPHP to her family, St. Petersburg, Russia, 1858. Pickens Papers, SCL-USC.

6. Prince Alexander Gorchakof, 1798–1883, a capable and respected Foreign Minister during the reign of both Nicholas I and Alexander II.

7. Stephen Graham, *The Life of Tsar of Russia* (London: Ivor Nicholson and Watson Ltd., 1935), 139–140.

8. Greer, *Leaves*, 68.

9. James Buchanan served as Minister to Russia during President Andrew Jackson's administration, 1829–1837.

10. LPHP to AEHG, St. Petersburg, Russia, 13 April 1860. D/L-G/H .

11. FWP to Milledge L. Bonham, October 1859. "Ante-Bellum Southerners in Russia", *Journal of Southern History*, Vol. 3, May 1937, 195.

12. FWP to Bonham, St. Petersburg, Russia, 14 October 1859. Pickens Papers, SCL-USC.

13. LPHP to AEHG, 18 January 1859. Pickens Papers, SCL-USC.

14. LPHP to AEHG, St. Petersburg, Russia, 20 December 1858.

CHAPTER TWELVE

1. LPHP to AEHG, St. Petersburg, Russia, 13 April 1860. Pickens Papers, SCL-USC.

2. Greer, *Leaves*, 69–70.

3. Ibid.

4. FWP letter to Milledge L. Bonham, St. Petersburg, Russia, circa 1859–60.

Pickens Papers, SCL-USC.

5. Graham, *Life of Tsar,* 50.

6. Graham, 40–42, 137–143.

7. Edward Crankshaw, *The Shadow of the Winter Palace* (New York: Viking, 1976), 198.

8. LPHP to her family, St. Petersburg, Russia, summer 1858. Pickens Papers, SCL-USC; Greer, *Leaves,* 70.

9. Ibid.

10. Ibid.

11. A replica of the Yellow Banqueting Hall was seen in the Exhibition, "The Palaces of St. Petersburg," at Jackson, Mississippi, 1996.

12. Greer, *Leaves,* 71; Letters to family, D/L-G/H.

13. John E. Bacon letter, St. Petersburg, Russia, 24 February 1859. Pickens Papers, SCL-USC.

14. Greer, *Leaves,* 71. (Johann Strauss, Jr., known as the "King of the Waltz," conducted the summer concerts in St.Petersburg, Russia, in the late 1850s.)

15. Tulle, a material somewhat like organdy and stiffened. Corsage refers to the bodice of a dress. A Grecian is a puff of tulle used in decoration.

16. Greer, *Leaves,* 71.

17. LPHP from St. Petersburg, Russia, to family. D/L-G/H

18. Greer, *Leaves,* 71.

19. Ibid.

20. Before her marriage to Tsar Nicholas I, the Empress was Princess Charlotte, daughter of Frederick William of Prussia. She assumed a Russian name at marriage.

21. FWP to EDH, St. Petersburg, Russia, 1858. D/L-G/H.

22. FWP to EDH, St. Petersburg, Russia, nd. D/L-G/H.

23. LPHP to AEHG, St. Petersburg, Russia, 13 April 1860. D/L-G/H.

24. Alexander II married Princess Wilhelmina Marie of Hess-Darmstadt in 1841. At marriage her name was changed to Marie Alexandrovna.

25. *The Private Mary Chesnut,* eds. C. Vann Woodward and Elisabeth Muhlenfeld, (New York: Oxford, 1984), 54.

26. Graham, *Life of Tsar,* 64–68.

27. LPHP to AEHG, St. Petersburg, Russia. 20 December 1859. D/L-G/H.

28. LPHP to AEHG, St. Petersburg, Russia. 9 May 1860. D/L-G/H.

29. Greer, *Leaves,* 70.

30. John E. Bacon to Milledge L. Bonham, St. Petersburg, Russia, February 1859. Pickens Papers, SCL-USC.

31. Pickens Papers, SCL-USC. This poem may be found in the Appendix.

CHAPTER THIRTEEN

1. LPHP to AEHG, St. Petersburg, Russia. 9 January 1959. D/L-G/H; Greer, *Leaves,* 75.

2. FWP to Milledge Bonham, St. Petersburg, Russia, 1859. Pickens Papers, SCL-USC.

3. FWP to EDH, St. Petersburg, Russia, 1859. Pickens Papers, SCL-USC.

4. LPHP to AEHG, St. Petersburg, Russia, 9 January 1859. Pickens Papers, SCL-USC.

5. John E. Bacon to Milledge Bonham, 24 February 1859. "Ante-Bellum Southerners in Russia," Milledge L. Bonham, Editor, *Journal of Southern History*, 1937. 3:191–193.

6. FWP to Bonham, St. Petersburg, Russia, 1859. Pickens Papers, SCL-USC.

7. John E. Bacon to Milledge L. Bonham, St. Petersburg, Russia, 24 February 1859. Pickens Papers, SCL-USC.

8. FWP to EDH, St. Petersburg, Russia, winter 1859. D/L-G/H; Greer, *Leaves*, 78

9. Greer, *Leaves*, 52.

10. Ibid.

11. Pickens-Dugas Papers, SHC-UNC.

12. AEHG to LPHP, Marshall, Texas, 29 April 1859. Pickens Papers, SCL-USC.

13. Statement from Douschka's granddaughter, Lucy Francis Pickens Dugas. D/L-G/H.

14. LPHP to AEHG, St. Petersburg, Russia, 6 July 1859. Pickens Papers, SCL-USC.

15. Ibid.

16. Ibid. Miss Lander was born 1835 in Salem, Massachusetts. Her works include busts of prominent Europeans and Americans. It is supposed that Miss Lander sculpted the busts of Lucy and Francis.

17. LPHP to AEHG, St. Petersburg, Russia, 1859. Pickens Papers, SCL-USC.

18. Ibid.

19. Ibid.

20. Rebecca Pickens married John E. Bacon during the first year of her father's residency in Russia. The marriage was said to have caused Francis embarrassment.

21. Jeannie (Jennie) Pickens to AEHG, Frankfort, Germany, 4 March 1860. D/L-G/H.

22. LPHP to AEHG, St. Petersburg, Russia, 1859. Greer, *Leaves*. 82. Pickens Papers, SCL-USC.

23. LPHP to AEHG, Schawlback, Prussia, 19 August 1860. D/L-G/H.

24. A reference to Pickens's earlier marriages.

25. LPHP to AEHG, St. Petersburg, Russia, n.d., Greer, *Leaves*, 82; Pickens Papers, SCL-USC.

CHAPTER FOURTEEN

1. LPHP to AEHG, St. Petersburg, Russia, nd. Pickens Papers, SCL-USC.

2. Greer, *Leaves*, 85.

3. Ibid., 80–81.

4. LPHP to AEHG, St. Petersburg, Russia, 20 December 1859.

5. Ibid.

6. Count Leo Tolstoy, *Anna Karenina* (New York: Random House, 1939). 160–161.

7. LPHP to AEHG, St. Petersburg, Russia, 13 April and 9 May 1860. Pickens Papers, SCL-USC.

8. LPHP to AEH, St. Petersburg, Russia, 13 April 1860. Pickens Papers, SCL-USC.

9. Ibid.

10. Greer, *Leaves*, 91. The actual quote reads, "Bless um pretty sould! Wont umyub um Mumes's flowers."

11. LPHP to AEHG, St. Petersburg, Russia, 9 May 1860. D/L-G/H.

12. Ibid.

13. Ibid.

14. AEHG to LPHP, Marshall, Texas, 14 May 1859. Pickens Papers, SCL-USC.

15. FWP to EDH, St. Petersburg, Russia, nd. Probably early in 1860. D/L-G/H. Fig brushes may have been an old home remedy.

16. Charles Edward Cauthen, "South Carolina Goes to War 1860–1865," *The James Sprunt Studies in History and Political Science* (Chapel Hill: University of North Carolina Press, 1950). 11.

17. FWP to B. F. Perry, St. Petersburg, Russia, 24 April 1859. Perry Papers, University of Alabama.

18. LPHP to EDH, St. Petersburg, Russia, 2 December 1859. Pickens Papers, SCL-USC.

19. Ibid.

CHAPTER FIFTEEN

1. LPHP to EDH, St. Petersburg, Russia, 1860. Pickens Papers, SCL-USC.

2. LPHP to AEHG, Schawlbach, Prussia, 19 August 1860. Greer, *Leaves*, 98.

3. Ibid.

4. LPHP to EDH, Schawlbach, Prussia, 31 August 1860. Pickens Papers, SCL-USC.

5. LPHP to EDH, Schawlbach, Prussia, 16 August 1860. Pickens Papers, SCL-USC.

6. LPHP to AEHG, Schawlbach, Prussia, 19 August 1860. Pickens Papers, SCL-USC.

7. LPHP to AEHG, St. Petersburg, Russia, 9 May 1860; Greer, *Leaves*, 94.

8. LPHP to AEHG, Schawlbach, Prussia, 19 August 1860. Pickens Papers, SCL-USC.

9. LPHP to EDH, Schawlbach, Prussia, 31 August 1860. Pickens Papers, SCL-USC.

10. LPHP letter to AEHG, Schawlbach, Prussia, 19 August 1860. Pickens Papers, SCL-USC.

11. LPHP to EDH, Schawlbach, Prussia. 16 August 1860. Pickens Papers. SCL-USC.

12. LPHP to AEHG, St. Petersburg, Russia, 13 April 1860; Greer, *Leaves,* 92; and LPHP to Beverly Holcombe, St. Petersburg, Russia, 29 June 1860. Pickens Papers. Duke University.

13. John Appleton of Massachusetts, a staunch Unionist, resigned his position as Minister to Russia at the outbreak of the American Civil War. *Dictionary of American Biography*, Vol. 1:329; The Historical Society of Pennsylvania, Collection James Buchanan Letters, Francis W. Pickens to President James Buchanan, St. Petersburg, Russia, 4 September 1860.

14. Frank C. Bowen, *Century of Atlantic Travel* (Boston: Little Brown & Company, 1930), 92–94.

15. Steven A. Channing, *Crisis of Fear: Secession in South Carolina* (New York: W. W. Norton, 1970), 269–71; John B. Edmunds, *Francis W. Pickens and the Politics of Destruction* (Chapel Hill & London: University North Carolina Press, 1986), 144.

16. Channing, *Crisis of Fear.*

17. Edmunds, *Francis W. Pickens.*

18. LPHP to AEHG, Schawlbach, Prussia, 19 August 1860. Pickens Papers, SCL-USC.

19. *New York Times,* 6 November 1860.

20. Margaret Leech, *Reveille in Washington, 1860–1865* (New York: Time Books Inc., 1941). 6.

21. FWP to President Buchanan, St. Petersburg, Russia, 4 September 1860. The Historical Society of Pennsylvania, Collection James Buchanan Letters.

22. W. A. Swanberg, *First Blood-The Story of Fort Sumter* (New York: Charles Scribner's Sons). 51.

23. *Mary Chesnut's Civil War,* 136.

24. William Seale, *The President's House* (New York: White House Historical Association, 1986), Vol. 1:349.

25. Seales, *The President's,* Vol. 1:349–350.

26. Chesnut, *Civil War,* 40.

27. Seale, *The President's,* 351.

28. Edmunds, *Francis W. Pickens,* 150.

29. Edmunds, 151.

30. *Edgefield Advertiser,* 28 November 1860.

31. *Charleston Courier,* 3 December 1860.

32. *Edgefield Advertiser,* 28 November 1860.

33. Ibid., 19 December 1860.

34. Edmunds, *Francis W. Pickens,* 153.

CHAPTER SIXTEEN

1. C. Vann Woodward, ed., *Mary Chesnut's Civil War* (New Haven & London: Yale University Press, 1981).

2. Landau: a four wheeled carriage with the top in two sections, each of which could be opened independently.

3. Clara Victoria Dargan's diary, 3 February 1863. Dargan-MacLean Papers No. M2321, Duke University.

4. FWP to Col. J. Davis, Charleston, South Carolina, 23 January 1861. Pickens Papers, SCL-USC.

5. Edmunds, *Pickens,* 154.

6. LPHP to General Harlee [Hardee?], Spring 1861, Pickens Papers, Duke University; A. P. Aldrich to LPHP, Richmond, Virginia, April 1861. Pickens Papers, SCL-USC.

7. President James Buchanan to Governor Francis W. Pickens, Washington, 20 December 1860. The Historical Society of Pennsylvania, Collection James Buchanan Letters.

8. Ibid.

9. W. A. Swanberg, *First Blood,* 85.

10. "Coast Guard Survey of 1860."

11. Chesnut, *Civil War,* 5.

12. *Harper's Weekly,* 12 January 1861.

13. Cabinet members: A. G. McGrath, Secretary of State; D. F. Jamison, Secretary of War; C. G. Memminger, Secretary of Treasure; W. H. Harlee, Head of Postal Department and Light Houses; and A. C. Garlington, Secretary of Interior.

14. Swanberg, *First Blood,* 107.

15. LPHP to Beverly Holcombe, Charleston, South Carolina. 1 January 1861. Pickens-Dugas Papers, No. 1492, SHC-UNC (It was not the *Harriet Lane* but the *Star of the West* that was sent with supplies).

16. *Harper's Weekly,* 19 January 1861.

17. FWP to Baron Stoekle, Charleston, South Carolina. 12 January 1861, Pickens Papers, Duke University.

18. Ibid.

19. *Leslie's Illustrated Newspaper,* 22 February 1861. Hill Memorial Library, Archival Library, Louisiana State University.

20. Randy J. Sparks, "Gentleman's Sport: Horse Racing in Antebellum Charleston," *South Carolina Historical Magazine,* 1992, Vol. 93, No. 1:21.

21. *Charleston Mercury,* 8 February 1861.

22. FWP to LPHP, Charleston, South Carolina, 23 February 1861. Pickens Papers, SCL-USC.

CHAPTER SEVENTEEN

1. *The Texas Republican,* 26 February 1861. Microfilm, Marshall Public Library, Marshall, Texas.

2. EDH journal, Greer, *Leaves,* 29.

3. Jefferson Davis note to Governor Pickens, Montgomery, Alabama, 18 March 1861. Pickens Papers, SCL-USC.

4. Excerpted from Ada Holcombe Aiken's unpublished memoir of Holcombe/Aiken families. Courtesy Dr. David Wyatt Aiken.

5. LPHP to EDH, 25 March 1861, Charleston, South Carolina. Pickens Papers, SCL-USC. "Bitters" is a concoction of bitter herbs and roots steeped in alcohol and was used in the nineteenth century for relief of indigestion and general malaise.

6. FWP to Jefferson Davis, Charleston, South Carolina. 23 January 1861. Pickens Papers, SCL-USC.

7. Clara Victoria Dargan, Dargan-MacLean Papers, No. M2321, Duke University.

8. Poem dated 8 April 1861 and letter Emily Haynes to LPHP, Charleston, South Carolina, 31 January 1862. Pickens-Dugas Papers, No. 1492, SHC-UNC.

9. Chesnut, *Civil War*, 639, 329.

10. FWP to General Evans, Charleston, South Carolina. 2 March 1861. Pickens Papers, SCL-USC.

11. *Official Records of the Union and Confederate Armies in the War of Rebellion.* Series 1, Vol. 1:25.

12. Ibid., 25, 60. It has often been wrongly reported that Governor Pickens gave the order to fire.

13. Ibid., 25, 34; Mrs. Julien Ravenel, *Charleston Its Place and Its People* (London: Macmillan Company, 1906), 492ff; *The Charleston Mercury*, 12 April 1861.

14. The gun fired on the *Star of the West* is sometimes thought to be the first shot fired in the War Between the States but the bombardment of Fort Sumter is usually credited as being the first shot.

15. Clara Victoria Dargan, Dargan-MacLean Papers, No. M2321, Duke University.

16. Patricia L. Faust, ed., *Historical Times Illustrated Encyclopedia of the Civil War* (New York: Harper & Row, 1986), 344.

17. Ravenel, *Charleston, Its Place*, 492.

18. *Official Records of the Union and Confederate Armies in the War of Rebellion.* Series I, Vol. 1:60.

CHAPTER EIGHTEEN

1. Aldrich meant General Joseph E. Johnston.

2. Lt. Col. A. P. Aldrich to LPHP, Richmond, Virginia, 29 April 1861. Pickens Papers, SCL-USC.

3. "Deed of gift absolutely to my beloved wife—F. W. Pickens, State of South Carolina Headquarters, May 4, 1861." Pickens Papers, Duke University.

4. Pickens-Dugas Papers, SHC-UNC.

5. FWP to LPHP, Charleston, South Carolina, 17 May 1861. Pickens-Dugas Papers, SHC-UNC.

6. Ibid.

7. "Legion" is an out-dated term possibly synonymous with the modern term, "Regiment."

8. *Charleston News and Courier*, 9 August 1899.

9. H. D. Allen, *American Numismatic Association*, "The Paper Money of the Confederate States, an interview with Major Richard S. Anderson," 10 January 1918.

10. From the notes of the late Miss Anna H. Smith of Marshall, Texas. D/L-G/H.

11. Speech recorded by John A. Chapman, A.M., in the "History of Edgefield County, from the Earliest Settlement to 1897." (Spartansburg, North Carolina: The Reprint Company. 1980).

12. Dock Owens of Company F, Holcombe Legion. Quoted by, Claud E. Fuller, *Confederate Currency and Stamps-1861–1865* (Tennessee: Parthenon Press, 1949), 49.

13. Ibid.

14. Chesnut, *Civil War,* 273n.

15. Dumas Malone, ed, *Dictionary of American Biography* (New York: Charles Scribner's Sons, 1934) Vol. 2.

16. Jane Petigru to LPHP, Charleston, South Carolina, 2 April 1861. Pickens-Dugas Papers, SHC-UNC.

17. Dumas, *Dictionary of American Biography.*

18. Chesnut, *Civil War,* 380.

19. FWP to LPHP, Edgewood, South Carolina. 26 July 1861. Pickens Papers, SCL-USC.

20. Ibid.

21. LPHP to EDH, Schawlbach, Prussia, 16 August 1860. D/L-G/H.

22. David Kennedy, *Birth Control in America, The Career of Margaret Sanger,* New Haven: Yale University Press, 1970, 45.

23. Daniel E. Sutherland, *The Expansion of Everyday Life 1860–1876* (New York: Harper & Row, 1989), 123–124.

24. Lucy Holcombe Pickens, Collected Writings. Pickens Papers, SCL-USC.

CHAPTER NINETEEN

1. Drew Gilpin Faust, *Mothers of Invention* (Chapel Hill & London: University of North Carolina Press, 1996), 180.

2. FWP letter to President Davis and Members of the Convention, State of South Carolina Headquarters, 8 January 1862, Pickens Papers, SCL-USC.

3. Chesnut, *Civil War,* 287.

4. Ibid., 275.

5. The Treasury Note Bureau of the Confederacy moved to the new College Hall of South Carolina College, September 1862. Pickens Papers, SCL-USC.

6. William West Bradbeer, *Confederate and Southern State Currency* (New York: R.Green, reprint, 1945), 246.

7. Bradbeer, *Confederate and Southern State Currency.* 215; *South Carolina News and Courier,* Charleston, 8 August 1899.

8. Authors and historians referred to in the period of 1915–1917: Dr. William Lee, Raphael Thian, Haseltine, and Dr. George W. Massamore.

9. Bradbeer, *Confederate and Southern State Currency,* 235; Arlie R. Slabaugh, *Confederate States Paper Money* (Wisconsin: Whitman Publishing Company, 1961), 38.

10. Mr. C. D. Allen in "The Paper Money of the Confederate States," from *Numismatic Magazine,* 1918; Bradbeer, *Confederate,* 236.

11. As told to the author by Lynda Crist, editor of *The Jefferson Davis Papers.*

12. Fred Reinfeld, *The Story of Civil War Money* (New York: Sterling Publishing Company, 1959), 62, 66; Grover C. Criswell and Clarence L. Criswell, *Criswell's Currency Series* (Florida: Criswell, 1957), 40–42.

13. Slabaugh, *Confederate States*, 38.

14. Unsigned letter but from content and salutation, the writer is thought to be Fleming Gardner. D/L-G/H.

15. Lieutenant General Wade Hampton, wounded at the Battle of Seven Pines, recovered to fight at Antietam and Gettysburg.

16. Chesnut, *Civil War*, 395.

17. Ibid., 342.

18. Ibid., 329.

19. Microfilm, Marshall Public Library, Marshall, Texas.

20. Chesnut, *Civil War*, 358.

21. "Bucket" letter to LPHP, Augusta, Georgia. nd. Pickens-Dugas Papers, No. 1492, SHC-UNC.

22. Ben McCulloch, born in Tennessee in 1811, Texas Ranger, United States Marshal, was a colorful and popular figure in early Texas history and second-ranking brigadier general in the Confederacy.

23. AEHG to her parents, Van Buren, Arkansas, 2 March 1862. Pickens-Holcombe Papers, SHC-UNC.

24. James McQueen McIntosh, born Fort Brooke, Florida 1828. His brother, John Baillie McIntosh was a brigadier general in the Federal forces.

25. William I. Shea & Earl T. Hess, *Pea Ridge, Civil War Campaign in the West* (Chapel Hill: University of North Carolina Press, 1992), 313.

26. EDH to AEHG, Marshall, Texas. 12 August 1862. Pickens-Dugas Papers, No. 1492, SHC-UNC.

27. *Historical Times Illustrated*, Patricia L. Faust, ed., 324–235.

28. EDH to LPHP, Marshall, Texas, 4 September 1862. Pickens Papers, SCL-USC.

29. General N. C. Yulee to LPHP, Homosassa, Florida. 12 March 1862. Pickens Family Papers, Special Collections, Leyburn Library, Washington & Lee University; LPHP to General Hardee [Harlee?] Columbia, South Carolina circa 1861, Pickens Papers, Duke University; A. P. Aldrich to LPHP, 29 April 1861, Richmond, Virginia, Pickens Papers. SCL-USC.

30. James McPherson, *Battle Cry of Freedom* (New York: Ballantine Books, 1981), 578, 628.

31. Robert M. McBride, ed, *Tennessee Historical Quarterly*, 1971, Vol. 30, No. 2:146–150; "La Grange-La Belle Village," John H. DeBerry.

32. Chesnut, *Civil War*, 338.

CHAPTER TWENTY

1. Clara Victoria Dargan diary, Dargan-MacLean Papers, No. M2321, Duke University.

2. Ibid.

3. Amandine Lucie Dupin wrote under the name, "George Sand," 1804–1876.

4. The Arthur Simkins family were related through marriage to Francis Pickens.

5. Clara Victoria Dargan diary, Dargan-MacLean Papers, No. M2321, Duke Uni-

versity.

6. Ibid., February 1863.

7. Ibid., 7 March 1863.

8. Ibid.

9. Ibid.

10. Ibid., 6 April 1863.

11. Ibid.

12. Ibid., 9 July 1863.

13. Ibid.

14. FWP to LPHP, Richmond, Virginia, June 1863. Pickens Papers, SCL-USC.

15. Mid-June 1863 Confederate troops were moving through the Shenandoah Valley north to Pennsylvania.

16. FWP to LPHP, Richmond, Virginia, June 1863. Pickens Papers. SCL-USC.

17. Clara Victoria Dargan diary, Dargan-MacLean Papers, Duke University.

18. Beverly Holcombe Robertson to LPHP, nd. or place. Pickens-Dugas Papers, No. 1492. SHC-UNC.

19. Edmunds, *Pickens,* 174.

CHAPTER TWENTY-ONE

1. From the poem *Evolution* by John Bannister Tabb.

2. Whitelaw Reid, *After the War, A Southern Tour* (New York: 1866); Francis B. Simkins & Robert H. Woody, *South Carolina During Reconstruction* (Chapel Hill: University of North Carolina Press, 1932), 21.

3. *Official Records of the Union and Confederate Armies in the War of the Rebellion,* Series I, Part II, Vol. 47:1198.

4. Ibid., 1199.

5. Ibid., 462.

6. Simkins & Woody, *South Carolina,* 16.

7. Robert O'Brien with Harold H. Martin, Editor, *The Encyclopedia of the South* (New York and Oxford, England: Facts on File Publications, 1985), 343–344.

8. E. Merton Coulter, *The South During Reconstruction 1865–1877* (Louisiana State University Press, 1947), 31–34.

9. Maurice Isserman, *Journey to Freedom, The African-American Great Migration* (New York: Facts on File, Inc. 1997), 10.

10. Leon F. Litwack, *Been in the Storm So Long* (New York: Vintage Books, 1980), 417.

11. Walter Prescott Webb, ed, *The Handbook of Texas,* Vol. II, (Austin: Texas State Historical Association, 1952), 939.

12. FWP to LPHP, Edgewood, South Carolina, 4 September 1865. Pickens Papers, Duke University.

13. FWP to Douschka, Edgewood, South Carolina, 1865. Pickens-Dugas Papers, No. 1492, SHC-UNC.

14. Signed application dated 18 August 1865. Pickens Papers, Washington & Lee University.

15. FWP to LPHP, Edgewood, South Carolina, 4 September 1865. Pickens-Dugas Papers, Duke University.

16. Benjamin F. Perry, *Reminiscences of Public Men* (Philadelphia: John D. Avil & Company, 1883).

17. FWP to LPHP, Edgewood, South Carolina, 1 September 1865. Pickens Papers, Washington & Lee University.

18. Edward P. Alexander, *Museum Masters, Their Museums and Their Influence* (Tennessee: American Association for State and Local History, 1983).

19. "Mabel," the character in Lucy's book, *Free Flag*, is patterned after herself.

20. LPHP to Clara Victoria Dargan, Edgewood, South Carolina, 2 June 1866, Pickens-Dugas Papers, No. 1492, SHC-UNC.

21. *The Encyclopedia of the South*, edited by Robert O'Brien with Harold H. Martin, (New York & Oxford England: Facts on File Publications, 1985), 343–344.

22. *Edgefield Advertiser*, 17 April 1867.

23. "The Whaley Family and its Charleston Connection," James Garner Patey, (The Reprint Company, South Carolina, 1992); "Pickens Families of the South," E. M. Sharp, Tennessee, 1963. South Carolina Historical Society.

24. LPHP to Clara Victoria Dargan, Edgewood, South Carolina, 5 June 1867. Pickens Papers, Duke University.

25. FWP to Stearnen in Augusta, Georgia, Edgewood, South Carolina, 1 July 1868. Pickens papers, SCL-USC.

26. *Edgefield Advertiser*, November 1868.

27. This legend is embellished in Elizabeth Boatwright Coker's novel, *India Allan* (New York: E. P. Dutton & Company, 1953), 189.

28. Franklin, *Reconstruction*, 91.

29. *The Edgefield Advertiser*, 2 December 1868.

CHAPTER TWENTY-TWO

1. LPHP to EDH, Edgewood, South Carolina. circa 1869. Pickens-Dugas Papers, No. 1492. SHC-UNC.

2. Clara Victoria Dargan, Dargan-MacLean Papers, No. M2321, Duke University.

3. LPHP to Hon. Jas. B. Campbell, Edgewood, nd. Pickens-Dugas Papers, No. 1492, SHC-UNC.

4. LPHP to EDH, Edgewood, South Carolina. circa 1869. Pickens-Dugas Papers, No. 1492. SHC-UNC.

5. Ellen Middleton to LPHP, Asheville, North Carolina. 2 February 1869. Pickens Family Papers, Washington & Lee University.

6. Douschka's letter to her aunt, Anna Eliza Holcombe Greer, Edgewood, South Carolina, 10 February 1881, D/L-G/H.

7. JTH to AEIIG, Edgewood, South Carolina, 8 November 1881. D/L-G/H

8. LPHP to Clara Victoria Dargan, Heybridge Lodge, North Carolina, 28 October 1870. Pickens Papers, Duke University.

9. Ibid.

10. LPHP to Clara Victoria Dargan, Edgewood, South Carolina, 12 December 1870. Pickens Papers, Duke University.

11. Harrison County, Texas, Courthouse Records.

12. LPHP to Hon. Jas. B. Campbell, Edgewood, South Carolina, circa 1873. Pickens-Dugas Papers, No. 1492. SHC-UNC.

13. AEHG to Eugenia Markoleta Greer, Marshall, Texas, 1 March 1874. D/L-G/H.

14. Harrison County, Texas, Courthouse Records, Book D:442; Book T:513; Book V:85. Deed Records, Book W:177, 291; Book Z:345; Book 113:362.

15. *The New Handbook of Texas.* 1990 Edition, Vol. 2:939.

16. AEHG to Eugenia Markoleta Greer, Marshall, Texas, January 1875. D/L-G/H.

17. FWP will, State Archives, Columbia South Carolina.

18. Note from Paul Hamilton Hayne in F. W. Pickens Papers, SCL-USC.

19. Lucy Holcombe Pickens, Collected Writings, F. W. Pickens Papers, SCL-USC.

20. LPHP to Miss Lucy Francis Pickens Dugas, Edgewood, South Carolina, circa 1898, SCL-USC.

21. LPHP to Mrs. Hudson, Edgewood, South Carolina, 9 November 1891, Mount Vernon Ladies Association. The Sweet Olive tree has a very pleasing scent. Ambrosia is a flower of the genus Aster.

22. Lucinda to LPHP, St. Marys Hall, 14 April 1875. Pickens-Dugas Papers, SHC-UNC.

CHAPTER TWENTY-THREE

1. *Reconstruction, An Anthology of Revisionist Writing,* Brenda Stallcup, Editor, (California: Green Haven Press, Inc. 1995), 416.

2. Leon F. Litwack, *Been in the Storm So Long* (New York: Vintage Books, 1979), 304.

3. John Hope Franklin, *Reconstruction: After the Civil War* (Chicago: University of Chicago Press, 1961), 167–168.

4. William Gillette, *Retreat from Reconstruction* (Baton Rouge: Louisiana State University Press, 1979), 316–317.

5. "First Lady of the South Carolina Confederacy," by Emily Bull, published in *The Proceedings of the South Carolina Historical Association,* 1982; Lucy Holcombe Pickens, unpublished manuscript by Raven Simkins Graydon, 1969; Elizabeth Coker, *India Allan* (New York: E. P. Dutton & Company. 1953).

6. Franklin, *Reconstruction,* 209.

7. Elizabeth B. Johnston, *Visitors Guide to Mount Vernon* (Washington, D. C.: Gibson Brothers, 1886), 1.

8. Attendance Roster for 1876, courtesy Mount Vernon Library. Also, Edward P. Alexander, *Museum Masters* (Tennessee: American Association for State and Local History, 1983), 184.

9. LPHP to AEHG, Mount Vernon, Virginia, June 1882. D/L-G/H.

10. AEHG letter to Flossie, Marshall, Texas, 26 January 1876. D/L-G/H.

11. LPHP to AEHG, Edgewood, South Carolina, 3 August 1881. D/L-G/H.

12. Patricia L. Faust, ed., *Historical Times Encyclopedia of the Civil War* (New York: Harper & Row, 1986), 54–55.

13. From unpublished notes of the late Miss Anna H. Smith of Marshall, Texas. D/L-G/H.

14. JTH to AEHG, Edgewood, South Carolina, 8 November 1881. D/L-G/H.

15. Letter from "M" to LPHP, presumably after 1884. Pickens-Dugas Papers, SHC-UNC.

16. Signed "L. H. Pickens" in family scrapbook, D/L-G/H.

17. Information from family members and noted in Holcombe/Greer family scrapbook. Also newspaper write-up dated 1893 from the Washington correspondent of the *Augusta Chronicle*. D/L-G/H.

CHAPTER TWENTY-FOUR

1. LPHP to Mrs. Hudson, Edgewood, South Carolina, 9 November 1891. Mt. Vernon Ladies Association.

2. Lucy Francis Pickens Dugas, born 1882 to Douschka Pickens Dugas and Dr. George Cuvier Dugas.

3. LPHP to Lucy Francis Pickens Dugas, Edgewood, South Carolina, 1895. Pickens Papers, SCL-USC.

4. Ellen Middleton to LPHP, Pickens-Dugas Papers, No. 1492, nd. SHC-UNC.

5. Lucy Holcombe Pickens, Collected Writings, 66. Pickens Papers, SCL-USC.

6. JTH to AEHG, Edgewood, South Carolina, 8 November 1881. D/L-G/H.

7. Philemon (Phil) Holcombe served in the Texas Cavalry from June 1862 to 20 May 1865. Confederate Pension Application.

8. JTH to AEHG, Edgewood, South Carolina, 8 November 1881. D/L-G/H.

9. Article by John R. Aull, 19 January 1930, Family scrapbook, D/L-G/H. Visit to Willowbrook cemetery by author.

10. Copy of broadside courtesy of SCL-USC.

11. Ibid.

12. "Oui" Louis Alexander Dugas, died later that summer (1898) of tick fever.

13. Letter (dated 1898) in unpublished 1969 manuscript of Raven Simkins Graydon, (daughter of Sallie Simkins). Courtesy of Augustus Graydon.

14. It has been said that Lucinda married the son of "Aunt" Betty, the cook at Edgewood, but no record has been found of this marriage.

15. Various unidentified newspaper obituaries. D/L-G/H.

16. *The Edgefield Chronicle*, 26 October 1898 and numerous obituaries in various but unidentified newspapers, D/L-G/H.

17. May 1900 Minutes of the Council, Mount Vernon Ladies Association.

Epilogue

1. Chesnut, *Civil War*, 287.

$\mathcal{B}$ibliography

ARCHIVAL SOURCES

Aiken, Ada Holcombe. "What I Remember" Collection of Dr. David Wyatt Aiken, New Orleans, Louisiana.

Clayton Genealogical Library, Houston, Texas.

Dargan, Clara Victoria. Dargan-MacLean, Papers. Special Collections, No. M2321, Perkins Library, Duke University. Durham, North Carolina.

Davis/Little Collection—Greer/Holcombe Families.

East Texas Baptist University Library.

Edgefield South Carolina 1900 census.

Edgefield South Carolina County State Archives.

Fayette County Tennessee Court Records.

Graydon, Raven Simkins. Memoirs. Augustus Graydon Collection, Columbia, South Carolina.

Hardeman County Tennessee Court Records.

Harrison County Texas Census Records: 1850,1860, 1870, 1880, 1900, 1910 and 1920.

Harrison County Texas Court Records.

Hill Memorial Library, Louisiana State University.

Historical Society of Fayette County Tennessee.

Historical Society of Harrison County Texas.

Holcombe, Dr. William Henry. Autobiography, Journal, and Notes. Collection of Dr. David Wyatt Aiken, New Orleans, Louisiana.

Howard-Tilton Memorial Library, Tulane University.

Hunt, John Wilkins II. *The Story of the Hunt Family that First Came to Hardiman County, Tennessee.* Memphis, Tennessee. 1938.

Mount Vernon Ladies Association, Mount Vernon, Virginia.

Official Records of the Union & Confederate Forces in the War of the Rebellion Vol. 47, Series I, part II. 50–53, 462, 1198, 1199.

Pickens Family Papers. Special Collections, Leyburn Library, Washington & Lee University, Lexington, Virginia.

Pickens Papers. South Caroliniana Library, University of South Carolina at Columbia.

Pickens, Francis W., Papers. Special Collections, No. M2321, Perkins Library, Duke University. Durham, North Carolina.

Pickens/Holcombe Letters. Augustus Graydon Collection, Columbia, South Carolina.

Pickens-Dugas Papers. No. 1492, Selected Items, Southern Historical Collection, Library of the University of North Carolina at Chapel Hill.

Pickens, Lucy Holcombe. Will. The State of South Carolina Archives, Columbia, South Carolina.

Records of East Texas, 1971. John W. Wilkins, Lufkin, Texas.

Sheppard-Weston Private Collection. Columbia, South Carolina.

Smith, Anna Greer. Notes on the Life of Lucy Petway Holcombe. Davis/Little Collection.

South Carolina State Archives.

State of Texas Federal Population Schedules, Seventh Census of the United States, 1850, Vol. II, transcribed by Mrs. V. K. Carpenter, Greenville, Mississippi. Century Enterprises, 1969.

The Historical Society of Pennsylvania .

United States Census, 1850.

PRIMARY PUBLISHED WORKS

Appletons' Illustrated Hand-Book of American Travel. New York: 1857.

Bremer, Fredrika. *The Homes of the New World, Impresions of America*. Vol. 3. London: Arthur Hall, Virtue & Co., 1853.

Caper, Henryk. *The Life and Times of C. G. Memminger*. Richmond, Virgina: 1893.

Clay-Copton, Virginia. *A Belle of the Fifties*. Doubleday, Page & Company, 1905.

Conyngham, Captain David P. *Sherman's March Through the South*. New York: 1865.

Davis, Varina. *Jefferson Davis, A Memoir*. Belford Company Publishers, 1890.

De Leon, T. C. *Belles Beaux and Brains of the 60's*. G. W. Dillingham Company, 1907.

"Famous Women of the South." *Times-Democrat*, (8 August 1899). Edgefield, South Carolina

Greer, Jack Thorndyke. *Leaves from a Family Album*, Holcombe/Greer. Waco, Texas: Texian Press, 1975.

Harper's New Monthly Magazine. Harper & Brothers, Vol. 4–5 (1852), Vol. 17 (1858), Vol. 19 (1859), Vol. 22–23 (1860–1861). New York.

Holcombe, Lucy Petway [H. M. Hardimann pseud.]. *The Free Flag of Cuba or the Martyrdom of Lopez*. New York: Dewitt & Davenport, 1855. Microfilm, Rice Library, PS 643 A64 Vol. II, Roll H-7.

Levering, Joseph Mortimer. *A History of Bethlehem, Pennsylvania-1741–1892*. Bethlehem Times Publishing Co., 1903.

Life and Liberty in America: or Sketches of a Tour in the United States and Canada in 1857–8. New York: Harpers & Brothers, 1859.

MacCorkle, William Alexander. *The White Sulphur Springs*. New York: Neale Publishing Co., 1916.

McPherson, Elizabeth Weir. *The Holcombes, Nation Builders, Their Biographies, Genealogies and Pedigrees*. Washington, D. C.: McPherson, 1947.

Perry, B.F., *Reminiscences of Public Men*. Philadelphia: John D. Avil & Co.,1883.

Phelps' Travelers Guide Through the United States. New York: Horace Thayer & Co., 1853.

Pickens, Lucy Holcombe. Collected Writings. Francis W. Pickens Papers, South Caroliniana Library, University of South Carolina at Columbia.

Poors, Ben Perley. *Reminiscences*. Hubbard Brothers Publishers, 1886.

Ravenel, Mrs. St. Julien, *Charleston—The Place and the People*. The Macmillan Company, 1906.

Reichel, William C., *A History of the Rise, Progress, and Present Condition of the Moravian Seminary for Young Ladies at Bethlehem, Pennsylvania with a Catalogue of its Pupils (1785–1858)*. Philadelphia: J. P. Lippincott & Co., 1858.

Trollope, Frances. *Domestic Manners of the Americans, 1832*. Reprint, Great Britain: BAS Printers, 1977.

Texas Almanac, 1850

Woodward, C. Vann, ed. *Mary Chesnut's Civil War*. New Haven: Yale University Press, 1981.

SECONDARY WORKS

Abbott, Richard H. *The Republican Party & the South 1855–1877*. Chapel Hill & London: University of North Carolina Press, 1986.

Abernathy, Thomas Perkins. *From Frontier to Plantation, A Study in Frontier Democracy*. Chapel Hill: University of North Carolina, 1932.

Able, Rene. "Fleur de Luce, Legends Lure, Linger Long." *The Edgefield Advertiser*, South Carolina. 29 May 1985.

Allen, H. D., "The Paper Money of the Confederate States." *Numismatis* 31:7, July 1919.

Alumnae Bulletin. Moravian Academy, Bethlehem, Pennsylvania. "A Seminary Girl of 1846."

Alvarez, Eugene. *Travels on Southern Antebellum Railroad—1828–1860*. University of Alabama Press, 1974.

Auchampaugh, Philip Gerald. *James Buchanan and His Cabinet, On the Eve of Secession*. Boston: J. S. Canner & Co., 1965.

Benner, Judith Ann. *Fraudulent Finance: Counterfeiting and the Confederate States: 1861–1865*. Texas: A Hill Junior College Monograph, No. 3: 1970.

Bergeron, Paul H. *Paths of the Past, Tennessee, 1770–1970*. Knoxville: University of Tennessee Press, 1979.

Billingsley, Betty and Terry Fish, "Huntland, A Southern Plantation Home" *Hard Times* (Hardeman County Times), Vol. 4:12, March 24, 1994.

Bleser, Carol. *The Hammonds of Redcliffe*. Oxford: Oxford University Press, 1981.

_____, ed. *In Joy and Sorrow, Women, Family and Marriage in the Victorian South 1830–1900*. New York, Oxford: Oxford University Press, 1991.

Bowen, Frank C. *A Century of Atlantic Travel—1830–1930*. Little, Brown and Company, 1930.

Bradbeer, William West. *Confederate and Southern State Currency*. Mt.Vernon, New York: 1915.

Brinnin, John Malcolm. *The Sway of the Grand Salon*. New York: Delacourte Press, 1971.

Bull, Emily. "Lucy Pickens, Queen of the South Carolina Confederacy." *South Carolina Historical Association*, 1982.

Burton, Orville Vernon. *In My Father's House Are Many Mansions—Family and Commu-*

nity in Edgefield, South Carolina. Chapel Hill: University of North Carolina Press, 1983.

Cary, John H. and Julius Weinberg, eds. *The Social Fabric, American Life from 1607 to the Civil War.* Little, Brown & Company, 1981.

Cauthen, Charles Edward. *South Carolina Goes to War 1860–1865.* Chapel Hill: University of North Carolina Press, 1950.

Channing, Stephen A. *Crisis of Fear: Secession in South Carolina.* New York: W. W. Norton, 1970.

Clark, Thomas D. *South Carolina, The Grand Tour 1780–1865.* University of South Carolina Press, 1973.

Clinton, Catherine. *The Plantation Mistress, Woman's World in the Old South.* New York: Pantheon Books, 1982.

_____ *Tara Revisited, Women, War & the Plantation Legend.* New York: Abbeville Press, 1995.

_____ *The Other Civil War-American Women in the Nineteenth Century.* New York: Hill & Wang, 1984.

Coker, Elizabeth B. *India Allan.* New York: E. P. Dutton & Co., 1953.

Coppock, Paul R., "South's Most Beautiful Woman."

_____. "La Grange Gave South Its Uncrowned Queen," *The Commercial Appeal of Memphis, Tennessee,* 10 June 1973. Reprinted in *Bank Note Reporter.* nd.

Corlew, Robert E. *Tennessee, A Short History.* University of Tennessee Press, 1981.

Coughlan, Robert. *Elizabeth and Catherine, Empresses of all the Russias.* New York: G. P. Putnam's Sons, 1974.

Coulling, Mary Price, *The Lee Girls,* Winston-Salem, North Carolina: John F. Blair, 1987.

_____. *Margaret Junkin Preston, A Biography.* Winston-Salem, North Carolina: John F. Blair, 1993.

Coulter, E. Merton. *The South During Reconstruction 1865–1877,* Vol. 8. Louisiana State University Press, 1947.

Crankshaw, Edward. *The Shadow of the Winter Palace.* New York: Viking, 1976.

Crist, Lynda Lasswell and Mary Seaton Dix, eds. *The Papers of Jefferson Davis.* Vol. 4, 1849–1852, Vol. 5, 1853–1854, Vol. 7, 1861, Baton Rouge & London: Louisiana State University Press, 1983, 1992.

Crute, Joseph H. *Confederate Staff Officers 1861–1865.* Clayton Library, Houston, Texas.

Crute, Joseph H., Jr. *Units of the Confederate States Army.* Derwent Books, 1987.

Dallas Morning News. Dallas, Texas, "The Only Texas Girl Pictured on Confederate Money." 19 May 1929 and 12 May.

Davis, William C. *Jefferson Davis, The Man and His Hour.* New York: Harper Collins, 1991.

DeBerry, John H. "La Grange, La Belle Village." *Tennessee Historical Quarterly,* Vol. XXX, Robert M. McBride, ed. 1971.

DeConde, Alexander. *A History of American Foreign Policy.* New York: Chas. Scribner & Sons, 1963.

Degler, Carl. *At Odds: Women and the Family in America from Revolution to Present*. New York: Oxford: Oxford University Press, 1980.

Dillman, Caroline Matheny, ed. *Southern Women*. New York: Hemisphere Publishing Corp., 1988.

Duffy, John. *Healers, A History of American Medicine*. Urbana: University of Illinois Press, 1979.

Edgefield Death Notices and Cemetery Records. Compiled by Carlee T. McClendon, Hive Press, Columbia, South Carolina, 1977

Edmunds, John B., Jr., *Francis W. Pickens and the Politics of Destruction*. Chapel Hill & London: University of North Carolina Press, 1986.

Encyclopedia of Southern Culture. Charles Reagan Wilson & William Ferris eds. Chapel Hill & London: University of North Carolina Press, 1989.

Farnham, Christie Anne. *The Education of the Southern Belle*. New York and London: University Press, 1994.

Faust, Patricia L., ed. *Historical Times Encyclopedia of the Civil War*. New York: Harper & Row, 1986.

Faust, Drew Gilpin. *Mothers of Invention—Women of the Slaveholding South in the American Civil War*. Chapel Hill & London: University of North Carolina Press,1996.

Foner, Eric. *Freedom's Lawmakers, A Directory of Black Officeholders During Reconstruction*. Louisiana State University Press, 1993.

Fox-Genovese, Elizabeth. *Within the Plantation Household, Black and White Women of the Old South*. Chapel Hill: University of North Carolina Press, 1988.

Franklin, John Hope. *Reconstruction: After the Civil War*. Chicago: University of Chicago Press, 1961.

Fuller, Claud E. *Confederacy Currency and Stamps*. Nashville, Tennessee: Parthenon Press, 1949.

Furnas, J. C. *The Americans, A Social History of the United States, 1587–1914*. New York: G. P. Putnam's Sons, 1969.

Gara, Larry. *The Presidency of Franklin Pierce*. Kansas: University Press of Kansas, 1991.

Gillette, William. *Retreat From Reconstruction 1869–1879*. Baton Rouge: Louisiana State University Press, 1979.

Glover, Lorrie M. "Bound by Words. "Published thesis, Clemson University, 1992.

Graham, Stephen. *A Life of Alexander II Tsar of Russia*. London: Ivor Nicholson & Watson, 1935.

Handbook of Texas, Vol. 2. Austin: Texas State Historical Association, 1952.

Herndon, Del Taliaferra. *Residences of Historic Interest in Marshall*. East Texas Baptist University.

Hill, Margot Hamilton and Peter A. Bucknell. *The Evolution of Fashion –1066–1930*. Reinhold Publishing Co., 1967.

Historical Sketch of the Moravian Seminary for Young Ladies at Bethlehem, Northampton County Pennsylvania, Founded 1785

Hubbell, Jay G. *The South in American Literature 1607–1900*. Durham, North Carolina: Duke University Press, 1954.

Hudson, Linda S. *Mistress of Manifest Destiny, A Biography of Jane McManus Storm Cazneau, 1807–1878.* Austin: Texas State Historical Association, 2001.

Isserman, Maurice. *Journey to Freedom.* New York: Facts on File, Inc., 1997.

James, Bessie Rowland. *Anne Royall's U.S.A.* Rutgers University Press, 1972.

Jones, Anne Goodwyn, *Tomorrow is Another Day, The Woman Writer in the South, 1859–1936.* Baton Rouge & London: Louisiana State University Press, 1981.

Journal of Southern History Vol. 3:1. Southern Historical Association. Baton Rouge: Louisiana State University Press, 1937.

Kane, Harnett T. *Plantation Parade.* New York: William Morrow & Co., 1945.

_____. *Natchez.* New York: William Morrow & Co., 1947.

Kennedy, David M. *Birth Control in America, the Career of Margaret Sanger,* New Haven: Yale University Press, 1970.

Lee, Rebecca Smith. *Mary Austin Holley, A Biography.* University of Texas Press, 1962.

Leech, Margaret, *Reveille In Washington 1860–1865.* New York: Time Inc., 1941.

Lewis, Kathleen, "The Woman Called Lucy." *Texas State Magazine,* 2 November 1952.

Litwack, Leon F. *Been in the Storm So Long, The Aftermath of Slavery.* New York: Vintage Books, 1980.

Malone, Dumas, ed., *Dictionary of American Biography. Vol.* 9. New York: Charles Scribner's Sons, 1932 & 1936.

"Marshall, Texas, C. S. A. 1861." *Marshall News Messenger,* Marshall, Texas: 26 February 1961.

May, Robert E. *John A. Quitman, Old South Crusader.* Baton Rouge & London: Louisiana State University Press, 1985.

McPherson, James M. *Battle Cry of Freedom, The Civil War Era.* Oxford: Oxford University Press, 1988.

Miller, Frances C. "Governor Francis Pickens and Lovely Lucy Subject of New Book." *The Citizens-News,* Edgefield County, 11 December 1986.

Mims, Nancy C. "The Mansion that Moved Away," Augusta Chronicle, Augusta, Georgia. 27 September, 1953.

Moore, John Hammond, ed. *A Plantation Mistress on the Eve of the Civil War.* Columbia, South Carolina: University of South Carolina Press, 1993.

Morton, Dorothy Rich and Charles W. Crawford, ed. *Fayette County Tennessee.* Memphis, Tennessee: Memphis State University Press, 1989.

Muhlenfeld, Elisabeth. *Mary Boykin Chesnut, A Biography.* Baton Rouge: Louisiana State University Press, 1981.

New Handbook of Texas Vol. 6. Austin: Texas State Historical Association, 1996.

Notable American Women 1607–1905, Biographical Dictionary. Vol. 3: 64–65. Cambridge: Harvard University Press, 1971.

O'Brien, Robert, ed., with Harold H. Martin. *The Encyclopedia of the South.* New York, Oxford: Facts on File Publications, 1985.

Parker, David. "Lucy Holcombe Pickens 'Cult' Continues." Edgefield, South Carolina: *The Edgefield Advertiser,* 29 May 1985.

Peterson, Jeanne M. *Family, Love, and Work in the Lives of Victorian Gentlewomen.* Bloomington, Indiana: Indiana University Press, 1989.

Plante, Ellen M. *Women at Home in Victorian America, A Social History.* Facts on File, Inc., 1997.

Quinn, Richard. "Save that Confederate Money, Boys." *Southern Partisan,* Spring Issue 1985.

Quisenberry, Anderson C. *Lopez's Expedition to Cuba 1850 and 1851.* Louisville, Kentucky: Filson Club Publication No. 21, John P. Morton & Co., 1906

Reinders, Robert C. *End of an Era, New Orleans, 1850–1860.* Gretna, Louisiana: Pelican Publishing Co.,1964.

Reinfeld, Fred. *The Story of Civil War Money.* New York: Sterling Publishing Co., 1910.

Robertson, Mary D.,ed. *Lucy Breckinridge of Grove Hill, The Journal of a Virginia Girl, 1862–1864.* Columbia, South Carolina: University of South Carolina Press, 1994.

Ruff, Nancy Blakely. *Harrison County, Texas, Caucasian Residents in 1880, and Texas Early Marriage Records 1839–1869.* Baltimore: Gateway Press, Inc., 1987.

Saxon, Lyle. *Fabulous New Orleans.* New York: Century Co., 1928.

Schuler, Stanley. *Mississippi Valley Architecture, Houses of the Lower Mississippi Valley.* Schiffer Publishing Ltd., 1989.

Scott, Anne Firor. *The Southern Lady: From Pedestal to Politics, 1830–1939.* Chicago: University of Chicago Press, 1970.

Seale,William. *The President's House, Vols. 1–2.* New York: White House Historical Association, 1986.

Shea, William L. and Earl T. Hess. *Pea Ridge: Civil War Campaign in the West.* Chapel Hill: University of North Carolina Press, 1992.

Sigerman, Harriet. *An Unfinished Battle, American Women 1848–1865.* New York, Oxford: Oxford University Press, 1994.

Simkins, Francis Butler, and James Welch Patton. *The Women of the Confederacy.* Richmond & New York: Garrett & Massie, Inc., 1936.

Simkins, Francis Butler, and Robert Hilliard Woody. *South Carolina During Reconstruction.* Chapel Hill: University North Carolina Press, 1932.

Smith-Rosenberg, Carroll. *Disorderly Conduct-Visions of Gender in Victorian America.* New York: Alfred A. Knopf, 1985.

Stalcup, Brenda, ed. *Reconstruction, Opposing Viewpoints.* San Diego, California: Green Haven Press, Inc., 1995.

Stampp, Kenneth M. and Leon F. Litwack. *Reconstruction, An Anthology of Revisionist Writings.* Baton Rouge: Louisiana State University Press, 1969.

Stern, Philip Van Doren. *Prologue to Sumter.* Indiana University Press, 1961.

Suchlicki, Jaime, *Mexico from Montezuma to Nafta to Chiapas and Beyond.* Washington & London: Brassey's Inc., 1996.

Sutherland, Daniel E., *The Expansion of Everyday Life 1869–1876.* New York: Harper & Row, 1989.

Swanberg, W. A., *First Blood, The Story of Fort Sumter.* New York: Charles Scribner's Sons, 1957.

Taylor, George Rogers. *The Transportation Revolution –1815–1860,* Vol. 4. New York: Rinehart & Company, Inc., 1951.

Tolstoy, Leo. *Anna Karenina.* New York: Random House, 1939.

Way, Fred, ed. *Steamboat Directory.* Columbus, Ohio: Ohio University Press, 1990.

Wiley, Bell Irvin. *Confederate Women.* New York: Barnes & Noble Books, 1975.

Williams, Ben Ames, ed. *Diary from Dixie, Mary Boykin Chesnut.* Boston: Houghton Mifflin, 1961.

Winther, Oscar Osburn, ed. *With Sherman to the Sea, The Civil War Letters, Diaries & Reminiscences of Theodore F. Upson.* Bloomington, Indiana: Indiana University Press, 1989.

Wolfe, Margaret Ripley. *Daughters of Canaan, A Saga of Southern Women.* Lexington, Kentucky: University Press of Kentucky, 1995.

Woodward, C. Vann. *The Burden of Southern History.* Baton Rouge and London: Louisiana State University Press,1968.

_____ & Elisabeth Muhlenfeld, eds. *The Private Mary Chesnut.* New York & Oxford: Oxford University Press, 1984.

Wyatt-Brown, Bertram. *Yankee Saints and Southern Sinners.* Baton Rouge: Louisiana State University Press, 1985.

Young, Marjorie W. "Lucy Pickens to be Recalled When Homes Tour Begins." *Independent,* Anderson, South Carolina, 27 March 1966.

PERIODICALS CONSULTED

Caddo Gazette, June 4, 1853.

Charleston Mercury, 1860–1861.

Charleston News-Courier, August 9,1899 (Obituary).

Columbus State, August 9,1899 (Obituary).

Edgefield Advertiser, 1860–61, 1867–69.

Fayette County Historical Society Bulletin, September 1981.

Frontier Times, Vol. I.

Marshall News Messenger, 1961.

Memphis Daily Eagle & Enquirer, 1851–52. 1858–60.

Memphis Weekly Appeal, 1858.

National Intelligencer, Washington, D.C., 1848.

New *York Times,* May 28–29, 1858, November 6,1860, August, September, 1881–1883.

Texas Republican, 1851, 1858, 1861, 1862, 1864.

Index

Abolitionist: 115, 120

Abner Perrin: Camp, UCV, 195

Activists: 121

Adriatic (ship): 118, 119, 120

Aiken (cutter): 128, 129

Aiken, South Carolina: 199, 200

Aiken Standard: 199

Alabama: 65, 127, 167, 172

Aldrich, A.P.: 142

Alfred (slave): 169, 175

Allen, H. D.: 150, 151, affidavits, 152

Alexander, C.H.: (friend), 11, 16

Alexander II: Emperor (Tsar) of
   Russia, 89, 93; Character, 94;
   attention to Lucy, 96-99, 115, 160;
   Gifts, 103, 143, 189; portrait, 104,
   159; Slaves versus serfs, 115, 132;
   aid, 131; assassination, 188

Alexandra Federovna: Dowager
   Empress, 98

Alexandrovna, Maria: Empress of
   Russia (Tsarina), 96; religion, 98;
   concern for Lucy and child, 99,
   103;

Amnesty: by President Johnson, 168

Anderson Lucy Maria. *See* Holcombe,
   Lucy Maria

Anderson, Robert: moves forces, 128,
   129; refuses to leave, 130, 131; Fort
   Sumter fired on, 138, 139

Anna Karenina: by Tolstoy, 112

Anthony, Susan B.: 24

Anti-bellum South: social standing, 5

Antionette, Marie: (French Queen), 2,
   47

Anti-slavery: societies; 24

Appamattox: 166, 168

Appleton, John: 119, 228n 13

Arsenal: United States, 128, 131

Atha, Mrs.; (family friend), 194

Aunt Betty:(slave), 171

Aunt Charlotte:(slave), 177

Auntie Viney:(slave), 30, 75, 111, 134

Austin, Stephen B.: 15

Austin, Texas: 16

Bacon, John E. (Judge): 87, 224n 2,
   106, 188

Bahia Honda Expedition: 44. *See also*
   Filibusters

Baldwin, Nannie, (second Mrs.
   Philemon Eugene Holcombe): 194

Baltic: (U.S. Steamer), 139

Bastrop, Texas: 16, 17

Battle of Brandy Station: 163

Battle of Pea Ridge: 155

Battery, The, 127: 138

Beatrice (slave): 30, 134

Beauregard, Pierre Gustav Toutant:
   fires on Fort Sumter, 138, 140

Bell, Colonel William; 55

Benjamin, Judah P.; 188

Berghman, Mrs. Lily: 187

Bess (slave); 171

Bethlehem, Pennsylvania; 15, 19, 50

Bickley, George Waashington Lamb:
   60, 61. *See also* Knights of the
   Golden Circle

Birth Control: 136, 146, 147

Bishop College: 180

Blacks: 14; in Emperor's Court, 90;
   protection, 133, 171, 172; during
   Reconstruction, 167, 184, 185;

Blanton, Duncan; 150

"Blue stocking": Lucy as, 22, 77

Bonham, Milledge: 69, 93, 102, 164

Bostic, Wesley (slave): 197

Breckenridge, John: 56, 120

Bremer, Fredericka; on women, 60

Brock, Mrs.: 19, 20

Brown, John: 115

Buchanan's Domestic Medicine: 33

Buchanan, James: 56; inaugural, 58, 59, 65; re Pickens, 69, 74, 76, 77, 90, 128; administration, 120, 121; Qualities, 121, 123

Bryan, George F.; 145

"Bucket": rebukes Lucy, 154

Burleson Street, Marshall, Texas: 32, 134

Butler, Maria Pickens, (Pickens daughter by first marriage): 163

Butler, Mathew Calbraith: 124, 163; post-war, 185, 178

Butler, Sallie Simkins, (family friend): 195

Byron, Lord: *Hebrew Melodies,* 75

Caddo Lake: 29

Calhoun, John: 65

Campbell, Robert Blair: 80, 223n4

Caroline (slave): 111, 169

Carolinians: 184, 185

Carpet-baggers: 172, 185

Cass, Lewis; 120

Castle Pinkney; 128, 129, 131, 136

Cedar Fields; cemetery, 195

Celah (slave); 30, 134

Chamberlain, Daniel H.: 185

Charleston Courier: 63, 65

Charleston Mercury; 136, 149

Charleston, South Carolina: 121, 125, 130, 136, 139, 190

Charley (slave); 75, 135

Chesnut, Mary Boykin (Mrs. James Chesnut, Jr.): ix; 145; on Lucy, 67; rivalry, 126, 149, 150, 152, 153; Faults Pickens, 129; re council, 149; post-war, 193; tribute to Lucy, 201

Chesnut, James, Jr.; 138, 140, 149

Citadel: 131

Clay, Clement; 193

Clay, Henry (Senator): 22

Clay, Virginia Clement: ix, 59; with Lucy, 77, 122; post-war, 193

"Clotilde": Lucy's ideal, 59, 220n 28

Columbia, South Carolina: 165, 166

Confederacy: flag of, 141; shortages, 148, 156, 176; Lucy's role in, 193, 195;

Confederate Blockade Runners: 148

Confederate Floating Battery: 139

Confederate Forces: 165, 166

Confederate Post Office: 167

Confederate Monument: 195

Congressional Reservation: 2

Constantin, Grand Duke: 98, 99, 102

Coste, Captain; secessionist, 129

Cousin Lollie (wife of Dr. William Henry Holcombe): 58

Cousin Willie. *See* Holcombe, Dr. William Henry

Creoles: 40, 41, 42

Crittenden, John J.: 45

Crittenden, William Logan: filibuster, 43; execution, 45, 46, 48

Cuba: 1, 40, 41, 42, 43, 44, 46

Cunningham, Anne Pamela; Founder of Mount Vernon Ladies Association, 169, 170, 187

Cunningham; Floride, friend, 145, 160

Currency; 20, 216n 8

Curtis, Samuel R.: 155

"Darbey." *See* Gardner, Fleming

Dargan, Clara Victoria (MacLean): Fort Sumter firing, 139; Edgewood, 159; on Lucy, 160, 161; "Mabel" revealed, 162, 163, 170, 179

Davis, Jefferson; 37, 40; on Fillmore, 46; as President of Confederacy, 122, 127, 135, 138, 145, 164, 169

Davis, Varina Anne, (Mrs. Jefferson Davis); ix; 122, 150, 151, 152; post-war, 194
Darlington Guards: 131
Democratic Governor; 186
Democratic Party; 3, 120
Deo Vindice (Confederate Motto); 148
Dis-Unionists: 105, 120
Donelson, Andrew Jackson; 56
Dortch, Robert; 28, 34
Douschka. *See* Dugas, Francis Eugenia Olga Neva Pickens
Dugas, Adrienne Dorothea Rebecca (granddaughter): 191, 192, 196, 199
Dugas, Francis Eugenia Olga Neva Pickens (daughter): mentioned; 145, 161, 167, 188; birth and christening, 103, 104; Letter to Uncle "Fee", 109—111; Childhood, 113, 116, 134, 135, 136, 140, 171, 173, 174; Traits, 177, 196; at St. Mary's, 181, 182; Edgewood, 184; Red Shirts, 185; Jeanne d'Arc of South Carolina, 186; marriage, 189; children, 190; Death, 191
Dugas, George Couvier, (husband of Douschka); 188, 189
Dugas, Louis Alexander (grandson): 191, 196
Dugas, Lucy Francis Pickens (grand-daughter): 151, 191, 192, 196, 199
Duncan, Jemine: 57, 220n 19, 85
Dunlap, W.C. (family friend): 85, 105

Edgefield Advertiser: 123
Edgefield Historical society: 195
Edgefield, South Carolina: 76, 159, 165, 175, 195
Edgewood: 68, 76, 107, 123, 142, 172, 175; described, 159, 162; intact, 166, 167; haven, 178, 188, 189,200
Education: for females in 19th century, 14

Elkhorn Tavern: 155
Emma Willard's Seminary; 14
Emperor. *See* Alexander II, Tsar of Russia
Endor, Witch of: 98
Ernest (slave): 134
Eve, Philoclea E.: friend of Lucy, 187

Fayette County, Tennessee: 2, 5
Fern Lake: 49, 60, 180
Filibusters: 1, 41, 44
Fillmore-Donelson Club: 56
Fillmore, Millard: on filibusters, 41, 44; criticized, 46; Know-nothing party, 56
First Presbyterian Church, Marshall, Texas: 32, 217n 16
Florida: (state), 127
Floyd, John Buchanan: 130
Folstoz, Count: 95, 96, 97
Fort Moultrie: 128, 131, 132
Fort Pickens: 139, 153
Fort Sumter: 128, 129, 132, 136; ultimatum, 138; shelled, 138, 230n 14, 139, 141; surrenders, 139, 148G
Fourteenth Amendment: 171
Frankfurt, Prussia: 106
Fredonia War: 16
Freedmen: 175
Free Flag of Cuba or The Martyrdom of Lopez: 43, 47, 48, 72

Gardner, Fleming: in Marshall, 53; as "Mr. Darbey," 53, 70; "Lady Bird" fantasies, 70; surfaces, 142, 145, 153; returns to "Lady Bird," 178, 192; death of Lucy, 197
Gary, Martin: with Red Shirts, 185;
Georgia (state): 127, 167
Gerard: 47
German Spa: 117
Gibbes, R.W.: knight errant, 137, 153

Gist, William H.: 120, 124, 133, 149

Gonzales, Ambrosio Jose: 41, 42; suspect, 48; post-war, 48

Gorchakof, Prince Alexander: 89, 224n 6; 94

Grant, Ulysses S.: 156; Vicksburg, 163; Appamattox, 166

Great Britain: antipathy to Russia, 131

Greer, Anna Eliza Holcombe, (Mrs. Elkanah Bracken Greer) (sister): mentioned, 2,14, 17, 23, 24, 33, 36, 63,69, 73, 74, 85, 91, 109, 134, 167; Birth 3; Beauty, 4, 12, 27, 28, 37; Talent, 10, 29; Education, 12, 18, 21, 25; Childhood, 13; Traits, 21, 60; Health, 21, 61, 96, 99; writes Senator Clay, 22;

Texas, 16, 26, 27; Marriage, 37; *Free Flag*, 47; Children,52; instructs Lucy, 60; Difficulties, 60, 118, 167, 178, 179, 180, 187, 189; on Douschka's birth, 104; to Battle-front, 154, 155; Death, 190

Greer, Anna Theodore (niece): 180

Greer, Beverly Holcombe (nephew): 52, 60, 61, 67

Greer, Elkanan Bracken (brother-in-law): 28; marriage, 37; character, 37, 47, 53; railroad, 52; Knights of The Golden Circle, 60, 61; at Pea Ridge, 155; Conscription Bureau, 156; Death, 187

Greer, Eugenia Markoleta (niece): 52, 61, 154, 180, 189

Grierson, Benjamin A.: 156

Gwin, Mrs. (friend): 70, 223n 2; 83

Hampton, Mary McDuffie (Mrs. Wade Hampton): 153

Hampton Legion: 141

Hampton, Wade: 153; Union advance, 165; Red Shirts, 185, 186

Hardeman, Henrietta Marie: ancestor, 47

Hardimann, H. M.: non de plume for Lucy Holcombe, 47, 58

Harlee, W.W.: 149

Harper's Ferry: 115

Harriet Lane (ship); 130, 139

Harrison County, Texas: 17, 26

Havana, Cuba: 44; 45

Hawley, Maria: 5; trusted, 6; 10; unwanted advice, 12

Hayne, Isaac: on council, 149

Haynes, Emily; friend, 137

Haynes, Paul: poet, 181

Henley, Lucien: 45, 48

Hermitage Museum. *See* Winter Palace

Herrara: Mexican President, 24

Hill, Henry Harvey: orders troops, 165

Holcombe, Amanda (Mrs. George Wyatt): aunt, 2

Holcombe, Anna Eliza. *See* Greer, Anna Eliza Holcombe

Holcombe, Beverly Lafayette (father): 23, 32, 38, 83; birth, 2; marriage, 3, 5; plantation owner, 5, 49; 109, 134, 180; characteristic, 9, 187; losses, 11, 12; reforms, 12; to Texas, 16, 17, 26; rejects Lucy's suitor, 72, 73; death 164

Holcombe, Emma Hilliard (first wife of Philemon Eugene Holcombe): 134, 194

Holcombe, Eugenia Dorothea Vaughan Hunt (mother): mentioned: vii, 16, 29, 32, 38, 60, 63, 76, 85; ancestry, 213n 9; Marriage, 3; children, 3, 4, 10, 11; on slavery, 5, 15, 26, Health, 5, 9, 10, 11, 12; on Miss Hawlery, 6, 10, 12; on Educatio, 9, 10, 12, 15, 20, 23, 50, 51, 52; religion, 9, 13, 22; as plantation mistress 8, 9, 11, 13, 14, 33, 167; hard times 11, 12, 28, 181; advises husband, 12; to Texas, 27, 28, 29, 30, 31, 56, 167, 168; concerns 21, 22, 25, 39, 52, 61, 63;

resents Pickens, 67; 71, 73, 74; heartbroken, 75, 134; urges Anna, 155; scolds Lucy, 156; finances 167, 179; Edgewood, 177, 179; Death, 180

Holcombe, Frances (Mrs. Thomas Watkins): aunt, 2

Holcombe, Helen, (sister): 26, 37, 85, 109 adoption, 10, 11; to Texas, 26, 30

Holcombe, John Theodore Hunt, (brother): mentioned: 7, 38, 74, 75, 85, 105, 109, 157, 190; birth, 4; traits, 4; Education, 50, 51; prodigal son, 52; influenced by, 61; moves in, 178; contributes 179, 180, 181, 186, 188; Douschka's wedding, 189; death of Anna Eliza, 190; death of Douschka, 191, 192; old times, 194; responsibility, 194; death of Lucy, 197; Edgewood, 199;

Holcombe Legion: 143, 144, 150, 164

Holcombe, Lucy Petway. *See* Pickens, Lucy Petway Holcombe

Holcombe, Lucy Maria Anderson: royal ancestor, 2

Holcombe, Martha Maria Edgeworh (sister): 4; "Ladybug" portrait, 4, 31

Holcombe, James Philemon (grandfather): war service, 1,2; marriage,2; with Moravians, 15; portrait, 31

Holcombe, Philemon Eugene (brother): 134,157,178, 180, 181, 199; birth, 4, affliction, 10; education, 11,50,75, 85; marries, 109; Confederacy, 194; death of Lucy, 197

Holcombe, William (ancestor): 1

Holcombe, William Henry (cousin Willie): 58, 60; student, 19; as doctor, 39; Swedenborgianism, 39; 218n 11; admires Lucy, 39

Homeopathic medicine: 39

Hood, Ned (slave): 30, 31, 49, 134

Hunt, John (maternal grandfather): 3, 5, 11, 13; will, 76

Immanuel Episcopal Church: La Grange, Tennessee, 13, 156

Imperial Palace, Russia: 88, 94, 97

Indians: 3, 15, 16, 17, 23

Ingleside: 3, 213n 11, 13; war time, 156

Jackson, Andrew: presidency, 3

Jackson, Mississippi; State House, 38

James, George S.: ordered to fire, 138

James Island: 131, 138

Johnson, Andrew: President, 167, 168

Johnson, Benjamin J.: 124

Johnson, Mary (slave): 189

Johnston, Joseph: 142, 230n 1

Judkins, Charles: Captain of Persia, 78

Keating & Ball Engravers; 150

Kent, Bishop of: at Westminster Abbey, 82

Ker, Victor: filibuster, 45

Kirkland, Samuel: 178; 197

Kirkpatrick, Alexander: 28

Knights of the Golden Circle: 60, 61

Know-Nothing Party: 56

Ku Klux Klan: 185

"Lady Bird" (Lucy): 53, 145

Lafayette, Marquis de: at Yorktown, 2, 42; with Moravians, 15

La Grange Female Seminary: 13

La Grange, Tennessee: 2, 213n 8, 3, 19, 26, 32; during war, 156

Lander, Miss, (sculptor): 105, 225n 16

Landskau, 99. *See also* Appendix

Lane, Harriet (niece of President Buchanan): 77, 122; as hostess, 123

Lee, Robert E.: 41, 142; Gettysburg, 163; Appamattox, 166
Lee, St. George S.; emigrates from Ireland, 26; with Lucy, 26, 28, 29; literary works, 34; concern for Lucy, 34, 35; "on the rack," 36, 55
Lincoln, Abraham: 167; "Black Republican," 120; President, 128, 141; on death of 194
Lind, Jenny; 37
livery; 81, 89, 95, 153, 174
Lone Star (of Texas): 143
Lopez, General Narciso: on Cuba, 40; meets Lucy, 40, 218n 14, 42; seeks leader, 40, 41, 43, 44; at Murillo, 44; refuses aid, 45; execution, 46; deceived?, 48
Loughrey, R.W.: 75, 76, 135
Louisiana: 127, 186
love feast: Moravian custom, 21
Lucinda (slave-maid of Lucy): mentioned::30, 63, 221n 3, 64, 74, 85, 97, 106, 134, 135, 145; as wedding Gift 76, 78; in Russia, 90, 96, 103; "trumpery," 109; love for Douschka, 113, 116; loyalty, 169, 173, 186, 189, 190, 196; as "Mamee," 181; writes to Lucy, 182; as "Duchess,", 183; heart-broken, 192; marries, 196, 235n 14; death, 197
Lucy Holcombe, (steam boat): 76, 223n 6

McCord, Louisa Susannah Cheves: 67
McCord, Wilhelmina: 57; 67
McCulloch, Ben: 155, 232n 22
McGowan, Captain: 131
McIntosh, James McQueen: 155, 232n 24
"Mabel": fictional character for Lucy, 47, 171
Magrath, Andrew G.: 164
Mamee. *See* Lucinda
Manassas: 148
manifest destiny: 24, 40

Marie Antionette (Queen): 2, 47, 175
Marriage Mart of the South, 61. *See also* White Sulphor Springs
Marshall House: Marshall, Texas, 32
Marshall, Texas: vii, 11, 26, 60, 71; business, 32; literary center, 32; railroad, 52, 54; politics, 56, 133, 134, 145 179
Mason, John Y.: 83, 84
Mathews, Mr. S. H.: (friend), 18, 21
Memminger, Christopher G.: 150
Memphis Eagle and Enquirer: 55, 80
Meserve, Frederick Hill: 151
Mexicans: 15, 23
Mexico: 61; boundary dispute, 23, 24;
Middleton, Ellen (Mrs. Harry Middleton): Lucy's friend, 144, 157
Miles, William Porcher: 137
Miliutin, Count Nicholas; 94
Mississippi River: 19, 27, 29, 38
Mississippi: 65, 127, 142, 169, 172
Mississippi Volunteers CSA: 37
Monmouth: 39, 40
Montgomery, Alabama: 135
Moravians: history, 15, 33, 50
Moravian Female Seminary: 20, 21, 84, 179, 187 Christmas Vigil, 24, 25
Moravian Seminary for Males: 50
Morgan, Wallace (slave): 175
Morris Island: 131, 136
Moses, Franklin Jr.: 137, 149
Mott, Lucretia: 24
Mount Vernon: 186
Mount Vernon Ladies Association: 169, 170, 186, 190, 195, 197
Mujik: Russian Serf, 113
Mumka: Russian wet-nurse, 104, 106
Munchausen, Baron: 53, 54
Murray, Mrs. (mother of W.L.Crittenden): 48

Nagadoches, Texas: 16
Napoleon, Louis III: 84, 224n 15

Nashville (steamer): 139
Natchez, Mississippi: 11, 28, 37, 38, 39
National Gallery; London, 81, 223n 5
Neva River: 88, 92, 99, 102, 116
New Harpers Monthly Magazine: 55, 56
New Orleans, Louisiana; 10, 15, 28, 29,
    36, 44, 46; as Crescent City, 57
New Orleans Delta News: 41
New Orleans Orphanage: 10, 16
New York Mutual Insurance Company:
    171, 172
New York *Journal of Commerce:* 121
New York Times: 78
Nicholas, Grand Duke: 98
Nicholas I: Tsar of Russia, 89, 95
Northern Subversives: 60
Nueces River: boundary dispute, 23

Oberlin College: 14
Old Hickory Plantation: 43
Old Knickerbocker Magazine: 34
O'Neall, John Belton, (Judge): 145
Ordinance of Secession: 125
Osuna, Duke de; admirer, 96, 111, 162
Owen, Dock: Holcombe Legion, 144
Owens, Allen F.: American Consul, 45

Pampero (fillibuster's ship): 41, 44;
    problems, 48
Parson's Brigade Texas Cavalry: 194
Patriarchal Southern Society: 56
Pea Ridge. *See* Battle of
Peck, Rev. Wiley B.: 3
Perry, Andrew (slave): 197
Perry, Benjamin F.: 145; as provisional
    governor, 167, 168
Persia (steamship): 77, 78
Peterhof: 89, 94, 95
Peter the Great: 92, 95
Petigru, James Louis: 144, 145
Petigru, Jane, (Mrs. James Louis
    Petigru): 144, 145

Pickens, Francis Wilkinson, (husband):
    mentioned: 87, 88, 91, 94, 107, 139,
    142, 159, 160; meets Lucy, 64,
    65;Background, 65; bares soul
    (almost), 66, 67, 68, 69; courtship
    by mail, 68——72; traits, 69, 74;
    accepts post and gives ultimatum,
    72; to Marshall, 73; wedding, 74, 75;
    Minister to Russian Royal Court 89,
    90, 93, 97, 98, 103; longs for heir,
    102; Russian winter, 102, 103;
    forbids Lucy, 105, 106; illness, 108;
    peace at the hearth, 109; Russian
    Easter, 113; delicacies from Texas,
    114, 227n 15; disturbing news, 114,
    115, 119; slaves versus serfs, 115;
    homeward bound, 119, 120; "ready
    at the first tap of the drum," 120;
    assures Buchanan, 122, 123; in
    political arena, 123, 124, 125;
    hastens the catastrophe to come,
    127; Palmetto Republic, 128; first
    blunder, 128; armed aggression,
    129; coastal defense, 130, 131, 132;
    applies to Russia, 131; "It is my
    destiny...", 133; fate of the Confed-
    eracy, 137, 138; Will, 142; a startling
    discovery, 145; a little blackmail,
    146, 168; controlled by council,
    149; tenure ends, 156, 158, 161; to
    Richmond, 163; advises Elkanah,
    167; 168; refused pardon, 168; fears
    prison, 169; surveillance 172;
    financial ruin and failing health,
    172, 173, 175; awaits pardon that
    never comes, 174; death, 175, 176;
    will 181
Pickens, Frank: illegitimate son, 69
"Pickens House": 200
Pickens, Jeannie Dearing, (Mrs.
    Mitchell Whaley): Lucy's step
    daughter, 76, 82, 84, 117, 132, 163;
    to school, 106; Love for Lucy, 107,
    137, 158; death, 173

Pickens, Lucy Petway Holcombe
(third wife): mentioned: viii, ix, 12,
16, 17, 24, 33, 39, 49, 52, 60, 61,
63, 163, 165, 166, 185; principles,
1, 37, 38, 56; ancestry, 1, 5; birth, 3,
81; personality, 4, 5, 28; beauty, 4,
28, 39, 55, 56; childhood, 6, 10, 11,
13, 14; devotion to mother, 7, 28,
38, 58, 84, 85, 180; plantation
demands, 8; education; 13, 18, 20,
22, 38, 84, 99; concern for others,
14, 23, 58, 182, 183, 193, 196, 197;
characteristics, 21, 25, 53, 55, 69,
70; health, 21, 117, 118, 136, 156
163, 179, 182, 193, 194; Homesick,
23, 81, 84, 86, 99, 100, 108, 118; as
"Blue Stocking," 22, 59, 77; final
school days, 24, 25; Southern
Belle, 26, 28, 29, 37, 38, 59, 100,
111; on "strong-minded women,"
25; to Texas, 26—28, 31; "admiration is a pleasant thing," 34, 35, 64,
69, 70, 125, suitors, 36, 38, 43, 46,
68, 53, 54, 55, 58, 68, 70; women's
role, 37, 55, 56; sister's marriage,
37, 56; politics, 38, 56, 120, 124,
160; General Lopez, 40—42, 218n
26, 48; Crittenden, 43; solace in
writing *The Free Flag of Cuba or
Martyrdom of Lopez*, 46, 47, 63;
blames Gonzales, 48; literary
efforts, 46, 47, 48, 51, 55, 57, 63,
71, 169, 181, 182; "Lady Bird" and
"Mr. Darbey," 53, 54, 70; writes to
New Harpers Monthly Magazine, 55,
56; Buchanan's Washington, 58,
59; "Clotilde"as ideal, 59; interest
in fashion, 59, 84, 96, 97, 98, 114,
119; on American Women, 60; The
Marriage Mart, captivates Pickens
and opts for higher stakes, 62—69;
courtship by mail, 69——72,
appeals to "Mr. Darbey," 70;
passport to fame and fortune, 72,

74, 75; "Blue stockings" surface,
77; refuses to embark, 77; 78;
letters from Europe, 80—81, 84—
85; Napoleon III, 84; in Russia,
87—90; St. Isaac's, 93; Royal
splendor versus the commonalty,
94; presented at court, 95—96;
attention of Tsar and Tsarina, 99,
225n 20, 255n 24; faults court
society, 100, 111, 112; pregnancy
and hopes for a son; 100, 102; a
royal demand denied, 103; birth
and christening of daughter, 103;
royalty forgives with diamonds and
portrait, 104; rumors and gossip,
104; mother ill and Lucy tries to go
home, 104; rebellion overruled,
106; Francis ill, 108; peace prevails,
109; attentions of Duke de Osuna,
111; disturbed by lack of recognition for women, 111; described by
Tolstoy, 112; Russian Orthodox
Easter, 112—114; Emperor's
attentions, 114; money worries,
115; to German spa, 117; 118;
advises Anna Eliza, 118; aboard
Adriatic, 119, 120; the decision that
changes her life, 121; challenge of
secession and South Carolina
politics, 125; loyal to the "Cause,"
127, 128; ignores threat, 129, "I am
where honor and duty demand,"
130; *Star of the West* appears, 131;
applies to Russia for aid, 131;
"Race Week" and off to Marshall,
Texas, 133, 134; calls on President
Davis, 135; delays train, 135, 136;
as Madame Governor, 137; firing
on Fort Sumter, 138, 140; poses as
sister-in-law, 142; helps the "Cause"
with Holcombe Legion, 142, 143;
Union friends beg favors, 145;
maintains autonomy, 147; indignant against controls, 149; rivalry

with Mary Chesnut, 149; a woman
of direction, 150; on Confederate
Treasury Notes, 150—152; criticized by "Bucket," 154; war-time
despair, 157; transforms
Edgewood, 158; confesses to Miss
Dargan, 162; death of father, 164;
comfort in religion, 164; threat
from Sherman's troops and fall of
Columbia, South Carolina, 166; as
plantation mistress, 167; applies to
Governor Perry, 168; as vice-regent
of Mount Vernon Ladies Association, 169, 170, 186, 187; belief in
the South, 170, 171; tragedies
mount, 173; raises spirits and
defies rabble, 174, 175; death of
Francis and the end of an era, 175,
176; Edgewood as a haven, 178;
death of mother, 180; problems
multiply, 180; returns to writing,
181, 182; loyalty of Lucinda, 182;
Douschka's wedding, 189; death of
Anna Eliza, 190; Lucy as "Dan",
191; death of Douschka, 191; "My
faithful servants," 191; loyalty to
the South 194; "Keep faith with the
past," 195; letter to Sallie Simkins,
196; Death, 197; will, 199; Lucy's
legacy, 200; a place in history, 201
Pickens, Marion Antionette Dearing,
(second wife): 158, 195
Pickens, Rebecca Simkins (Mrs. John
E. Bacon): 76, 82, 94, 106; and
marriage, 107
Pickens-Salley House: 199
Pierce, Franklin: as President, 84
Plantation: demands of, 8, 9, 167
Point Coupee: 29
Poland, Mr.: 180
Politics: 38, 56, 120, 124, 160
Polk, James Knox: 23, 24; Manifest
Destiny, 24, 64
Polk, Thomas N.: letter from Texas, 16

Powers, Hiram (sculptor): 37
Pro-slavery expansionists: 40, 41
Provost Marshall: 172

Quai de la Cour, St. Petersburg: 99
Quitman, John A.: 39; with filibusters,
40, 41, 44, 47; as mutual friend, 57

Race Week: 132, 133
Ravenel, Mrs. St. Julien: 139
Rebels: 185, 186;
Reconstruction: 167; a troubling issue,
169; improves, 172, 175, 178, 186
Reconstruction Act: passed, 171
Recreational Clubs: 185
Red Shirts: 185, 186
Religion: 9, 13, 103, 112
Republican Radicals: 172, 185, 186
Republic of Texas: 15
Rhett, Barnwell; 124
Rhett Guards, CSA: 131
Richard, Mr. A.E.; re portrait of Lucy,
104
Richardson Guards, CSA:131
Richland Rifle Company, CSA:131
Richmond, Virginia:141
River Styx: Eugenia's fantasy, 29
Robertson, Beverly Holcombe
(cousin): 23, 38, 68, 70, 71; on
Gettysburg, 157, 164; Edgewood,
178; Death of Lucy, 197
Robertson, Martha Maria Holcombe,
(aunt); 23
Royal, Jackson (slave): 197
Rubini, Monsieur: voice teacher, 99
Russia: 95,131, 132
Russian Activists: 115
Russian Aristocracy: re Lucy, 112
Russian Court: 84, 112, 189
Russian Fleet: at New York, 132
Russian Orthodox Church: 98, 113

St. Andrew's Hall, Charleston: 125
St. Charles Hotel, Charleston: 57
St. Isaac's Church, Russia: 92, 93
St. James Park, London: 80, 81
St. Mary's Hall: school, 181
St. Michael's Church, Charleston: 139
St. Petersburg, Russia: 88, 92, 102, 132
Sallie, Eulalie: 199; on Edgewood, 200
Salem, North Carolina: 15
Samovar: 91, 161
San Augustine, Texas: 16
San Jacinto Battlefield, Texas: 17
Scalawags: 172, 185
Schawlbach: German Spa, 117
Scott, Robert Kingston: 174
Secession: 61, 115, 120, 121
Seneca Falls, New York: 24
Serfs: 94, 132
Seymour, Thomas Hart: 87, 224n 2, 88
Shakespeare, William: 69, 82
Sharecroppers: 169, 185
Shelby, Joseph: at Wyalusing, 167
Sherman, William Tecumseh: 104, 166
Shreveport, Louisiana: 29
Shultz, Rev. Henry: Moravian School,
    20, 21; "Undine" 23; 109;179
Sigur, Laurent J.: 41; plantation, 43
Simkins, "Colonel" Arthur: 161
Simkins, Mrs. Arthur: 160, 232n 4
Simkins, Mrs. S. McGowan: 151
Simkins, Sallie: family friend, 64
Simpo, Archie(slave): 197
Simmons, John Jr.(slave): 197
Simmons, John Sr. (slave): 197
Slabaugh, Arlee: 152
Slavery: in the South, 8; political battles
    over, 24; as a grand empire, 61, 122
Slaves. *See also* Blacks: children of, 5;
    treatment, 5, 33; as an oppressive
    system, 8, 166, 167, 169; Compared
    to serfs, 94; post-war, 184, 185
Slidell, John: 24
-Smith, Anna Holcombe, (great grand
    niece): 33, 36, 189

South, The: 148; in ruin, 166; as a
    Kingdom, 193
South Carolina: 125, 131, 141, 166,
    187, 196
Southern Belle: 37, 57, 58
Southern Democrats; 185, 186
Southern Parlor Magazine: 57
Southern Planter Class: 99
Southern Rights Club: 60
Stage Coach: 6, 8, 19, 31
Stanton, Elizabeth Cady: 24
Staples, Rev. Moses W.: 32
Star of the West (steamer): 131
Stettin: 85, 87, 106
Stevens, Colonel P. F.: 131, 143
Stoess, Mrs.: 151
Strauss, Johan: court musician, 96,
    225n 14
Suffrage; 167
Summerson, Sir John; 81
Sun Hotel, Bethlehem, PA: 19
Swanson's Landing, Texas: 29
Sweat., Margaret J. K.: Lucy's friend
    187, 197
Swedenborgianism: 39, 218n 11
Sweet Springs Hotel: 63, 68

Taylor, General Zachary; 24
Texas Republican: 37, 75, 153
Texas, State of: admitted to Union, 23;
    boundary dispute, 24; new state, 26
Texas Western Railroad: 52, 54
Thomas, Daniel (slave): 130, 197
Thrasher, John: 46
Tolstoy, Count Leo: 111, 112
Tom (slave): 76, 78, 87, 90, 103, 108
Tompkins, A.S.: 151
Touhey, May Margaret, (great grand
    niece): 194
Trescott, William Henry: 122; 128
Trinity Episcopal Church, Edgefield:
    175, 190, 193, 197
Trump, Mrs. N. W.: 151

Tsar. *See* Alexander II
Tsarina. *See* Alexandrovna, Marie
Tschoop: Mohican Indian, 23
Tyler, John: President, 64

Undine: 109
Union blockade: 61, 148
Union Forces: 164, 165, 166
Unionists: 105, 121
United States Government: 40
University of South Carolina: 200

Van Buren, Arkansas: 155
Van Dorn, Earl: 155, 156
Vicksburg, Mississippi: 27, 28
Vickers, Pleasant: 217n 12
Virginia, State of: 141
Volunteers, CSA: 130, 131, 136, 143

Walker, Leroy Pope: 138
Washington, D.C.: 58, 59, 121
Washington, George: 154, 186, 187
Washington, John Augustine, Jr.: 169
Washington Light infantry: 131

Washington Race course, Charleston, S.C.: 133
Waterproof, Louisiana: 58
Westover, at Woodstock, Tennessee: 5
Whaley, Edward Mitchell: 173
Wheeler, Joseph: 166
Whigs: political party, 3; 51
White Diamond: novel, 48, 219n 14
White Sulphor Springs: 61, 62, 65
Wigfall, Charlotte (Mrs. Louis Wigfall): 122, 123
Wigfall, Louis T.: 71; a bitter rival, 122;
Willis, Nat (family friend): 26
Willowbrook Cemetery, Edgefield, S.C.: 175, 195
Wilson, Rev. T. B.: in Marshall, 75
Winter Palace, (now the Hermitage Museum): 92, 99, 114
Witch of Endor: 98
Woodstock: location, 6; loss of, 38
Women's Suffrage: 24
Wright, Joseph A.: 84, 85
Wyalusing: 33, 217n 20, 37, 54, 73, 74, 156, 167; sold, 179, 180
Wyley, Charles Spalding: 48
Wyatt, George, (uncle): 12